peak district : climbing

over 850 classic routes and boulder problems

peak district : climbing

over 850 classic routes and boulder problems

John Coefield and Jon Barton

peak district : climbing

Published by **Vertebrate Publishing**

ISBN 978-1-906148-06-5

Cover : Amanda Skeldon on Sunset Crack (VS 4c), Froggatt. **Photo :** Alex Messenger
Back cover : Niche Arête (VS 4c), Castle Naze.
Photo : John Coefield
All other photos as credited.

Design and typesetting by **Vertebrate Publishing**
Illustrations copyright Simon Norris/**Vertebrate Graphics Ltd** used courtesy of MLTUK.

www.**v-publishing**.co.uk

Every effort has been made to achieve accuracy of information in this guidebook. The authors, publishers, distributors and copyright owners can take no responsibility for: loss or injury (including fatal) to persons; loss or damage to property or equipment; trespass, irresponsible climbing or any other mishap that may be suffered as a result of following the route descriptions or advice offered in this guidebook. Climbers must use judgement to ensure challenges are within their abilities, and accept the consequences of these decisions. The inclusion of a route or boulder problem in this guidebook does not imply you have the right to climb it.

Climbing is a dangerous activity.

This guide, including its area coverage, route count and ethos, has been produced with the acknowledgement and kind support of the **BMC Guidebook Committee**. It is hoped that it will serve visitors to the area and those new to the sport to get to know the Peak District, and be the perfect introduction to their superb range of definitive guides.

contents

foreword

photo : Pete O'Donovan

I've lived in the Peak District for many years and I don't think I'll ever tire of that run up to Stanage and the quality of the climbs and boulder problems once you get there. The Peak is a special place, often for the small things like the way the sun burns through the clouds over Mam Tor, spraying gold across the length of Stanage, and the eastern edges farther south.

Thinking back, the apprenticeship I served as a young climber on the gritstone edges and limestone crags of the Peak District stood me in good stead for the years to come. Routes at places like Stoney and Wildcat, although perhaps slightly more worn these days, have a certain timeless quality, an enduring testament to days gone by and challenges for days yet to come. The routes build character and sharpen technical skills that can be applied to climbs around the world.

This book contains so many excellent and classic routes as well as some of the finest bouldering in the world. I've often thought about which climb is my favourite, and reading through these pages I'm reminded of many excellent days out, but whether my favourites turn out to be yours I don't know. The enjoyment really is contained within the initial adventure, the leap of faith, the voyage of discovery; it is only then when you reach the top, sit down and gaze across the golden sky that you can truly reflect on what it is to be a rock climber.

See you out there one day.

Ron Fawcett.

Ron Fawcett
Hathersage, February 2008

Introduction

This book has been bubbling away beneath the surface, in one form or another, for several years. Bringing it to fruition has been at times a difficult process, but it is clear from the finished work that it meets our original brief and slots neatly into an already dense array of guidebooks to the Peak District area.

In producing the book we have tried to place the emphasis on a safe approach to rock climbing and, importantly, an ethical one, as this is what ultimately makes UK climbing so rich and unique.

Traditional climbs are well covered, across the lower grades and on both gritstone and limestone. In addition, we have included sport routes, as they represent the logical and accepted path of development of many of the limestone crags in the Peak District.

This guide is intended to dovetail neatly with our existing guide to Peak District bouldering and we hope that, like its ancestor, it will inspire and inform in equal measure.

Enjoy!

John Coefield and Jon Barton
February 2008

Acknowledgements

A word of thanks is necessary for everyone who helped out with this guidebook:

All the photographers who submitted images: Adam Long (**www.adamlong.co.uk**), Ian Parnell (**www.ianparnell.com**), Pete O'Donovan (**www.podimaging.com**), David Simmonite (**www.davidsimmonite.com**), Dave Parry (**www.beardownproductions.co.uk**), Alex Messenger, Keith Sharples (**www.keithsharplesphotography.com**), Mike Robertson (**www.wildartproductions.com**), Nick Smith (**climbers.net**), Stuart Littlefair (**www.darkpeakimages.co.uk**) and Jerry O'Donnell. A big thanks in particular to Keith as he shot at least 80% of the crag photographs.

Everyone who helped with the guide by offering feedback, suggestions, agreeing to be photographed, proofreading, route-checking etc etc etc: Libby Peter, Steve Long, the Staff at the BMC, Simon Wilson, Adam Long, Andy West, Helen Kean, Paul Firth, Simon Watchman, Keith Sharples, Niall Grimes, Alan James, Rupert Davies, Jason Myers at Wild Country, Neil Bentley and Iain Whitehouse at The Foundry, Sam Whittaker at The Climbing Works, Eadaoin Hutchinson at The North Face, Neil McAdie and Jennifer Dargue at Equip UK, Colin Boothroyd at Entre-Prises and of course 'big' Ron Fawcett.

And finally, the team who put the book together: Oliver Jackson, Nathan Ryder and John Coefield.

what to do in an **emergency**

Getting medical help

In the event of an accident that requires medical assistance, dial 999 and ask for Police – Mountain Rescue.

Give them details of the accident and your location, including the OS reference of the crag you are at (*see the introduction section for each crag*).

Do not contact Mountain Rescue directly – the Police will co-ordinate the Mountain Rescue team and, if necessary, the air ambulance.

First aid

There are basic principles to First Aid, the first of which is the most important as without it you can do little to help a casualty.

- Ensure your own safety.
- If spinal or head injuries are suspected in the casualty then do not move him or her without professional help, other than to maintain breathing and circulation.
- If breathing has stopped, clear airways and begin CPR. Do not stop until a professional diagnoses death.
- Stop bleeding by applying direct pressure.
- Summon help.

Supporting mountain rescue

The local mountain rescue teams operate on a voluntary basis. To support their efforts, please do contact them:

- **Edale Mountain Rescue**
  (covering most of the Eastern Edges)
  www.edalemountainrescue.co.uk

- **Kinder Mountain Rescue**
  (covering, you guessed it, Kinder)
  www.kmrt.org.uk

- **Oldham Mountain Rescue**
  www.omrt.org

- **Buxton Mountain Rescue**
  01298 812 232
  www.buxtonmrt.org.uk

- **Staffordshire County Air Ambulance**
  01384 241 133
  www.countyairambulance.com

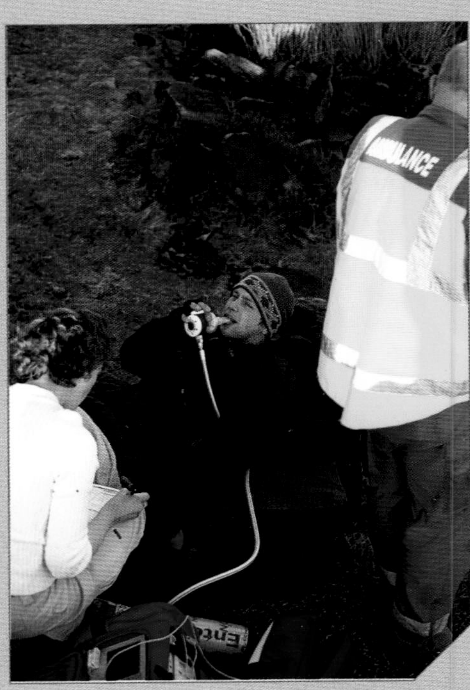

ENTRE PRISES
Bolt-on holds
Training boards
Bouldering Walls
Leading Walls
Mobile Towers
Ice Walls
Artificial caves

getting **started**

Types of climbing:

Lead climbing: The first climber leads a rope up the route. Protection is provided from below by clipping the rope into runners placed while climbing. Should the leader fall, the belayer controls the fall with a belay device and the last piece of protection placed should hold the leader, backed up by the runners placed prior to this.

Sport climbing: In sport climbing, the anchors are already in place in the rock, in the form of bolt anchors – but bear in mind that bolts do age and corrode, so **always** check them very carefully before relying on them. The climber clips a quickdraw into these as he/she climbs and then passes the rope through this as protection. In sport climbing, the climbing is generally quite safe and therefore the climber can focus on the technical and physical difficulties of the climb.

Top roping (and bottom roping): A safety rope is provided above the climber to minimise the distance they might travel in a fall. This is a common practice when belaying groups of novice climbers. Unfortunately, it can lead to the monopolisation of areas of crags, as top ropes can be in place for hours as many novices attempt the route. In top roping, the rope is provided from above and the belayer is also located above the climber, who ascends to the top of the route towards the belayer. In bottom roping the rope passes through a karabiner at the top of the climb and comes back down to the belayer who is located at the foot of the climb – similar to top-rope climbs at indoor walls. 'Top roping' has evolved into a generic term to describe both top and bottom roping. Sometimes very hard or dangerous routes are top roped prior to leading, a practice known as head-pointing – or 'cheating' by climbing purists.

Soloing: This is the ascent of routes without a rope and gear for protection.

Bouldering: Bouldering has risen dramatically in popularity in recent years, with the Peak District offering some of the best in the country. It is the pursuit of short, difficult, usually safe challenges, where the emphasis is placed entirely on the technical aspects of individual moves. There are no ropes and no gear, only climbing shoes, chalk and bouldering mats. Bouldering mats are portable crash pads designed to prevent broken ankles, muddy feet and to minimise erosion beneath boulder problems.

photo : Alex Messenger

Climbing: Essentials

Belay: Belay can refer to the belayer, who controls the climbing rope using a friction device (a belay device). It can also refer to the safety anchors a climber places at the top of a climb before belaying the second climber up the route.

Runner/Protection/Gear/Anchor/Piece:
There are lots of terms that describe the equipment designed to protect rock climbing. Climbers frequently refer to placing runners, good protection (pro), bomber gear (very good protection), solid anchors or placing several 'pieces'. The language varies but the terminology refers to the same thing.

An introduction to gear

Ropes: Pretty obvious really, but there are many different kinds. A single, 50m rope will be fine for most climbing found in the Peak District, but double ropes are essential to protect routes that follow wandering lines, and their competent use is generally much better for traditionally protected climbs. Double ropes should not be used for sport climbing, however, and do require additional belaying skills, since two ropes must be independently managed through a belay device.

Ropes can be dry-treated, which protects the outer sheath and increases the life of the rope. This comes at a premium, though, and you can expect to pay a little bit more for treated string.

It is also possible to purchase static rope which can be used for setting up top rope belays, and for abseiling. However, static rope should not be used for climbing on as it has no shock absorbing properties and can cause injury.

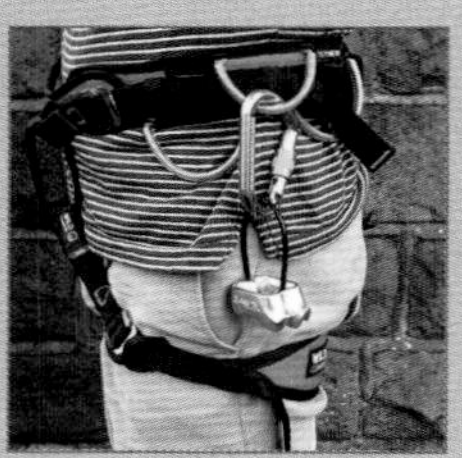

Harness: Back in the days of yore, climbers would wrap the rope around their waist, tied with a bowline knot. Given the high safety standards to which climbing equipment is now manufactured, we enjoy much more comfortable, safer harnesses with an array of features to make the climbing experience more enjoyable. Dependent on the particular style, most harnesses are fully adjustable with control over the fit of both waist and legs. They come with plenty of well-placed gear loops for racking gear and they are designed to be easy to use, light and comfortable.

Belay devices: There are several different belay devices on the market, although they all do essentially the same important job – controlling the rope. The most common devices are able to control both single and twin ropes, and can also be used for abseiling, which means only one device need be carried.

Rock boots: Rock boots (or shoes) are essential for climbing to any standard. Brand and model are less important than a good fit and comfort. They should be clean before starting each climb, and once a hole appears in the sole, get the boot resoled or replaced.

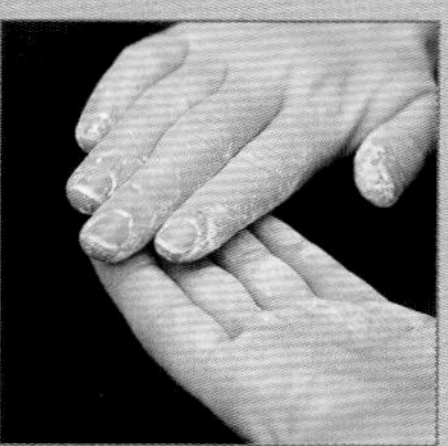

Chalk/chalkbag: Rock boots ensure climbers' feet stick to the rock and to counteract the sweat that hands and fingers produce a chalk compound (magnesium carbonate) is used to dry hands. A small chalkbag is worn around the waist allowing quick access mid-route.

Helmet: As most of the climbs in this book are vertical or slabby, a fall can often result in head injury. **Get a helmet, make sure it fits and wear it all the time!** A lot of climbers don't bother, but particularly for new climbers getting to know their limits, or indeed pushing their grade, a helmet on the head is one less thing to worry about when gravity wins the day!

Karabiners/snapgates ('krabs'): The basic screwgate karabiner is probably the most essential piece of climbing equipment after ropes. Karabiners can be used to belay without a specialist belay device, and, with only a single gate and a rope, a very effective belay can be set up. It all comes down to experience with ropes and good rope technique. Karabiners without a screwgate are often referred to as snapgates.

Quickdraws: A quickdraw is an extender for runners with a snapgate at either end of a Dyneema® or nylon tape sling. They are commonly placed on wires to allow the rope to be clipped, and are essential for sport routes, as one snapgate is clipped to the bolt while the rope is clipped through the other.

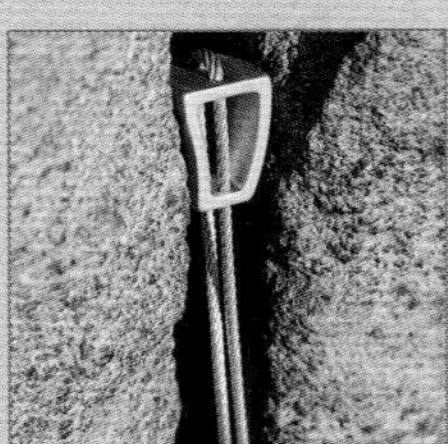

Wires/nuts: Wedge-shaped sections of steel on a threaded metal wire, which slot into tapered sections of cracks, breaks or pockets to hold a leader in the event of a fall. An essential addition to the well-equipped leader's rack.

Hexes: Larger than wires, hexes are useful in larger cracks from hand to fist size. They complement camming devices well in odd-shaped cracks where cams may not necessarily fit. More properly called hexcentrics, they are originally named after their six-sided shape.

Camming devices/ Friends: These actively cam into cracks and breaks to provide protection. The more parallel the sides of the crack or break the better; however, cams do work very well in tapered and angled cracks, as the force they exert increases as load is placed on them. Friends, one of the generic terms given to camming devices, are the original camming device produced by Wild Country.

Slings: Traditionally made of nylon cord, slings are now commonly produced from a lighter, thinner and stronger material known as Dyneema®. Available in many different sizes, they are incredibly useful for setting up belays at the top of climbs, for threading chockstones or to extend runners, thereby minimising rope drag *en route*.

Nut key: It is not uncommon for bomber runners to be 'well placed' (a.k.a. stuck). To aid gear retrieval – important in limiting the damage to your/your leader's wallet – these nifty little devices can be used to fiddle out well-placed gear. Several different styles are available depending on the manufacturer, although they all do essentially the same job.

Recommended rack

A set of wires, a small selection of larger protection, such as hexes, and a set of cams from **1** to **3** should suffice for most of the routes in this book. In addition, five to ten quickdraws, a couple of longer slings, two screwgates and a few spare krabs are a good bet. As you progress, some smaller cams and micro wires will also come in handy.

Basic climbing techniques

Laybacking: This is a useful technique when there are no horizontal holds to pull down on. Cracks or arêtes can be leaned away from and feet placed high on the edge of the arête or opposing wall of a crack, to provide friction for upward movement.

photo : Ian Parnell

Bridging: With either blank corners or corners with cracks, the climber spans across the corner to make use of both sides.

photo : Mike Robertson

Mantelshelf: To gain positions on flat holds and shelves, often at the top of routes, the climber presses down with his or her hands and arms until the arms are straight, while running the legs up behind to place a foot on the ledge.

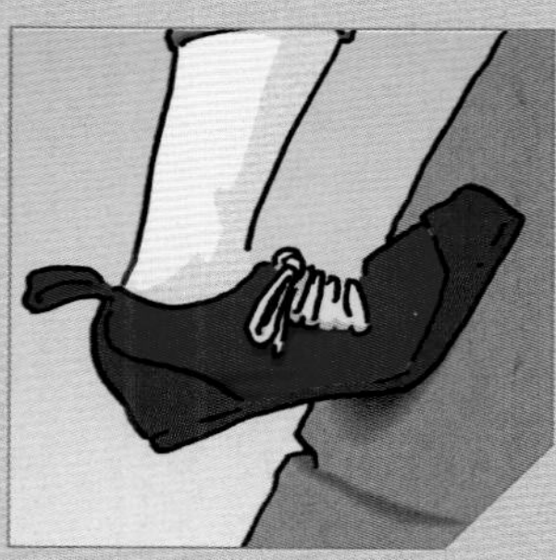

Smearing: In the absence of footholds, a flat foot is placed on the rock with the surface area of the shoe, the pressure placed on it providing the grip.

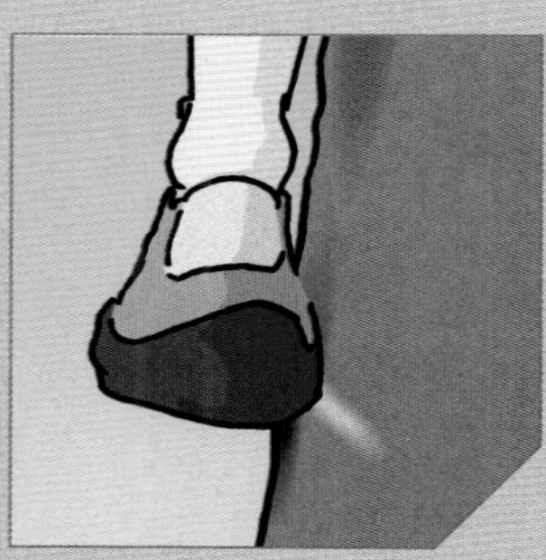

Edging: On small edges, the side of the shoe is used to gain maximum hold.

Illustrations from ***Rock Climbing***, published by MLTUK

Communicating with your partner

A few simple phrases can help to ensure clear and safe communication with your climbing partner.

Belayer *(after threading the rope into the belay device)*: "Climb when ready"
Climber *(aware that the belayer is ready and it is now safe to begin climbing)*: "Climbing"
Belayer "OK"

Climber *(after reaching the top of a route and placing anchors to make him/herself safe)*: "Safe"
Belayer *(aware that the climber has completed the route and has made him/herself safe by placing and clipping into anchors on the summit)*: "Off belay"

About the rock

Gritstone: Millstone grit, as found on the eastern edges of the Peak District, is a deltaic sediment, formed on river beds, and made up of coarse sand grains with small stones (pebbles) thrown in for good measure. It was previously quarried to produce millstones for flour mills and grindstones for Sheffield's world-famous steel and cutlery industry. Remnants of the quarrying age can found scattered around the Peak.

Limestone: Limestone is a sedimentary rock, exposed in beds or reefs in various locations around the Peak, although the entire area is underlain by a huge limestone deposit. It was formed in warm shallow seas from deposits of animal skeletons or corals and is typically exposed in river valleys, by quarrying, in collapsed caverns, gorges or reef mounds or wherever the land has eroded down enough.

Where to go and when

Generally speaking, gritstone is best climbed in the autumn, winter and spring, when the sun is out, the midges are on holiday and the friction is optimum. Limestone is best in the summer and autumn, when the moisture has seeped away. Of course, a breezy day on an exposed eastern edge may be lovely in August, and worse than Everest's South Col in December. Where possible we have tried to give advice on conditions in the introduction to each individual crag.

PHOTO: KEITH SHARPLES PHOTOGRAPHY
THE
FOUNDRY
RUTLAND
ROAD
A61
BARNSLEY
MOWBRAY
STREET
TESCO
METRO
MEADOWHALL
M1 - J34
SAVILLE STREET
THE
FOUNDRY
CORPORATION STREET
UNIVERSITY
SHEFFIELD
CITY
CENTRE
A57
PARKWAY TO
M1 - J33
A57
GLOSSOP
MIDLAND
TRAIN STATION
A625
HATHERSAGE
A61
CHESTERFIELD

a note about **grading**

British grades

Traditional British grades are split into two parts: the adjectival grade (VDiff or HVS, for example) and the technical grade (4a or 5b, for example). The adjectival grade describes the overall difficulty of a climb and may refer to how well protected it is, how sustained it is and ultimately how hard it is. From around HVD and upwards it will be supplemented with a technical grade, informing you of the hardest move, or sequence of moves. VS 4c and HVS 5a describe routes that are not overly bold, sustained, or technical at the grade. A grade of HVS 4c indicates that the moves themselves are not particularly tough for HVS, so the route must be either bold or sustained. This is usually confirmed by cross-referencing the grade with the description.

UK Adjectival Grade	UK Technical Grade (approx)	French Grade
Moderate		1
Difficult		1, 2, 2+
Very Difficult		2, 2+, 3–
Hard Very Difficult	4a, 4b	2+, 3–, 3, 3+
Mild Severe	4a, 4b	3–, 3, 3+
Severe	4a, 4b, 4c	3, 3+, 4
Hard Severe	4a, 4b, 4c	3, 3+, 4, 4+
Mild Very Severe	4a, 4b, 4c	3+, 4, 4+
Very Severe	4a, 4b, 4c	4, 4+, 5
Hard Very Severe	4c, 5a, 5b	4+, 5, 5+, 6a
E1	5a, 5b, 5c	5+, 6a, 6a+
E2	5b, 5c, 6a	6a+, 6b, 6b+
E3	5c, 6a	6b, 6b+, 6c
E4	6a, 6b	6c, 6c+, 7a
E5	6a, 6b 6c	7a, 7a+, 7b
E6	6b, 6c	7b+, 7c, 7c+
E7	6c, 7a	8a, 8a+
E8	6c, 7a	8b, 8b+

Example 1: *Sunset Slab* (HVS 4b) at Froggatt is given 4b as it features climbing that might ordinarily be found on a VS. Since there is little protection, the route is given HVS to inform prospective leaders that it is a serious route.

Example 2: *Fern Crack* on the Upper Tier at The Roaches is given HVD 4b. This informs the leader that it is an HVD, but with a very difficult, well-protected move somewhere on the route. The leader can infer that, if it was a sustained sequence of 4b moves, or if the move was bold, the route would more likely be graded HS or even VS.

French grades (used in sport climbing)

French grades are single numerical grades that refer to the overall difficulty of a climb, without any particular reference to how sustained it may be or the technical difficulty of the hardest move or moves. It is assumed that, as a bolted route, it will be relatively safe. Nevertheless, care should still be exercised on sport climbs.

photo : Dave Parry

Font grades
(used in bouldering)

Comparable with French sport climbing grades, Font grades, named after the world famous Fontainebleau bouldering area in France where they were developed, also refer to the overall difficulty of a boulder problem. They can be interpreted differently; for example, if a Font 6a has many moves, say 12, then the boulderer can infer that the individual moves are perhaps not that difficult; if a Font 6a problem is only two moves long, then it can safely be assumed that one or both of those moves are very difficult for the grade.

As with our ***peak district : bouldering*** guide, we have opted to use Font grades here, as they provide a very accurate way of grading boulder problems, and in particular the authors have a vast amount of experience in using the system. If you've been climbing a little while but are new to bouldering and/or Font grades then fear not: this system isn't as hard to understand as it might first appear.

Being able to climb VDiff on gritstone equates to about Font 3+; Severes may be anything from 3+ up to Font 5; HVS might run up to 5+; if you're pushing the toughest HVSs (say 5c) or breaking into E1, then this might be up to 6a – but these comparisons are quite general. As boulder problems tend to be close to the ground, they provide a great opportunity to push your technical ability, so you might be a solid Severe leader but find you can boulder Font 6a! The thing to do is just get on some and see how you get on – you're bound to surprise yourself.

Font Grade	V Grade
3	V0-
3+	V0-, V0
4	V0, V0+
4+	V0+
5	V1
5+	V1, V2
6a	V2, V3
6a+	V3
6b	V3, V4
6b+	V4
6c	V4, V5
6c+	V5, V6
7a	V6
7a+	V7
7b	V7, V8
7b+	V8, V9
7c	V9
7c+	V10
8a	V11

access and conservation

Access

Seasonal climbing restrictions

Several crags and sections of crags in the Peak District are subject to seasonal climbing restrictions due to nesting birds. Access representatives from the BMC have developed an excellent working relationship with their colleagues in the RSPB and the Peak District National Park Authority to negotiate how climbers and nature can co-exist in harmony.

Millstone

Every spring, Millstone is a popular nesting spot for Ravens. They tend to nest in the same areas, usually around the Twikker bay. Also, in spring 2007, a Tawny Owl nested in a route adjacent to Great North Road.

When birds are nesting and restrictions are in place, signs will be placed at the foot of buttresses/routes advising climbers of the situation and requesting that they do not climb in the area.

Stanage

Localised restrictions can often be found on buttresses, usually around the Popular End, during the nesting season for Ring Ouzels. As is the case at Millstone, signposts are placed at the foot of affected buttresses/routes advising climbers of the situation.

Seasonal restrictions are also posted in the rock counter at **Outside** in Hathersage, and full details of all current access arrangements can be found online at the BMC's Regional Access Database: **www.thebmc.co.uk/bmccrag**

CRoW

This section is intended to provide a brief synopsis of the Countryside Rights of Way Act 2000. If you would like to read about the Act in more detail we would recommend visiting the BMC website at: **www.thebmc.co.uk**

The Countryside Rights of Way Act 2000 came into force on a phased basis in England on 31 October 2005. The Act gives right of access on foot to open country, which includes mountain, moor, heath and down.

photo : John Coefield

The CRoW Act does not mean that you can go anywhere on open access land, and landowners do retain control over a number of important restrictions and exclusions, including:

- The right to exclude dogs
- The right to restrict access to a particular linear route
- The right to refuse access for any reason for up to 28 days a year (not including national and bank holidays, or more than four Saturdays or Sundays in total, or any Saturday from 1st June to 11th August, or any Sunday from 1st June to 30th September)

Applications can also be made to close CRoW land for specific reasons including:

- land management;
- fire risk;
- public safety;
- nature conservation;
- national security.

Restrictions cannot be applied to established Rights of Way and the BMC and other local access forums must be consulted before any significant closures. As such, the BMC spends a great deal of time ensuring as much of the Peak District remains open to climbers for as much of the year as possible.

General access

Just because a crag is featured in this book does not necessarily mean that you are allowed to climb there. For up-to-date information about access to individual crags please read the notes in the crag introductions or alternatively refer to the BMC's Regional Access Database at: **www.thebmc.co.uk/bmccrag**

Conservation

As is the case with any other users of the National Park, climbers will inevitably have some impact upon it. Our effect is often minimal due to the conscientious nature of 99% of climbers but the issues that can be attributed to us include:

- footpath erosion;
- rock erosion;
- chalk;
- nature preservation;
- chipping;
- litter.

Footpath erosion

Most crags are accessed on foot using established rights of way: footpaths, bridleways and byways. Footpath erosion can be minimised by sticking to established paths and not veering off them, which will gradually widen them. The areas at the foot of crags are showing signs of wear and tear and in some instances, such as under several of the Stanage Plantation boulders, remedial work is now underway to control the side-effects of the increasing popularity of climbing.

Rock erosion

Although we'd perhaps like to think it is not the case, our rock is a finite resource and lots of little climbers scampering all over it week after week, in their little rubber shoes and chalky white hands, will slowly affect how the rock ages. In places the hard outer crust, the patina, wears away revealing the softer rock below which can then be quickly ground down leaving unsightly scars and forever damaged climbs. Similarly, years of action polishes the rock; the friction that many of us lay in bed dreaming about disappears to leave a glassy sheen. This is wear and tear but there are steps we can take to minimise this:

- Ensure boots are clean before climbing; climbing in dirty/muddy boots which have grit particles stuck to the sole are ideal for polishing rock and generally accelerating the aging process.
- Avoid climbing on areas of rock shortly after wet weather. Some gritstone buttresses, particularly around the Cratcliffe area and the western Peak, can be quite vulnerable when damp.
- Do not top-rope or lead groups on popular routes. Leave popular routes for small parties to enjoy in a traditional leader–second relationship.

Chalk

The traditional approach to climbing in the UK ensures virtually nothing is left behind after a route is completed; gear is placed to protect the leader and then removed by the second. However, the primary lasting visual indicator of our presence is the white handprints we leave up and down, left and right, all over the rock. Chalk is commonplace in climbing and has allowed new levels of difficulty to be climbed. However, we should endeavour to use only what is needed, clean up any spillages and remove any associated marks, such as 'tick marks' placed with chalk while bouldering.

Nature preservation

By adhering to the Countryside Code, you will be doing your bit to help the natural environment of the Peak flourish.

Chipping

Chipping is the practice of either creating or improving a hold artificially. There is no place in rock climbing for chipping, but unfortunately there has been a spate of it on gritstone recently. If you discover what you believe to be recent chips, we recommend that you contact the Access and Conservation team at the BMC.

Litter

A bit of an egg sucking lesson this one. Although it should fall under 'The Basics', many climbers do seem to have an aversion to taking their litter home with them. We all have a responsibility to treat our crags with respect and it takes no effort to take home any litter you generate, including food wrappers, finger tape and cigarette butts. Even a discarded half eaten sandwich is litter, it attracts magpies and crows, who then go on to predate on indigenous moorland species.

Crag Care Fund

The BMC has proposed money for a Crag Care Fund, to be spent on tools, professional time, crag furniture (for example, stiles, fences etc) and anything else associated with keeping crags open and in good condition. The aim is that the fund should be self-financing through events, sponsorship and donations. Find out more at **www.thebmc.co.uk**

Countryside Code

- **Be safe – plan ahead and follow any signs**
- **Leave gates and property as you find them**
- **Protect plants and animals, and take your litter home**
- **Keep dogs under close control**
- **Consider other people**

history

Peak District Climbing

A Potted History

It is true to say that climbing in the Peak District started with James W (Jimmy) Puttrell back in the late 19th Century. The industrial setting of Wharncliffe, situated to the north of Sheffield, was his original forcing ground, but he made his mark on most, if not all, of the major Peak District crags. Routes such as *Mississippi Chimney* and the *Hollybush Gully* at Stanage bear his stamp, as does *Nursery Slab* at Froggatt.

Puttrell was a member of the Sheffield, Manchester and Derby-based Kyndwr Club (Kyndwr being the proper spelling of Kinder). The group's membership, both prior to and after the club was formed, was responsible for much climbing activity between the three city points of the Peak District triangle. They made little impact on the western edges, however, including the virgin rock of The Roaches.

Fear not though, as the prodigious team of Siegfried Herford, Stanley Jeffcoat and John Laycock were on hand to ensure the western edges did not go on empty-hearted. Jeffcoat chipped in with his eponymous *Chimney* and *Buttress* routes on the Upper Tier of The Roaches, Laycock added the *Central Climb* to Hen Cloud with the aid of AR Thompson, and Herford established the *Great Chimney*, also at Hen Cloud. The team also made forays to the Kinder Edges, leaving behind *Herford's Route* on The Pagoda, among others.

Significantly or otherwise, there is little recorded activity during the period of either World War, with the exception of a flurry at Stanage during the first year of the Great War. Climbing did take place at these times, but, as much focus was placed on simply practicing on the outcrops for the greater challenges of the European Alps, it is unfortunately likely that many first ascent details were never recorded.

WWII came and went and larger numbers of people began to visit the moorland of the Peak District following the formation of the Peak as the first national park in 1951. The moors were no longer the reserve of the landowners and upper classes, and were thrown open to the residents of the towns and cities bounding the park.

Around the same time, the legendary Rock and Ice Club, formerly the Valkyrie Club, began to flex its muscles, particularly in the form of the world famous duo of Joe Brown and Don Whillans. We have a lot to thank these two for. They combined their creativity, adventure and innate ability to produce hard and often bold routes at a time when much of the modern protection we now take for granted did not exist.

Take a stroll along The Roaches and look up in wonder: *Saul's Crack* (Brown), *The Sloth* (Whillans), *Matinée*, *The Mincer* (the two of them). Then head over to Stanage: *The Right Unconquerable* (Brown), *Terrazza Crack* (again, the two of them). Now imagine climbing any of those routes without a full rack of cams or wires. Bonkers. Of course, this is only a very small selection of routes below E1 – they established many, many routes well into the mid-extremes.

The latter half of the 20th Century saw gaps plugged, 'last great projects' fall to new and upcoming talent, and the increasingly frequent

production of guidebooks informed the leisure climber of what had and had not been done.

However, that's not all – oh no. Two major shifts were to follow that had a significant effect on the shape of British climbing today. First, stronger climbers, training specifically in the gym, started to explore the limestone crags, notably Stoney in the '70s. Then, during the '80s, climbers saw the potential of the limestone crags of Cheedale and other valleys, adopting techniques learnt in the south of France. This new approach elevated the Peak's limestone routes to some of the most challenging in the world. The likes of Tom Proctor, Pete Livesey, Ron Fawcett, Jerry Moffatt, Ben Moon and today Steve McClure have, like Brown and Whillans in their day, kept the Peak as a forcing ground in world climbing. In recent years, this quest for difficulty has energised a new generation of climbers, focussing on smaller climbs or boulder problems.

Sport climbing, where routes are protected with *in-situ* bolts, brought with it a new style of climbing which permitted focus to be placed on the physical and technical aspects of the climbing, while danger and derring-do took a back seat. Levels of fitness shot up, which also had a positive effect on trad climbing, and everyone wanted to chew down on a piece of this tasty new pie while sporting the most garish lycra available on the market.

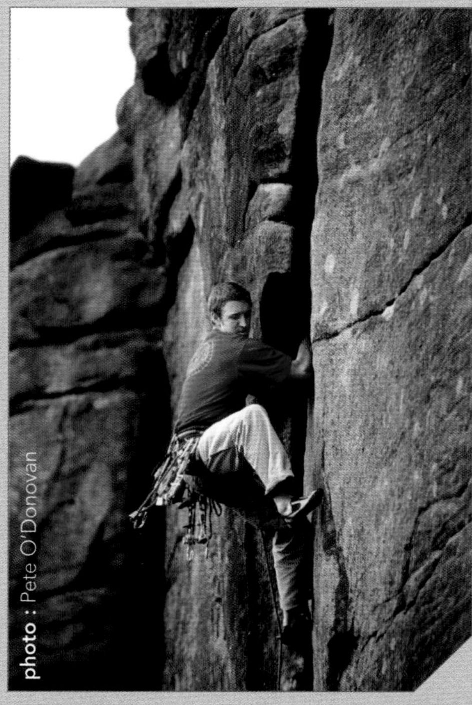

photo : Keith Sharples

Horseshoe was one of the first mid-grade venues to receive the bolt in the '80s, and was followed by other such venues, including Harpur Hill. Much of this work was carried out by Gary Gibson, who invested a great deal of his own time, money and effort into bringing this style of climbing to the masses. A round of applause, please.

Mid-grade sport climbing in the Peak has maintained its popularity and Horseshoe certainly is still a popular venue on weekday evenings, or if a weekend 'burn' is required to get the arms going.

As far as bouldering is concerned, climbers have been exposing themselves on miniature bits of rock for decades, however this was always just as practice for the bigger rocks. These days bouldering is well and truly established as an activity in its own right. The first guide to bouldering in the Peak District was produced by Allen Williams in the mid '90s and we're now onto a fourth version, jam packed with over 1000 problems. Although much of the history is reserved for the harder problems, it is worth mentioning that many routes now considered boulder problems were climbed some time ago, the classic highball *Crescent Arête* at Stanage being the perfect example. Gabe Regan made the first ascent in 1976.

So, there you go, a potted history. There's much more to read about, and lots of anecdotes to tell, but these have also been recorded many times over elsewhere so we'll leave you to discover them for yourself.

A Potted History... Potted

Jimmy did heaps of stuff back in the day, while sporting a moustache. Then came Joe and Don who were tough guys and talented climbers to boot. They set new standards and established many classics, including *The Right Unconquerable* and *The Sloth*. Time doesn't stand still though, and neither do clichés. Along came sport climbing and spandex, which were both cool until the '80s ended, and they were replaced by bouldering.

Suggested further reading:
The BMC Definitive Guidebooks.

area map

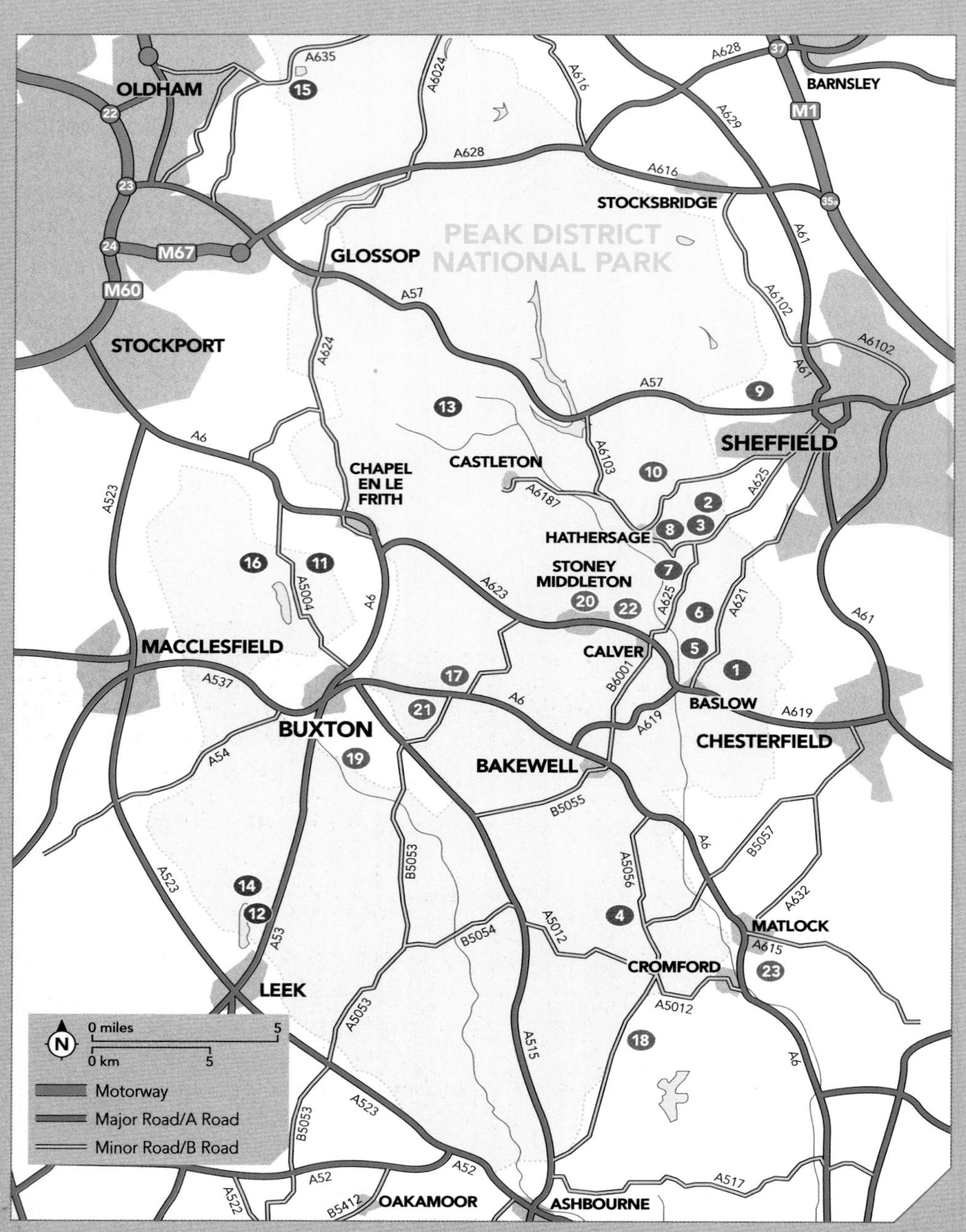

OLDHAM
A635
15
A6024
A616
A628
37
BARNSLEY
M1
A629
22
A628
A616
23
STOCKSBRIDGE
35a
PEAK DISTRICT
NATIONAL PARK
24
M67
GLOSSOP
A61
M60
A6102
A57
STOCKPORT
A624
A6102
A61
A57
9
13
SHEFFIELD
A6
CASTLETON
A6103
CHAPEL
EN LE
FRITH
10
A625
A523
A6187
2
3
8
HATHERSAGE
16
11
STONEY
MIDDLETON
7
A5004
A6
A623
20
22
A625
6
A621
A61
MACCLESFIELD
5
CALVER
1
A537
17
B6001
A6
BASLOW
A619
21
A619
BUXTON
CHESTERFIELD
A54
19
BAKEWELL
B5055
A6
B5057
A5056
B5053
A523
14
A632
4
12
MATLOCK
A5012
B5054
A53
A615
CROMFORD
23
LEEK
A5012
A5053
18
A6
A515
0 miles
5
0 km
5
Motorway
Major Road/A Road
Minor Road/B Road
A523
B5053
A52
A52
A517
A522
B5412
OAKAMOOR
ASHBOURNE

BMC CRAG CODE

www.thebmc.co.uk

Access Check the Regional Access Database (RAD) on www.thebmc.co.uk for the latest access information

Parking Park carefully – avoid gateways and driveways

Footpaths Keep to established paths – leave gates as you find them

Risk Climbing can be dangerous – accept the risks and be aware of other people around you

Respect Groups and individuals – respect the rock, local climbing ethics and other people

Wildlife Do not disturb livestock, wildlife or cliff vegetation; respect seasonal bird nesting restrictions

Dogs Keep dogs under control at all times; don't let your dog chase sheep or disturb wildlife

Litter 'Leave no trace' – take all litter home with you

Toilets Don't make a mess – bury your waste

Economy Do everything you can to support the rural economy – shop locally

BMC Participation Statement — Climbing, hill walking and mountaineering are activities with a danger of personal injury or death. Participants in these activities should be aware of and accept these risks and be responsible for their own actions and involvement.

eastern crags

- Birchen Edge
- Burbage North
- Burbage South
- Cratcliffe Tor and Robin Hood's Stride
- Curbar
- Froggatt
- Lawrencefield
- Millstone
- Rivelin
- Stanage

Flying Buttress (VDiff), Stanage **photo :** Pete O'Donovan

birchen edge

Access

Long pigeon-holed as a novice crag, the truth is, a day out at Birchen is bloody good fun! This crag is home to a large collection of amenable routes and a large number of these are top quality.

If you're operating at VS, then aim to tick off the trilogy of *Topsail, Sail Buttress* and *Powder Monkey Parade*. If you're after something a little easier then seek out *Trafalgar Crack* or *Monument Chimney*. Regardless, a trip through the *Telescope Tunnel* should be on everyone's list.

It's an eastern edge so we don't need to tell you that the rock is good quality, but beware of the polish in places, mainly in the lower halves of routes. The rock is fairly quick-drying and catches plenty of sun, but it can be a little too hot mid-summer.

Parking is available in the National Trust car park adjacent to the Robin Hood pub, and is often busy. Please do not park in the pub car park. Once parked, head back out to the minor road and wander up it a short distance to a stile. Cross this and follow the path on the edge of the woodland, bearing left at an obvious fork. This will lead you to the main area close to Trafalgar Wall.

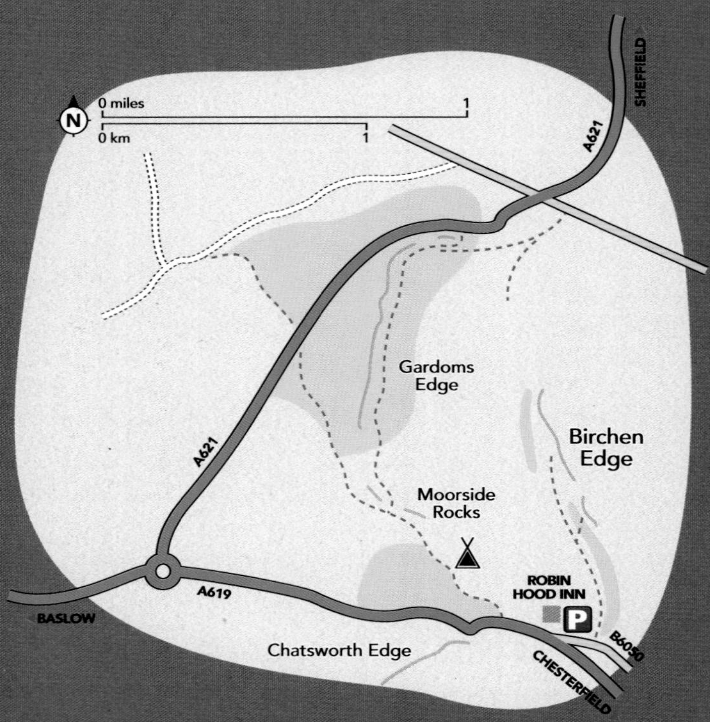

Sail Buttress (HS 4b) · **photo** : Ian Parnell

the **routes**

The Crow's Nest

The first route gives the area its name, easily identifiable by the prominent tower at the left-hand end.

1» The Crow's Nest **VS 4c // 14m // ✪✪**

Climb the crack on the left-hand side of the tower and traverse to the centre of the upper slab. Pad up this delicately to a precarious reach at the top.

2» The Funnel **Diff // 12m // ✪✪**

The deep chimney gives a 'traditional' climbing experience.

3» Kiss Me Hardy **VDiff // 12m // ✪**

Climb the short wall right of The Funnel to gain access to a ledge. Surmount the large block with interest and tackle the upper crack that splits the buttress.

4» Emma's Dilemma **S 4a // 14m // ✪✪**

A direct line up the buttress, following the varied crack, with a steep and challenging finish.

Nelson's Slab

Another fine buttress with a good selection of moderate routes.

5» Telescope Tunnel **Mod // 14m // ✪**
If you only do one route on the edge, make sure it is this one! Climb the easy initial chimney before summoning all your strength and caving experience. Enter the slot and squirm up and into the crag. Close your eyes and you could emerge anywhere. How does Hawaii sound? New Zealand...?

6» Porthole Direct **VS 4b // 12m // ✪✪**
Start in the centre of the wall, right of the chimney and climb up into the corner passing the porthole. From here gain a ledge and finish with difficulty to the left.

7» Nelson's Slab **VS 5a // 14m // ✪**
From the right-hand edge of the slab, make a series of strenuous and difficult moves in the niche to get established on the slab proper. Traverse left for several metres before finishing directly.

Sail Buttress

Home to some of the best routes at Birchen, including its namesake.

8» Sail Buttress HS 4b // 14m // ✪✪

From below the undercut steep arête, climb up and right to a ledge. Traverse the deep horizontal crack leftwards to gain the easier upper slab. The route is polished in places, but this does not detract from the quality of the climbing.

9» Sail Chimney S 4a // 14m // ✪✪✪

Super classic squirming through the slippery groove into the true chimney above.

10» Topsail VS 4c // 12m // ✪✪✪

The buttress to the right has a roof split by a crack at half height. Approach this directly using a crack, passing thread protection, and pull through the bulge confidently on good holds. The upper slab is much easier.

11» Monument Chimney VDiff // 14m // ✪

Start on the left and head right into the attractive groove which is followed throughout towards the monument.

Monument Buttress

This leaning wall is home to some of the crag's harder routes, including *Orpheus Wall* with its baffling crux.

Note: Climbers are asked NOT to use Nelson's Monument as a belay or abseil anchor.

12» Orpheus Wall HVS 5c // 14m // ✪✪✪

A technical sequence, but short-lived and well protected with medium sized cams. Climb the thin crack to reach the leaning wall and the Friend-friendly horizontal slot. Puzzle enthusiasts should have no trouble on the next move (top tip: place several limbs quite close together). Finish more easily.

13» Monument Gully VDiff // 14m // ✪

Jam the initial crack before getting stuck into the steep upper crack. It is possible to lasso a jammed chockstone but the effort involved can often outweigh its potential value.

The Promenade

Another popular buttress, with the namesake route being a particularly good introductory route for beginners.

14» The Promenade Mod // 15m // ✪✪

Follow the left-hand side of the slab to the break before traversing rightwards to finish up the tower.

15» Powder Monkey Parade
HS 4b // 17m // ✪✪✪

A superb climb with three contrasting sections. Squeeze up the slippery short chimney to a standing position on the chockstone. Traverse rightwards across the face with just the right amount of exposure and protection before padding up the centre of the well-positioned finishing slab.

Trafalgar Wall

This large fine slab is home to a number of low-grade classics, characterised by undercut starts and low crux sections.

16» Camperdown Crawl
VS 4c // 14m // ✪✪✪

A good introduction to finger-jamming up the thin low crack with perfect protection. Finish more easily up the wall above.

17» Trafalgar Crack VDiff 4a // 14m // ✪✪

From below and right of the prominent upper crack, gain the centre of the ramp line and trend left to gain the crack.

18» Trafalgar Wall VS 4b // 14m // ✪✪✪

From the lowest point of the ramp, head directly up the slab with a delicate approach required in the upper half.

Kismet Buttress

Some way right of the main area of Birchen is this often-overlooked buttress of some stature. The two routes here tackle the central groove with alternative finishes. There is plenty of further climbing between *Trafalgar Wall* and *Kismet Buttress* but we'll leave you to discover that for yourselves.

19» Horatio's Horror S 4a // 14m // ✪✪

Enjoyable jamming up the corner leads to the roof and a poor rest. Levitate left from here to finish up the continuation corner.

20» Nelson's Nemesis VS 4b // 16m // ✪✪✪

Start as for the previous route and continue to the same poor rest. From here traverse right with a tricky foot swap to reach the base of the upper crack. Power up this to ledges and an exit on juggy flutings.

burbage north

One half of an impressive double-act, the northern stretch of Burbage has a bountiful supply of friendly and approachable routes, together with extensive bouldering at all grades.

Although the edge itself feels relatively long, the climbing is clumped into concentrated groups dotted along the edge. The selection here provides a good taster for what else is on offer and is intended to cater for all abilities.

The rock at **Burbage** is among some of the coarsest on the eastern edges, but is of excellent quality and is bullet-hard. Due to the exposed nature of the edge, it is rarely, if ever, dirty and provides a good option on a mild day where the wind can take the sting out of the heat, although it is best avoided if the wind is blowing on a cold winter's day.

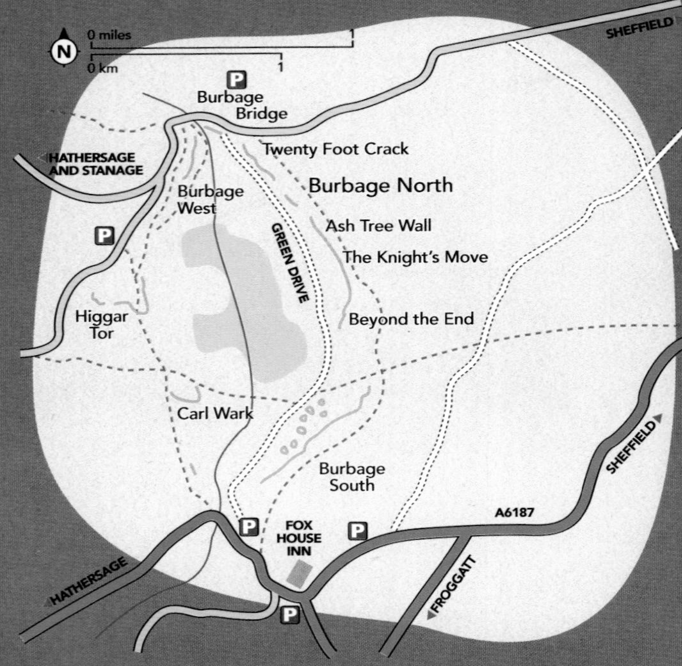

Access

There is considerable parking at the two Burbage Bridge car parks and the edge is most easily approached from the wide path that runs parallel to, and below, the edge. There are no access issues associated with Burbage North.

Andy Weston on Ash Tree Wall (S 4a) **photo**: John Coefield

the **routes**

Twenty Foot Crack

1» The Chant **HVS 5a // 6m // ✪**
A short route that packs in the climbing and the quality. Follow the overlap to a prominent horizontal slot on the right. A tricky, well-protected move from here will bring the apparently distant top within reach.

2» Twenty Foot Crack **S 4b // 6m // ✪**
Jam or layback the perfectly formed crack.

Triangle Buttress

3» Triangle Buttress Direct **S 4a // 7m**
The very blunt arête is started just to the left. Taken directly, the start is a more difficult 5b.

4» Triangle Crack **VDiff 4a // 7m**
After a tough start the corner crack eases somewhat.

5» Leaning Wall **S 4a // 8m**
Traverse in from the left to gain the broken, upper crack system. A direct start is more commonly made at VS 5a via a short fingery sequence.

6» Little White Jug **VS 4c // 8m // ✪✪**
The steep wall culminates in an unladylike pull over the top.

7» Steptoe **Mod // 7m**
Chunky, honest climbing up the wide broken crack with no hidden surprises.

Banana Finger Area : bouldering

The following two problems are found 50m right of **Triangle Buttress.**

1» Banana Finger // 6a

A Peak District classic. Traverse the thin break leftwards to a stiff move up to the upper break.

2» Banana Finger Direct // 6a

The direct start can be frustrating until you learn the knack. Placing your left hand at the very top bit of the starting hold helps!

Helen Kean on Overhanging Buttress Arête (Mod) **photo** : John Coefield

Overhanging Buttress

8» Overhanging Buttress Direct

S 4a // 10m // ✪

A polished start gives way to enjoyable open climbing on the upper slab.

9» Overhanging Buttress Arête

Mod // 10m // ✪

Delicate, but never alarming, the arête is pleasant throughout. A good first lead.

Remergence Area

10» The Grogan **HVS 5b // 8m // ✪✪**
Tough as old boots, the thin crack line will require 110% effort if you're to stand any chance of succeeding. Good, small protection will allow you to focus on the technical and physical difficulties.

11» Pulcherrime **VS 4b // 8m // ✪**
Pleasant hand-jamming and good protection in equal measure on this small yet enjoyable crack.

12» Slanting Crack **VDiff // 8m**
The crack to the right is awkward, yet never difficult.

13» Mutiny Crack **HS 4c // 12m // ✪✪✪**
Classic. After a tough start the route relents with good protection throughout and holds when and where required. Belay close to the holly tree.

Remergence Area : bouldering

1» Arête Problem // 6b
The left-hand prow of the block, starting on the low break. A 6c variation avoids the good hold in the upper break and instead uses slopers just above.

2» Remergence // 6b
Another Peak classic. From painful pockets below the roof, pull over to gain the crescent shaped hold and edges above, before commencing the mother of all rockovers.

20m to the right of the **Remergence** wall is the delightful **Tiny Slab**.

3» 4
The left-hand side of the slab.

4» 5
Just left of centre.

5» 5+
Just right of centre.

6» 6b
The awkward right-hand edge of the slab demands excellent technique.

Paul Firth on Bilberry Crack (VDiff) **photo :** John Coefield

Ash Tree Wall

14» Wall Corner **HVD // 10m**
The juxtaposition of a corner within the arête provides a blocky route with a big feel.

15» Ash Tree Wall **S 4a // 12m // ✪✪**
A classic of the edge, the line of least resistance meanders up the *Ash Tree Wall*, starting at the polished fist-sized crack in the centre. Trend left to the chunky flake and follow this to the open upper groove.

16» Ash Tree Crack **VDiff // 12m // ✪✪**
The line is obvious, the level of physical exertion required perhaps less so. Well protected throughout the big crack is deservedly popular.

17» Bilberry Crack **VDiff // 12m // ✪**
The next crack right swallows up good gear before a steep finish above the large ledge.

Adam Coefield on Cleo's Edge (5+) **photo** : Dave Parry

Safe Bet Area : bouldering

Andy Banks on Safe Bet (6b+) **photo** : John Coefield

1» Cleo's Edge // 5+
A superb arête with a tricky start.

2» Roof Goofe // 6b
Looks easy doesn't it? Climb the small roof to a demanding mantelshelf.

3» Pocket Passer // 5+
Pop to the pocket and continue more easily.

4» Jetty Bulge // 6b
Somehow climb the bulge to the right.

5» Safe Bet // 6b+
A classic spook-fest. Layback the left-hand side of the highball arête.

Hollyash Wall

18» Green Crack **VDiff // 12m // ✪**
As honest as the day is long; good protection, good climbing – what are you waiting for?

19» Hollyash Crack **VS 4b // 12m // ✪✪**
A good companion to the previous route, particularly if you're in search of more of a challenge. Approach it from the outside, get inside it – it's up to you.

20» The Knight's Move **HVS 5a // 14m // ✪✪✪**
Bottom of the grade, this is a good route for a VS leader keen to move to the next level. Follow the large pockets at the left-hand end of the big roof to a flake line and continue directly – and ever so slightly to the right – through the upper bulges and cracks.

21» Great Crack **VS 5a // 14m // ✪**
Ensuring your arms and legs aren't exposed, disappear behind the huge holly tree. Follow the crack to the roof, traverse out to the lip and romp up the upper crack.

22» The Big Chimney **HVD // 12m // ✪**
Follow the wide fissure to the capping stone and escape right. A leftwards finish is S 4a.

23» Big Chimney Arête HS 4b // 12m // ✪
Good protection compensates for the feeling of exposure on this delightful arête.

Obscenity Area

24» Brook's Layback HS 4b // 8m // ✪✪
If only the corner crack were longer! Employ whatever tools are at your disposal; swiftly layback or jam like Bob Marley.

25» Obscenity VS 4c // 11m // ✪✪✪
Get stuck into the wide crack. Big gear will certainly come in handy.

26» Amazon Crack HS 4a // 11m // ✪✪
Not the brute its neighbour purports to be, yet still no pushover. Plenty of jams and plenty of gear make this a thoroughly enjoyable outing.

E Also of note is the slabby open corner a few metres to the right; *Long Tall Sally* (E1 5b). Delicate climbing requiring faith in friction, backed up with just enough protection, make the route a common introduction to the Extreme grade (*see page 147*).

Nicotine Stain (6b) **photo :** John Coefield

Nicotine Stain Area : bouldering

1» The Enthusiast // 6a+
The puzzling left arête and wall.

2» Nicotine Stain // 6b
The thin seam up the centre of the wall was previously E1 6b. With pads it's a classic highball test of technique that sees many failures.

Beyond the End Area : bouldering

3» Beyond the End // 3+
The right arête of the small wall is worth the walk.

50m right again are **The Three Bears** with a good selection of easy problems:

4» Daddy Wall // 3

5» Daddy Bear Arête // 3+
Climbed on the left. On the right it is 4.

6» Mommy Wall // 4+

7» Mommy Bear Arête // 4
On the left. On the right it is 3+.

8» Baby Bear Wall // 3+

9» Baby Bear Arête // 3

Sarah Clough on Amazon Crack (HS 4a) **photo :** Nick Smith

VDiff to VS

A selection of routes that ride the rollercoaster from VDiff to VS in five simple steps.

Eastern Grit – Burbage North

The following five routes at Burbage North give an honest progression through the grades on escapades of varying styles. Despite the differences in style, good protection is something they all have in common.

VDiff: Ash Tree Crack
A popular and well-protected blast up a friendly big crack.

HVD: Wall Corner
The blocky arête is never desperate and has ample protection.

S: Ash Tree Wall
The initial crack is tricky but well protected. The blocky upper groove and corner are immensely enjoyable.

HS: Amazon Crack
Sometimes sparse protection restricts you from climbing something that technically is well within your ability. Plenty of gear on this route allows you to focus on, and enjoy, the climbing.

VS: Obscenity
Not the easiest VS on grit, but topping out on this will give you an enormous sense of achievement. Again, well protected but this time with big gear.

Western Grit – The Roaches

The routes at The Roaches, and particularly on the grand **Upper Tier**, tend to vary in style from their cousins on the eastern edges. The big outings described here reward confident leaders with an overwhelming sense of accomplishment.

VDiff: Prow Corner
No nonsense, well-protected climbing up the leaning corner crack.

HVD: Black Velvet
The hardest move on many routes is actually racking up and setting off. Once off the ground, you begin to flow and focus purely on what you're doing. A big line through the right hand side of the **Black and Tans** wall – just rack up and get going. The climbing is HVD and no harder.

S: Hollybush Crack
A good, old-fashioned traditional climb. If you're in a T-shirt, put a long-sleeved top on. Not to protect your arms, but so that you can roll your sleeves up and get down to business.

HS: Damascus Crack
A thinner, more delicate crack than the previous affair. There is still plenty of gear allowing you to focus on the matter at hand.

VS: West's Wallaby
A good well-protected expedition with a little bit of everything. We'd recommend going for the direct version – safe as houses and much more rewarding.

burbage south

The second of two significant edges in the hugely impressive Burbage Valley, Burbage South is world famous for its concentration of cutting-edge traditional routes at the hardest grades, yet it is also home to a concentration of excellent quality crack climbs, upon which this selection is based.

If you're keen to develop your crack skills, then this will be a good laboratory, offering all manner of widths and angles that require varying techniques and levels of tenacity.

As is the case at Burbage North, the rock is some of the coarsest on the eastern edges and is, of course, of excellent quality. Unlike Burbage North, 'the South' faces north-west and therefore receives only the briefest glimpse of afternoon sun. Consequently it can be unpleasant and green after damp weather, but the flipside is that it can provide respite from the sun on warmer, sunnier days.

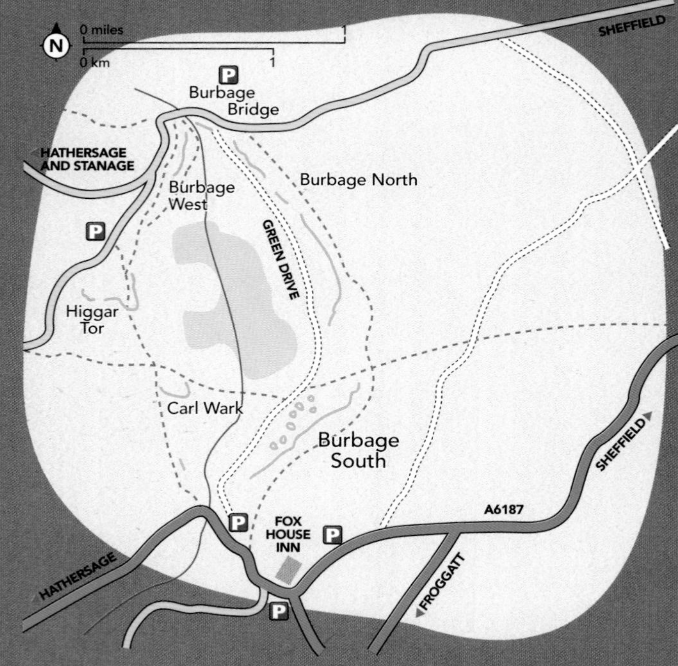

Access

A number of parking options are available, but we would advise you only use the Fox House car park if you intend to be a customer post-climb. The most convenient parking is adjacent to a stile around 200yds up the road from the Fox House. From here follow the footpath directly across the moor. Once arriving at the edge head right with the Northern Quarry the first area reached.

Simon Wilson on Problem 26 (5+) **photo :** Adam Long

the **routes**

The Tower

Cracks, cracks, cracks. You should be getting pretty good at them after this little lot!

1» Every Man's Misery VS 5a // 6m // ✪✪
Alliteration aside, the short slot succumbs to a self-assured, single-minded leader set on a slippery, yet successful squirm.

2» Roof Route VS 4c // 8m // ✪✪
Visually appealing, the climbing doesn't disappoint on this sustained, yet well-protected, corner crack.

3» Gable Route HVS 4c // 8m // ✪✪
A wonderful excursion up the right-hand side of the buttress, taking in the wide crack and upper arête and slab.

4» Charlie's Crack HVS 5b // 10m // ✪
Found the other routes OK? Our hardest in the area begins with a tough, well-protected start up the arcing crack and is complemented with delightful moves on the upper arête.

5» Tower Crack HVS 5a // 12m // ✪
The excellent steep crack leads to a ledge and the well-protected, exhilarating finale.

photo : John Coefield

The Keep

The tall, brooding prow is flanked by two tall crack lines:

6» Brooks' Crack **HVS 5a // 14m // ✪✪✪**

A big, sustained route and ultimately very rewarding.

7» Byne's Crack **VS 4b // 14m // ✪✪✪**

A good crack-climbing exercise at the grade. The right-hand crack will feel easier for the more proficient jammers out there but is well-protected for all.

The Staircase Area

A good little area with four contrasting routes.

8» Reginald **VS 4b // 9m // ✪**

Ooh you are awful! More cracking (!) fun in the deep recess.

9» No Zag **HVS 5b // 8m // ✪**

The initial crack is steady, the continuation perhaps less so...

10» The Staircase **HS 4b // 8m // ✪**

The big Lego block wall has a tricksome move at half height unless you are on the tall side of short, in which case it will feel easy. Shorties fear not, the move is well-protected and the alternative to the big reach is an over-too-soon stylish layaway.

11» The Drainpipe **HS 4b // 9m // ✪✪**

Straightforward, honest climbing up the crack system in the corner.

Central Section : bouldering

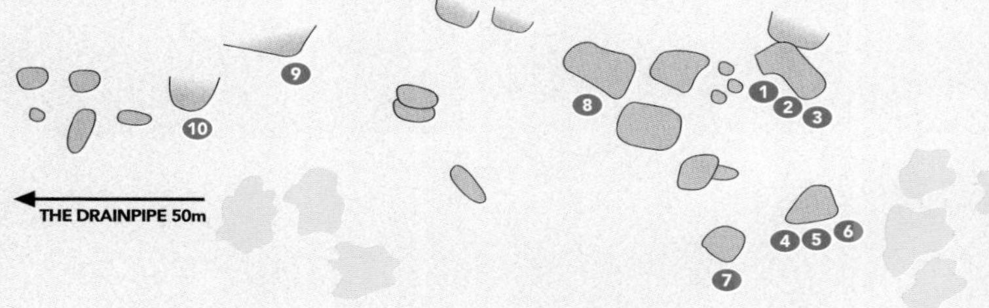

1» 7 Ball // 6c
Sit start right of the groove and traverse up and left into the groove and rib.

2» Middle Wall // 4+

3» Corner Pocket // 6a
The arête. A low start is 6b.

Just below the edge is an easy-angled slab:

4» 5+
Just right of the left arête, avoiding the arête and groove.

5» 5
The centre of the groove.

6» 4
The right-hand side of the slab.

7» 4
The arête to the left. From sitting it is 5.

8» Curving Crimps // 6a+
The wall left of the arête requires some steely pulls.

9» Birch Tree Arête // 6a+
A superb arête.

10» Scratcher Sitdown // 6b+
Tackle the front of the small block front-on from a sit-down start.

Andy Grieve on David (HVS 4c) **photo** : Mike Robertson

David and Goliath Area

The larger crack in the centre of the buttress is *Goliath*, but it's also E5 unfortunately.

12» David
HVS 4c // 8m // ✪✪

Don't worry, appearances can be deceptive – the wide corner fissure is not as tough as it looks, although it does require a confident approach for the committing layback.

Northern Quarry

Despite first appearances, there is great climbing to be had in this dark recess.

13» Hades HVS 5b // 11m // ✪

A sustained and technical exercise up the corner.

14» Fox House Flake VS 4b // 14m // ✪✪

A classic of the edge and rightly so. The delightful lower flake crack sweeps up to the finishing corner.

15» Dunkley's Eliminate VS 4c // 9m // ✪

Let's finish with a flutter shall we? Gain the ledge via a variety of starts and enjoy tremendous exposure on the upper arête.

Dean Grindell on Pock Man (5+) **photo** : Ian Parnell

Burbage South Boulders : bouldering

The bouldering found on the fine collection of blocks below the edge is among some of the best in the Peak.

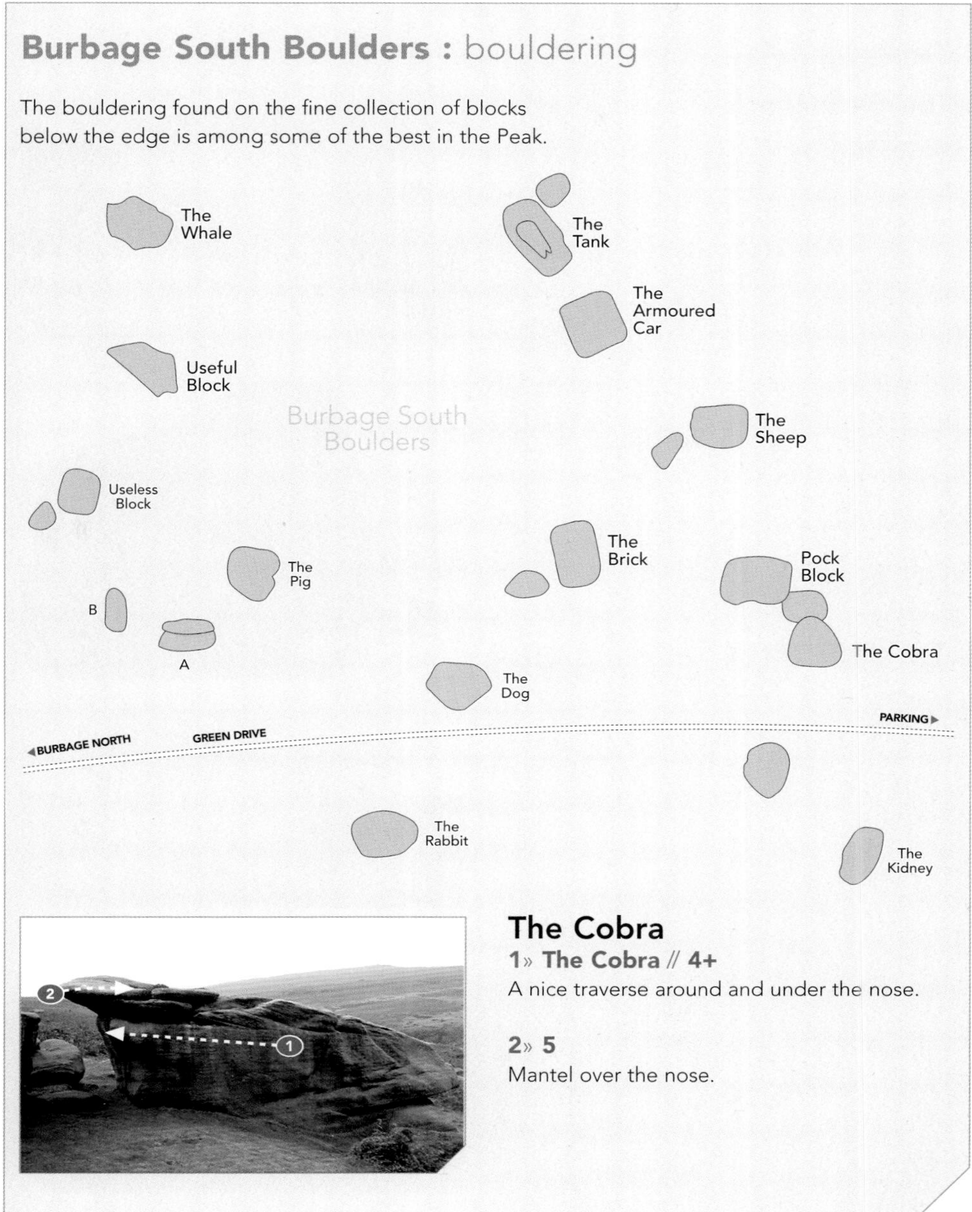

The Cobra

1» The Cobra // 4+

A nice traverse around and under the nose.

2» 5

Mantel over the nose.

Burbage South Boulders : bouldering

The Pock Block

3» Puck // 5+
The blunt arête on shallow dishes.

4» Pock // 5
The centre of the pock-marked wall.

5» Pick // 3+
The arête on large features.

6» Pock Man // 5+
The delicate slab.

7» 3+
Mantel into the slot.

The Brick

8» 4
The arête above the slot.

9» 4
The centre of the wall.

10» 4
The arête.

11» 4+
The slab just right of centre. Slightly left again is also 4+.

12» 5+
The steep double arête on the boulder next to **The Brick**. The centre of the slab to the left is 3+.

Burbage South Boulders : bouldering

The Sheep

13» 5
Layback the arête on its left all the way.

14» The Sheep // 6c+
The curving crack and slopey pocket is a frustrating classic.

The Armoured Car

A good boulder with several problems and variations all around Font 4.

15» 4
The arête and flakes.

16» 5
Traverse the face leftwards from the right arête to rock around the lip at the far end. Two problems can be climbed up the short wall through the traverse at 4+.

The Tank

17» 4+
Sit start the short prow adjacent to **The Tank**.

18» Tiger // 6a
Pull on sidepull pinches and slap the (coarse) top.

19» 3+
The big chunky flake.

20» Panzer // 6b+
Traverse the top of the boulder – left to right.

21» 6a+
Jump to the out-of-reach hold and top out.

22» Chieftain // 5
The delightful rib.

Stephen Coughlan on Chieftain (5) **photo :** David Simmonite

Burbage South Boulders : bouldering

The Useful Block

23» 4+
The short rib. The crack to the left goes at the same grade.

24» 3+
The crack in the front of the slab.

25» 5
The slab is one of the best problems on the boulders.

26» 5+
The sharp-quarried arête climbed on the right.

27» 6b
The wall on crimpy, crumbly edges.

The Whale

28» 5
A rising, rightwards line along the arête/top of the boulder.

29» 5
The wall past a pocket.

30» 5
The wall past the big break.

cratcliffe tor & **robin hood's** stride

The outcrops of Cratcliffe and Robin Hood's Stride should be top of the list if you're keen to pack in a few routes and bouldering in the same day. The boulders on and around Cratcliffe provide a good circuit, with problems that are particularly enjoyable in the lower grades. Once warmed up, dive into your pack and dig out the rope and rack and head down to the crag itself. It may not be laid out before you in the same way as the likes of Stanage or Froggatt, but it is home to several star routes, including *Owl Gully* and *Suicide Wall* – the latter simply one of the best routes in the Peak District.

Also included for interest's sake is the **Inaccessible Pinnacle** at Robin Hood's Stride. Although the summit can be approached by a number of means, we've chosen the *Short Climb* here to provide a point of focus – this is also the original route up the pinnacle. Had a good day? Make sure you head over and summit on this miniature mountain.

The crags can be slow to dry after rain, but the boulders can dry quickly in a fair wind. Be aware that, while it may be raining further north, these popular spots sometimes provide an oasis of dry, if such an analogy is possible!

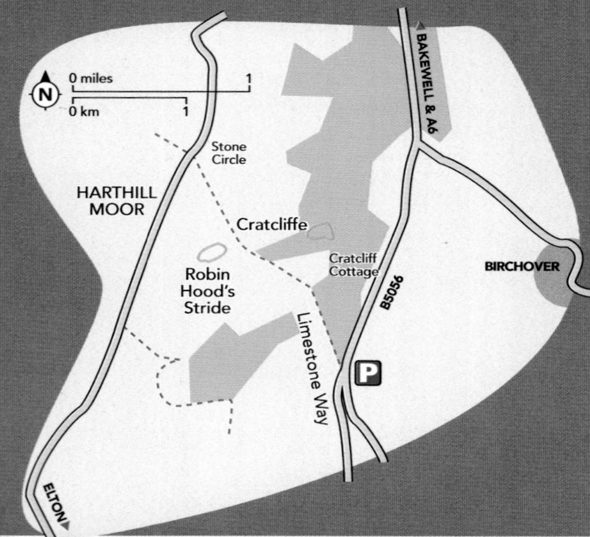

Access

Parking is available on the B5056 between Bakewell and Winster. Be sure your car is well off the road, but be mindful not to block access to the farm. Follow the large gravel track up the hill; Cratcliffe is to your right and Robin Hood's Stride to your left. Continue up the track to the trees and head right or left from here. DO NOT attempt to access Cratcliffe through the farm situated halfway up the track.

Richard Barson on Problem 6 (5+) at Gratcliffe **photo :** John Coefield

the **routes**

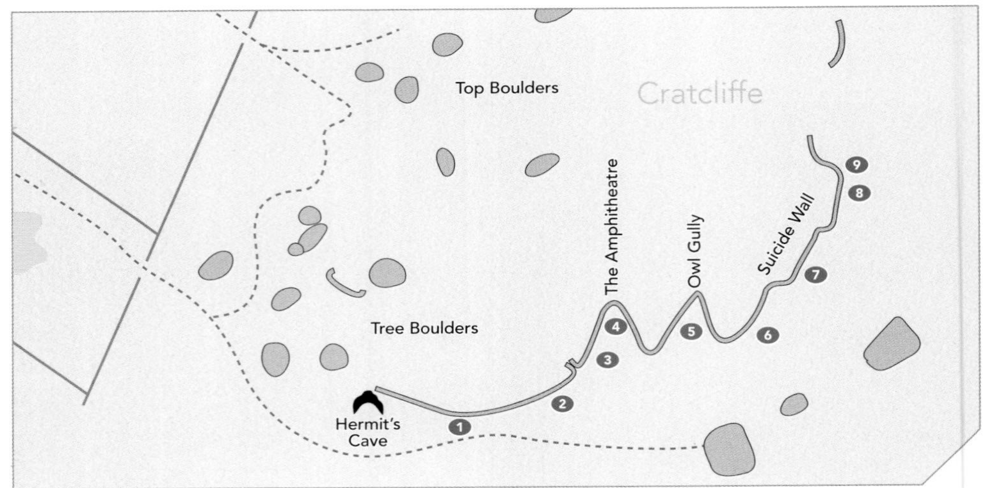

Hermit's Cave Area

The following routes start just right of the old Hermit's Cave.

1» Hermitage Crack **VS 4c // 8m // ✪**

Start at the foot of a large groove (itself *Hermitage Groove*, VDiff) and climb the curving crack rightwards. Descend to the left.

2» The Giant's Staircase **HVS 5a // 18m // ✪**

A series of huge steps, best approached with back-to-back mantelshelves, gives access to a crack and corner. Follow the crack before pulling left onto another step and the hardest mantelshelf of all to finish.

The next route starts from **The Amphitheatre**, accessed by scrambling easily up to the mid-height ledge.

3» Elliott's Unconquerable **HVS 5a // 8m**

A wonderful little jamming exercise up the leaning crack after a tricky, undercut start.

E *Elliott's Right-Hand* (E1 5b) takes the flake and wall to the right of the previous route.

Owl Gully

Further down the hill, **Owl Gully** falls open before you, offering a small collection of quality climbs at all levels. The first route begins to the left of the left arête of the gully.

4» Weston's Chimney **VDiff // 16m**

The corner can be green and slippery, but is enjoyable enough when in condition. A belay stance can be taken before the continuation crack in the right wall.

5» Owl Gully **VDiff // 20m // ✪✪**

The eponymous gully is followed in its entirety to a finish on the right.

E *Fern Hill* (E1 5c) is the most amenable of a number of routes on the gully walls themselves, but is perhaps not a good first E1.

Suicide Wall (HVS 5a) **photo : Adam Long**

Suicide Wall

Not really suicidal at all, the routes here are well protected with superb, exposed climbing on the upper wall. The route of the same name is the best here, and a contender for the best HVS in the Peak District.

6» The Bower, Route 1 **HS 4b // 11m // ✪✪**

A good pitch that climbs to and terminates at the obvious Bower half way up the wall. The easiest finish here is HVS 5a (*Suicide Wall*) and so HS climbers are advised to abseil from the tree, or bivouac there until climbing skills improve enough to continue. Start just right of the arête and gain a flake to the right. From here, make a precarious move to a ledge. Follow this to the slabby corner that is followed to the tree and the The Bower.

7» Suicide Wall **HVS 5a // 30m**

Stunning. It is possible to split this classic into two pitches by taking a belay in *The Bower*, however we'd recommend would-be ascentionists be ruthlessly selfish and lead it in one pitch. Climb the crack and groove through the tree and blast up a short hand-jamming crack to the right-hand edge of *The Bower*. Exhale. Inhale. From here, hand traverse rightwards to the thin crack and layback this to a niche, before pressing on up the wider crack to finish with a flourish over the final juggy lip.

8» Sepulchrave **HVS 5a // 18m // ✪**

Zig-zag climbing up the diagonal cracks in the right-hand side of the wall. Climb a crack and niche to gain the first break and hand traverse this leftwards and eventually back right before getting stuck into the wide finishing crack.

9» North Climb **S 4a // 10m // ✪**

Climb the polished corner to half-height before traversing left to an airy finish up the arête.

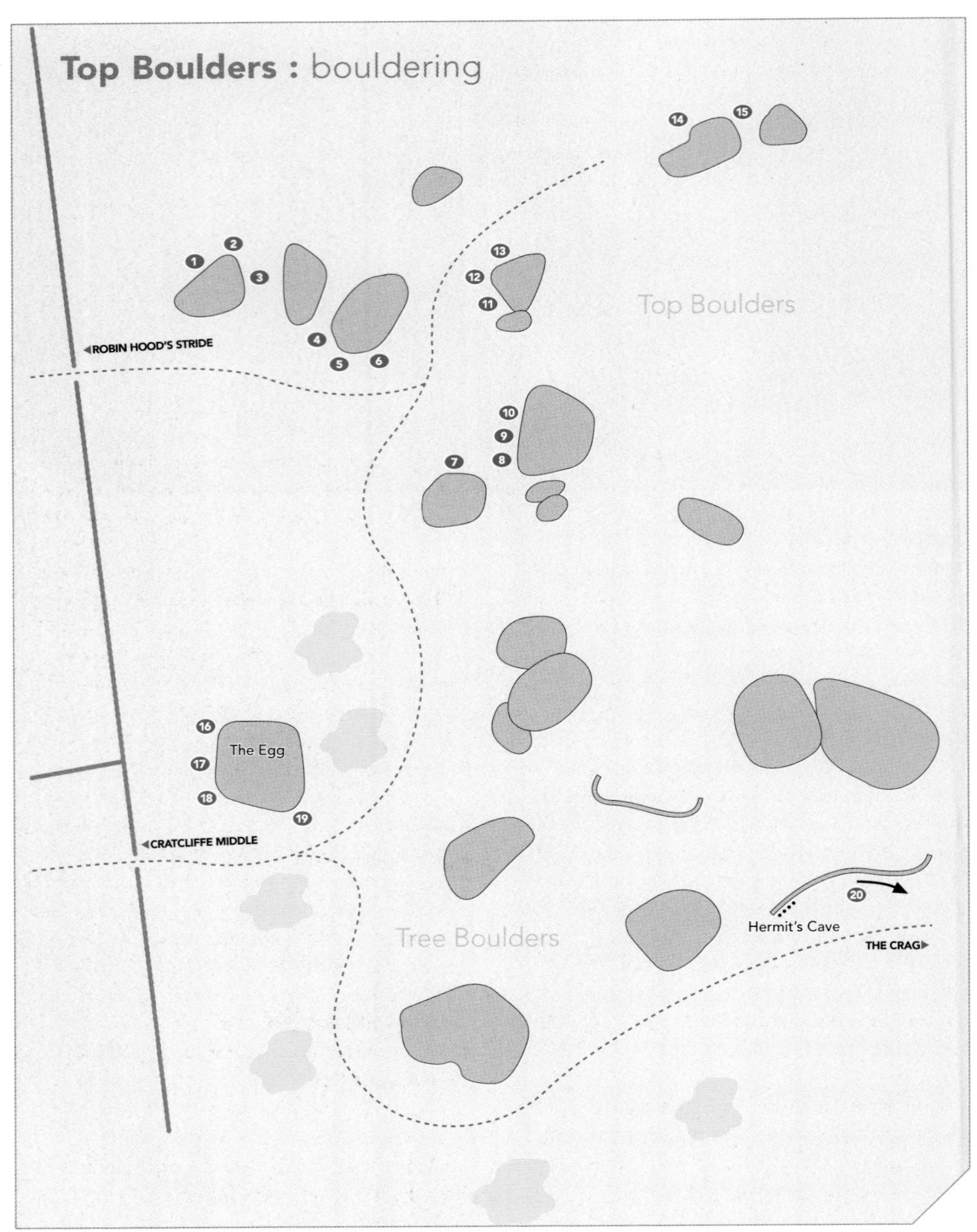
Top Boulders : bouldering
14
15
1
2
3
13
12
11
Top Boulders
ROBIN HOOD'S STRIDE
4
5
6
10
9
8
7
16
The Egg
17
18
19
CRATCLIFFE MIDDLE
20
Hermit's Cave
Tree Boulders
THE CRAG

Located on the main plateau, above the crag, the top boulders offer a good selection of problems with nothing too high from the ground. The landings are generally good and as such it is as good a place as any to start your bouldering career.

1» 3+
The scoop.

2» 4+
The left-hand side of the arête.

3» 4+
Up and at them. Into the runnel.

4» 4
The short flake.

5» 5+
The left-hand side of the arête.

6» 5+
Climb the rib on the left using the delightful next-to-nothing pinch. The grade assumes the left arête isn't used, although it is still an excellent 4+ with the arête. Be warned, this problem can feel/be impossible in warm weather.

7» 4
Pad up the left-trending rampline.

8» 5
The right arête and pocket.

9» 5+
Pockets up the centre of the tall wall.

10» 5
The left-hand side of the slab.

11» 4+
The slab using the chip. It is naturally more difficult without the chip – 5+?

12» 3
The chipped arête.

13» 4
The chipped slab. Try it without the chips too.

14» 6b+
Struggle up the groove.

15» 6b
Sit-start the arête. The footholds are in bad shape, so the grade varies – please don't try it when damp as it will only deteriorate further.

The Egg Boulder

16» 5+
The left-hand slab.

17» 5
The central slab above the scoops.

18» 6a+
Super-classic grit up the blunt arête.

19» 5+
The right arête using the flake.

The Hermit's Cave

Down towards the main crag and routes is the **Hermit's Cave**.

20» 6b
Traverse right from the bars along various natural and hermit-made features.

Emma Flaherty on Problem 34 (6b) at Robin Hood's Stride **photo :** John Coefield

Robin Hood's Stride – The Route!

The following route at **Robin Hood's Stride** is included to add variety rather than being of any great quality.

10» Short Climb **VDiff // 5m† //** ✪

(*†Depending on your classification of 'floor'*)
The original route to give access to the *Inaccessible Pinnacle*, the highest point on **Robin Hood's Stride**. Scramble up the rocky platform on 'top' of the Stride. From here approach the eastern (shortest) face of the Pinnacle and ascend a series of cracks to get stood on the top. **Note that descent is by climbing back down the same way.**

Robin Hood's Stride : bouldering

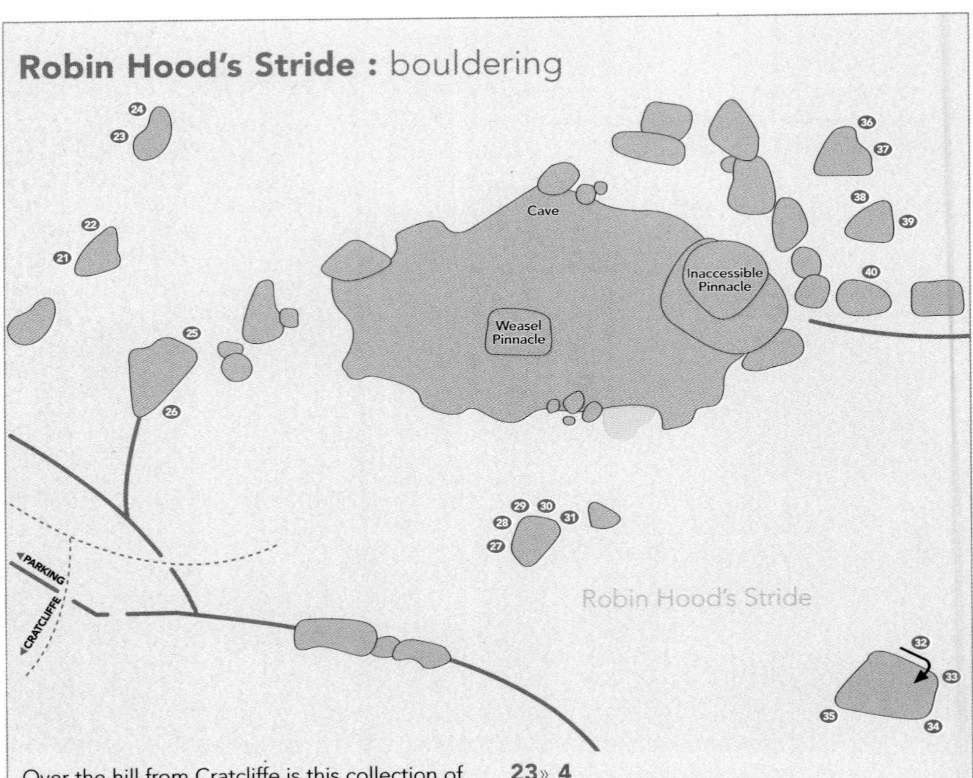

Over the hill from Cratcliffe is this collection of lumpy lumps, piled on top of each other and scattered around the surrounding hillside. The first problems can be found down and left of the stride as you approach from the central track between the two crags.

21» 5
The slab and cracks.

22» 3
The left-hand side of the slab and bulge.

Further left again is another slab.

23» 4
Climb the centre of the slab passing a sloping ledge.

24» 5
The flake and slab.

The large chipped slab up the hill is a pleasant 3. Right of this is a meaty hanging crack:

25» Boysen's Crack // 6c
A classic tussle up the off-width.

26» 6b
The rounded arête just right of the fence.

Robin Hood's Stride : bouldering

Around to the right of the stride is a tall leaning boulder.

27» 6a
Pull on and climb eroding chips.

28» 6c
Undercut the wall to the crack, share and finish. 6a if the left arête is used.

29» 4
The wide crack.

30» 4+
The wall.

31» 4
The wall and arête.

Isolated in the south-west corner is an angular boulder with several classic problems.

32» 5
Pull on at the left-hand side and traverse the slab leftwards to top out up the arête.

33» 4+
The short arête.

34» 5
The classic stepped arête climbed on its right. On the left it is 6b. The short steep slab to the right is 7a if climbed directly.

35» 6b+
The nose feature approached from the hole.

Heading back towards the Stride, and hopping over a small drystone wall leads to the final area.

36» 6a
The bulging arête.

37» 6c
Mantel onto the projecting nose.

The arête to the left is *Jerry's Arête* (7a), started using blobs on the arête and the thin crack in the left wall. Finish by laybacking the left-hand side.

38» 5
A rising line up the right-hand side of the block.

39» 6b+
Pull into the scoop and exit using the right arête. Spooky. 6c+ if climbed directly throughout, or 6a if the left arête is used.

40» 6a
Up and left is a concave wall. Use lovely little gratton crimps to climb this to an involved top-out.

...rbar

Access

Park at the Curbar Gap car park (Pay and Display) or in roadside bays slightly down the hill (the latter more convenient for the bouldering). A wide track runs along the top of the crag with smaller paths dropping down to the various buttresses. The bouldering is most easily approached by walking downhill from the lay-bys and taking a path along the bottom of the boulder field just above Warren Lodge.

The eastern edge of Froggatt continues towards, and ultimately evolves into, Curbar, but with the change of name comes a noticeable change in style. Often taller and steeper, Curbar offers a different challenge and one that will reward the confident leader.

Again, the rock is hard and of excellent quality with peculiar, horizontal pebble bandings occurring in places. Routes to seek out include *P.M.C. 1* (HS) and the bowed fissure of *The Peapod* (HVS). There are also several excellent E1s for leaders confident at HVS wishing to progress into the extremes. We have made reference to these in the text.

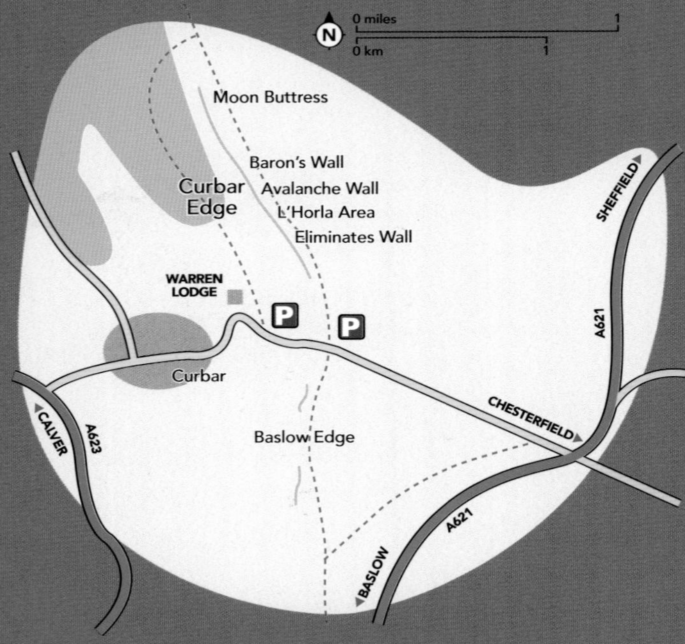

Mick Carron Green Crack (HVS 5b) **photo :** David Simmonite

the **routes**

Moon Buttress

Home to some of the great classics of Peak District climbing. Unfortunately most are classic hard routes, such as the central arête *The End of the Affair* (E8 6c) – very inspirational stuff.

1» Sorrell's Sorrow HVS 5a // 12m // ✪✪✪
Great Scott. Big arms, big ideas, big gear. In fact bring anything you have at your disposal with 'big' in the title for this attractive and uncompromising crack, particularly 'big' effort.

2» Amphitheatre Crack Diff // 8m // ✪✪
The wide crack gives a pleasant layback experience.

Apollo Buttress

This jutting, bulbous buttress houses one excellent VS and overlooks another.

3» Two Pitch Route VS 4c, 4c // 16m // ✪✪

1: From the very bottom of the buttress, follow a large crack to a ledge and traverse rightwards along this to a belay on the right.

2: From here, the finishing crack gives superb jamming.

Below and slightly south of **Apollo Buttress** is a jutting mini-buttress that contains the following route – well worth seeking out.

4» The Brain VS 4c // 18m // ✪✪

Climb the lower slabby wall heading right to the ledge at the base of a groove. From here the traditional finish is straight up the groove, but an alternative finish takes an obvious traverse line to the arête at half-height at the same grade. This finish is highly recommended.

Baron's Wall

The walls in this area were quarried a long time ago, but certainly don't climb like quarried grit. They offer short, sharp technical wall climbs with the first route just left of the narrow gully.

5» Baron's Wall **HVS 5b // 8m // ✪**

A reachy start on the right gives access to the initial crack and the continuation in the upper wall.

The following route is on the larger central wall.

6» Wall Climb **VS 5a // 10m // ✪**

The steep groove is accessed from slightly to the left and then climbed directly.

To the right is a gentle gully, *Calver Chimney* (Mod). The wall to the right is:

7» Calver Wall **VS 4b // 8m // ✪**

A straightforward start gives way to pleasant jamming in the upper crack.

Avalanche Wall

A more noticeably quarried bay provides two of Curbar's finest low-grade routes: *Avalanche Wall* and *P.M.C. 1*.

8» Avalanche Wall **HVS 5a // 12m // ✪✪**

Two cracks split the centre of the wall; follow these in their entirety.

9» Owl's Arête **VS 4b // 14m // ✪**

The prominent right arête of the wall has a tricky section at mid height, but no nasty surprises.

10» P.M.C. 1 **HS 4a // 16m // ✪✪✪**

The cracks in the sidewall lead to a ledge and a possible belay position. From here, head diagonally rightwards up and across the upper wall to an exhilarating finish.

11
12
14
15

L'Horla Area

Although the route that gives this area its name is actually E1, there is enough here to keep the sub-E1 leader busy, including a couple of star HVSs that are the very essence of the big-and-butch style for which Curbar is famous.

11» Slab Route **S 4a // 10m // ✪**

From the centre of the slab, follow the steepening line of shiny holds to a steep exit left of the pinnacle.

12» Bel Ami **VS 4b // 16m // ✪✪**

Follow the steep jamming crack right of Slab Route, before surmounting the pinnacle via the short, exposed arête. Escape off the back.

13» Green Crack **HVS 5b // 10m // ✪✪**

From the ledge, step across the void to gain access to the attractive curving flake. Follow this past poor rests to an easy finish on juggy flutings.

14» Maupassant **HVS 5a // 10m // ✪✪**

Jam the initial crack before getting stuck into the steep upper crack. It is possible to lasso a jammed chockstone, but the effort involved can often outweigh its potential value.

E The route to the right is the E1 *L'Horla*. An awkward groove gives access to a steep and strenuous finish. Solid at E1. Be warned this is not an ideal contender for an introduction to the grade.

Claire Reading on Maupassant (HVS 5a) **photo** : Keith Sharples

Mellee Rafe on The Peapod (HVS 5b) **photo:** Mike Robertson

Eliminates Wall

The biggest section of the crag, sliced vertically by several attractive cracks. The first is the E1 *Left Eliminate*, the next one with the pod-shaped fissure is:

15» The Peapod **HVS 5b // 18m // ✪✪✪**
Super-classic, the pod is gained via a short crack and climbed via traditional back-and-footing chimney technique until it again narrows. The upper crack is awkward, but soon eases. The trick is to know which way to face – many recommend facing the opposite of right…

16» Alpha **HVD // 10m // ✪**
The groovy tombstone is almost the crag's last hurrah before the car park.

Susan Hatchell on Strawberries (6b) **photo :** Ian Parnell

Curbar : bouldering

Trackside

A classic warm-up boulder, and one that remarkably either stays dry or dries quickly after rain. In addition to the problems listed below, there are also some fun escapades around the back.

1» 6b+
The crack and various pockets lead upwards, or not. The arête/prow to the right is the frustrating but classic 7a *Trackside*.

2» 5
The crack.

3» Strawberries // 6b
This can feel easy or impossible, regardless of the abilities of the climber. Lay and press off the thin, discontinuous cracks.

4» 4+
The wall right of the pockets.

5» 5+
The left-hand side of the front face using the pockets.

6» 5
The short crack from the low break.

7» 5+
Around the arête, past the ledge, is a short wall. Mantel up past the slot. With the arête it's a 4.

8» 4+
Link the lower flake into the smaller, upper flake.

9» 3
The crack.

10» 3
The right-hand side of the short arête.

Fiona Fullwood on Mini Prow (5). **photo**: John Coefield

Curbar : bouldering

Gorilla Warfare Slab

11» The Arête // 4
The same grade on either side.

12» The Slab // 4
The slab past the crescent hold.

13» The Groove // 3
The leftward-leaning groove is great. It is also possible to traverse right-to-left above the lip, finishing up the arête, at about 5+.

Further up, you'll find the dirty, dank pit of **Gorilla Warfare** – a great first 7a which starts sitting on the large flake in the centre and traverses right along spikes to a smile shaped sloper above a large block before topping out. The large crack is *Off width*, about 5.

Mini-Prow Boulder

14» Mini Prow // 5
The prow.

15» Mini Crack // 3+
The crack.

16» Mini Arête // 3
The arête.

17» Mini Traverse // 6a
Traverse the thin back wall around the front and finish up *Mini Prow*.

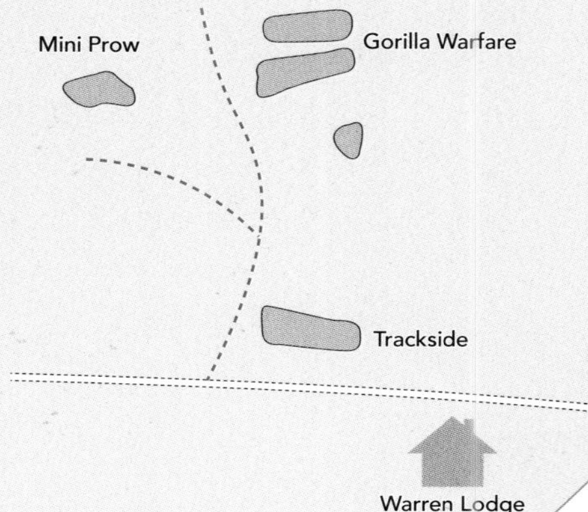

the next step

Adam Coefield on Jerry's Arête (7a) **photo :** John Coefield

font 7a

Springboard into the Font 7s.

A selection of 7a's to try now that you are a seasoned rock gymnast.

01 » The Green Traverse **7a** // ***Stanage Plantation***
Warning: This will feel like the living end until you do it. Practice the middle move, keep persevering and the link will come.

02 » Trackside **7a** // ***Curbar***
A Curbar testpiece, many rock over on the heel, Others prefer to use a toe...

03 » Hamper's Hang **7a** // ***Stanage Apparent North***
Perhaps lacking in line, but a Peak rite of passage nonetheless. **Tip:** The big pebble on the lip is less useful than appearances suggest.

04 » Gorilla Warfare **7a** // ***Curbar***
Super classic, steep sideways yarding.

05 » Jerry's Arête **7a** // ***Robin Hood's Stride***
A tricky start with an exciting finish. One of the best.

froggatt

Access

The crag is best approached from roadside parking close to a series of bends on the B6054. You'll find it shortly after the Grouse Inn, if you're approaching from Sheffield, or shortly after you emerge from the ascent through trees, if you've approaching from Calver. If there is no space beside the road, then an additional car park can be found down a minor road, just before the Grouse, heading back towards Sheffield. The approach on foot takes approximately 20 minutes – look out for the Pinnacle Boulders directly above the Valkyrie Area.

Classic grit, Froggatt continues the brand of quality gritstone climbing that meanders south along the eastern edges of the Peak District. With Stanage, it is probably one of the primary reasons climbers visit the national park.

A pleasing mixture of natural and quarried gritstone, Froggatt is big on variety, which bodes well if you're a developing climber keen to polish your technique. The quarried rock at the right-hand end is among the first in the Peak to dry after rain, due to its exposed nature and the sun-trap potential. However, the flip side is that on anything approaching a summer day, Froggatt can be HOT.

Get involved in pure, bold gritstone padding on *Sunset Slab*, or gather your marbles and focus your energies on more complex challenges, such as the delightful *Tody's Wall*, or the room-for-two multi-pitch experience on the fabled *Valkyrie*. Regardless, you will not be disappointed after a day out here.

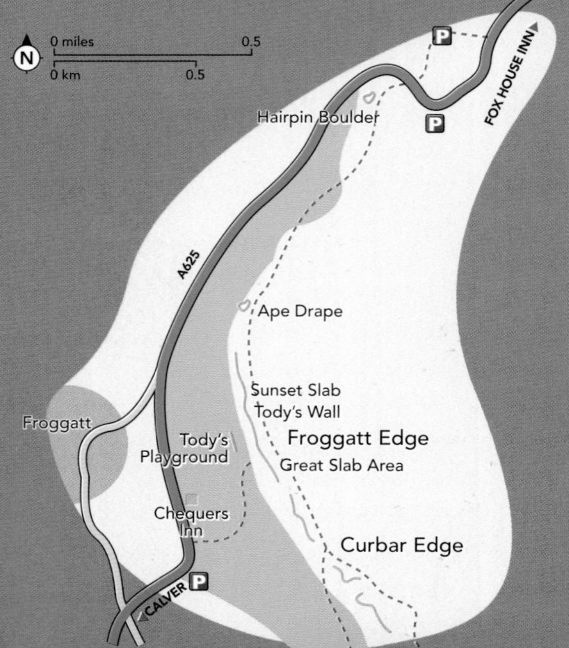

Dieter Cole on Chequers Buttress (HVS 5a) **photo** : Adam Long

Peter Rolls on Sunset Slab (HVS 4b) **photo :** Pete O'Donovan

Sunset Slab

The first three routes can be found on the famous (or infamous) **Sunset Slab**.

1» North Climb **HVD // 12m // ✪**

A good, honest challenge up the left-hand crack. This route is over 100 years old!

2» Sunset Slab **HVS 4b // 14m // ✪✪✪**

As bold as a bull's onions, this route is proof that routes can be far more mentally difficult than physically difficult. Start up the crack, just right of centre and trace it back left as it slowly fizzles into the ramp line. Pad delicately up to the blunt flake system and layback this with increasing exposure.

3» Sunset Crack **VS 4c // 12m // ✪✪✪**

You can now place all the gear you didn't use on the previous route. The crux is low, passing the bulge, but the route will hold your interest above.

Tody's Wall

4» Heather Wall **S // 16m // ✪✪✪**
A superb jamming experience. Access the wonderful upper crack from the tricky low section.

5» Tody's Wall **HVS 5a // 18m // ✪✪✪**
There's a bit of everything on this essential Peak HVS. From the centre of the bay, gain the protruding block and somehow stand on it. An unlikely move from here (face right) will grant you access to the upper slab and delightful finishing crack.

Today's Playground : bouldering

A wonderful spot, located underneath the path that runs below the crag. The finishes are high, but are all equipped with big jugs. Endless variations are available for the keen.

1» 4
Climb the wall behind the tree.

2» 5+
Gain the upper flakes from the blank wall below.

3» 4+
Climb directly to the pocket, finishing on jugs.

4» 6a
Use poor edges in the centre of the wall to reach good edges and eventually jugs above. Finish left or right.

5» 5
Use small flakes to gain the upper rail.

6» 5
Gain the big flake from directly below.

Richard Mayfield on Pitch 1 of Valkyrie (HVS 5a, 5a) **photo** : Keith Sharples

The Pinnacle

Home to one of two famous multi-pitch routes of the same name (the other is at The Roaches). Do them both and decide for yourself which is best!

6» Valkyrie **HVS 5a, 5a // 20m // ✪✪✪**

Excellent multi-pitch climbing, with two wonderfully contrasting pitches. Descent from the pinnacle is by a short abseil down the back from the big summit ring.

1: Jam the rightward-slanting crack to the horizontal ledge and shuffle right to a solid but awkward stance on the arête.

2: Step right from the belay and head for a short crack (good gear). Head back left to a crux mantelshelf before the easy upper slab.

7» Diamond Crack **HS 4b // 8m // ✪✪**

Advance your jamming up the crack system in the bay right of *Valkyrie*. Tiring, but well protected.

The Pinnacle : bouldering

Underneath the **Valkyrie Pinnacle** is a couple of problems on the quarried walls, while a wonderful set of low-grade problems on freestanding natural boulders can be found on the plateau above.

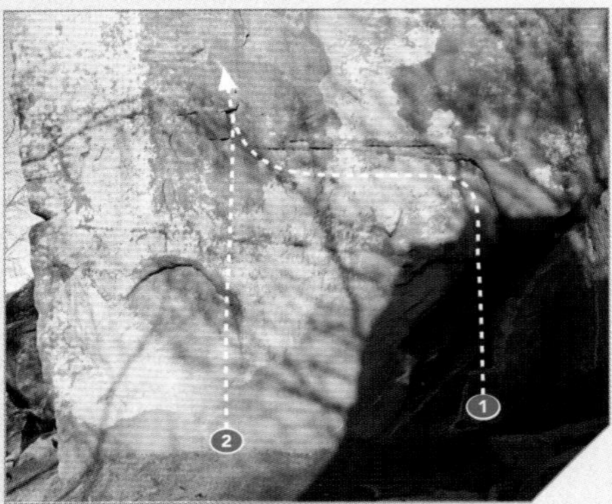

1» Oedipus Traverse // 6b
From the cave on the right, traverse the thin break leftwards to finish on the flake. Jump off.

2» Oedipus Direct // 6b+
Climb directly to the flake from the curving arch. Tough for midgets. Jump off.

Pinnacle Boulders

A good spot for beginners. The first problems are on the lone boulder nearest the track.

3» 4+
The left side of the blunt arête. The right-hand side comes with a 'no fun' alert.

4» 4+
The pocketed wall finishing over the bulge.

5» 5+
Climb through the scooped recess.

6» 3+
Easy ledges.

7» 3+
The rippled wall facing the edge.

8» 3+
The blocky arête. The small steep wall to the right on little holds goes at the same grade.

9» 4
The rippled groove.

The following problems are found on the two blobby boulders closer to **the Pinnacle**.

10» 5
Sit-start on diagonal jugs beneath the nose of the lower boulder and pull out to fine flakes on the upper boulder.

11» 5+
From a sit-start on the shelf, pull up to smaller flat holds.

12» Come Together // 4
The fabulous fissure.

13» 4+
Climb the left edge of the crack.

14» 5
The groove left of the arête is excellent.

The Pinnacle : bouldering

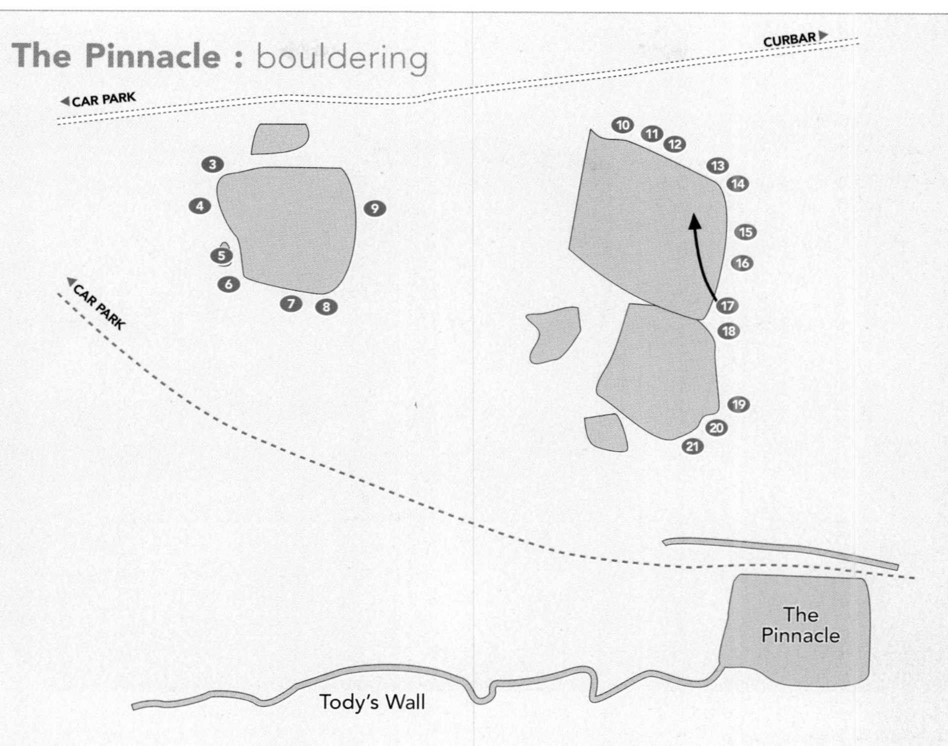

15» 6a
The bulge just left, with an awkward high step.

16» 5
The small seam is lovely.

17» 3
The gentle ramp. Also doubles as a way down, so beware oncoming traffic.

The final problems are on the second of the two blobs.

18» 4+
Mantel over the low nose. Through the easy section of the roof just left is 4.

19» 5
Traverse the lip of the roof leftwards to finish up the next problem.

20» Air Bear // 4+
The excellent crack.

21» 4+
The wall to the left on flat holds.

Great Slab Area

Home to Froggatt's most famous offerings: infamous, hard-and-high slab routes that are unfortunately all too often the recipients of top-roping. The first group of routes is found on the left-hand section. Try each one in succession and push your grade.

8» Slab Recess **Diff // 16m // ✪✪**

Climb the cracks to the right of a short wall (**Joe's Slab**) before trending left to the terrific flake in the centre of the face, which leads all too soon to the top.

9» Allen's Slab **S // 16m // ✪✪**

From the same start as the previous route, continue a little further up the crack system, before breaking out along the attractive rising crack to the right. Finish on good holds before the next crack along. The crack all the way is *Gamma* (VDiff).

10» Trapeze Direct **VS 4c // 12m // ✪✪**

An easy initial crack leads to a bulge (crux). Empty your rack into the crack and get involved – don't worry – jugs await! Finish more easily.

11» Nursery Slab **Mod // 10m**

The next crack system to the right is blocky and polished in places, but also good practice for the novice.

Joe's Slab : bouldering

Another little playground that features three quite contrasting problems. To descend, reverse the blocky twin cracks right of the slab (the start of *Slab Recess*).

1» The Arête // 6b
Harder than it looks. Success usually revolves around a mantel of the slight bulge, using the arête as and when required.

2» Joe's Original // 6a
From flat holds right of centre, move up to another before working left to gain and finish using the large crescent feature.

3» The Undercuts // 6b
Take a very direct line right of *Joe's*. Avoid **a)** the crack and b) any holds near *Joe's*. Build your feet above the lip, and using the small undercuts, get into a position to jump for the ledge. Then jump.

The following two boulder problems are also worthy of note:
Leggit (6b) is a thin slanting crack line found in a bay down and left of *Sunset Slab*.

Ape Drape (6c+) is a classic sideways shuffle found on a steep block before the beginning of the crag proper, or about 50m before the classic *Strapadictomy*, if you have a definitive guide handy.

Green Gut Area

A short distance further on the quarrying steepens in angle. The first right-angled bay on the left is home to the famous *Brown's Eliminate* (E2 5b) and several more moderate offerings, including:

12» Green Gut
HS 4a // 14m // ✪✪✪

Superb climbing straight up the corner crack.

13» Pedestal Crack
HVS 5a // 14m // ✪✪

The first crack to the right is a sterner challenge, particularly passing the roof at three quarters height.

Chequers Buttress

14» Chequers Crack HVS 5b // 12m // ✪✪✪
Tough. One of the hardest routes in this book. The finger crack in the lower half is the crux, with much easier jamming in the upper half.

15» Chequers Buttress HVS 5a // 14m // ✪✪✪
Follow the ramp to the right before taking on the sidewall diagonally leftwards to a crux sequence that gets you established on the arête. Follow this to finish in a fine position.

16» Solomon's Crack VDiff // 12m // ✪
Follow the ramp as for **Chequers Buttress** but instead continue into the wide upper crack.

17» Janker's Crack HS 4b // 10m // ✪
From the low crack enter the upper crack with difficulty, and often a little blue language.

18» Janker's Groove VS 4c // 10m // ✪
Start as for the previous route but head right and enter the right hand groove/crack line.

faith in friction

photo : John Coefield

Disclaimer: Don't worry, this tutorial is almost entirely free of SCIENCE, even though we do have cupboards full of evidence waiting to be unleashed on the climbing community.

Friction FAQ

We should all know what friction is – if not, reach for the dictionary. But how does this relate to the merry rock dance we insist on doing?

Friction in climbing basically takes the standard to its extreme. It's the force we generate between our shoes and hands, and 'The Rock', how 'sticky' it feels and consequently how easy things feel. Certain factors commonly have an adverse effect on friction, including:

- rain;
- sweat;
- rain;
- hot weather;
- dirty boots;
- rain;
- confidence.

Unfortunately, rain, rain and rain are something we get a lot of in Blightly and there is very little we can do about it other than going climbing indoors (see page 314 for a list of local climbing walls). However, we do have options with regard to the other factors.

Rock boot rubber is designed to provide extremely high friction on rock. If shoes are dirty, their ability to adhere to the rock is significantly reduced. Furthermore, dirty boots can accelerate polish on popular routes as bits of muck stuck to the boot quite literally grind away at the rock surface.

For our sweaty hands, climbers commonly now use chalk (magnesium carbonate), introduced into the sport in the '70s by legendary American boulderer, John Gill. Gill was a gymnast by training and was more than familiar with the practice of using the white stuff to improve grip for gymnastic activities.

In common with rain, rain and rain, hot weather limits the number of venues we can climb at. To overcome this, we can choose venues that catch the wind or are in the shade. A winter's day at Wimberry, for example, can feel as though even hell has frozen over, yet when Stanage is baking in the midsummer sun, the former, with its exposed, north-facing aspect and propensity to catch the wind will be a sound bet. When grit is too warm and slippery, limestone will most likely be in good condition, so Stoney, Staden or one of the sport climbing venues might be worth considering.

Climbing without holds

Voilà! The basics. The buzz of grit, and indeed the rock's 'X' factor, stems from Homo sapiens' ability to ascend rock when there is almost nothing to hold onto!

Here are a few classics to seek out to test to the limit your faith in friction:

- *Sunset Slab*, Froggatt – ultimate, heart-in-mouth, low-grade, slab padding
- *Hargreaves' Original Route*, Stanage – pad and mantel your way up the breaks, and don't lean back!
- *Rib Chimney*, Hen Cloud – oppose the sides with all your might, and all your back, and all your everything else
- *Herford's Route*, Kinder – the friction is the only thing stopping you falling off, seriously
- *Sifta's Quid*, The Roaches – a route where friction actually hinders upwards progress
- *Flight Exam Right-Hand*, The Roaches Skyline – good introductory smearing on immaculate rock

photo : John Coefield

lawrencefield

A warm, friendly atmosphere makes Lawrencefield a popular venue on all but the hottest of days. Much of the climbing is concentrated around the picturesque Pool Area, which is convenient as this provides an excellent base for a day out at this crag.

As is the case with much of quarried gritstone, the rock lends itself to positive climbing on angular features – corners, arêtes – with a plentiful supply of crack systems that will waste no time in gobbling up your rack.

It is worth noting that the crag can be hot to the touch on anything approaching a summer day as the main pool area receives little wind and is directly in the sun. Furthermore, and like neighbouring Millstone, immediately after periods of heavy rain the rock – and particularly the cracks – can become very sandy. Just something to watch out for.

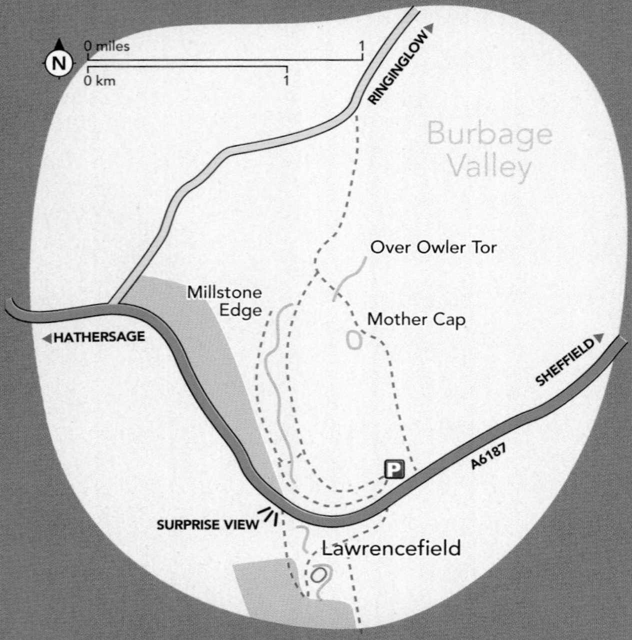

Access

The most convenient parking can be found at the Surprise View Pay and Display, located on the A6187. This can be busy on weekends, particularly if the weather is remotely good and/or during holiday periods.

From the car park, walk back towards Surprise View corner. Cross the road, cross over a stile and follow the path towards the valley. A path leads down the side of the main pool area, depositing you at the left-hand routes first of all.

Crag-top belays

Note that many of the belay anchors at the top of the crag are provided by the refurbished fence posts set some way back, or by iron stakes buried in the ground around the Pool Area.

Jon Winter on Meringue (HVS 5a) **photo :** Ian Parnell

the **routes**

The Pool Area – Left

The first routes are located on the left-hand walls as you face the large pool and back wall that dominate the quarry.

1» Summer Climb HS 4b // 15m // ✪

Climb the large stepped corner with good protection throughout.

2» Three Tree Climb HS 4b // 21m // ✪✪

Follow the groove system before veering right, just below the top to finish up a crack around the arête.

3» Pulpit Groove VDiff // 27m // ✪

A smashing excursion across much of the left wall.

1: Start as for the previous route and trend diagonally up and right through the groove system to a good thread belay in the pulpit.

2: Step out of the pulpit and follow the scoop to a large shelf and a final belay at the tree.

E Before the next route, the thin, finger crack of *Great Peter* (E1 5c), is a strenuous, sustained test of crack technique. It is well protected and is worth bearing in mind if you're 'on one'.

4» Great Harry VS 4c // 21m // ✪✪✪

A Lawrencefield classic. Jam and bridge the wide corner crack, passing the pulpit, to finish up the final corner. Take care topping-out as there is some suspect rock.

The Pool Area – Back Wall

The back wall is home to a number of stern, extreme challenges and one excellent VS.

5» Excalibur VS 4c // 21m // ✪✪✪

An outstanding lead, the upper section in particular being an absolute delight. Climb the grassy groove before embarking upon the well-protected corner crack.

Dave Landman on Limpopo Groove (VS 4b) **photo** : Ian Parnell

Gingerbread Slab

A popular buttress, the friendly slab can be busy with top-ropers on nice weather weekends. Once atop the slab, escape can be made up a chimney at the left-hand side.

6» Limpopo Groove **VS 4b // 9m // ✪✪**
The groove is a little polished but is well protected, so fear not.

7» Gingerbread **VS 4c // 9m // ✪✪**
The precarious left edge of the slab was HVS in a previous life. Gear arrives at half height, but be prepared for a flutter.

8» Meringue **HVS 5a // 9m // ✪**
The thin crack is a tough nut to crack, particularly the slippery start.

9» Snail Crack **HVD // 18m // ✪**
No surprises on the blocky crack line. Finish up easy rock. A good route for beginners.

10» Nailsbane **VDiff // 20m**
The leftward-leaning crack line finishes as per the previous route.

millstone

Access

One of the tallest crags on grit, Millstone is the place to be if you're after big routes with plenty of exposure. Furthermore, drink in the views over Hathersage and the Hope Valley on a spring or autumn afternoon and it is the finest cure for any malaise.

Like the vast majority of quarried gritstone, Millstone is angular, lending itself to climbs that pursue a variety of striking features: arêtes, corners, cracks. The climbing is generally excellent, with good honest moves and good protection throughout.

The positive nature of the climbing and the holds will perhaps feel less alien to the traditional 'slope' found on other gritstone edges, but this is often balanced out by a leader's ability (or lack thereof) to jam competently on many of the cracks.

The most convenient parking can be found at the Surprise View Pay and Display located on the A6187. This can be busy on weekends of good weather, and particularly during holiday periods.

From here, walk back to Surprise View corner and pick up the track that runs directly to the crag from the corner. There was once a time when you could park directly beneath the routes!

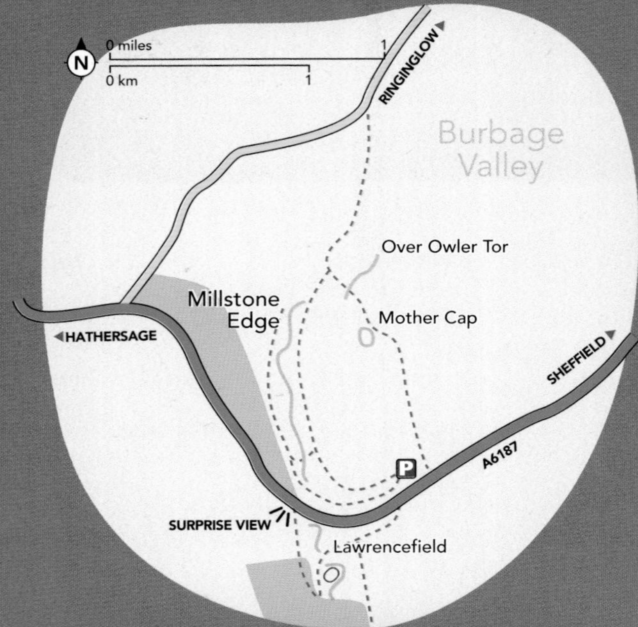

Crag-top belays

Note that many of the belay anchors at the top of the crag are provided by the refurbished fence posts set some way back, or by iron stakes buried in the ground.

John Sharratt on Bond Street (HVS 5a) **photo :** Mike Robertson

the **routes**

North Bay

The far (northern) end of the edge gives the first group of routes. It is worth bearing in mind that the edge becomes less busy the further you head along it from the car, so if you're keen on escaping the crowds around the Embankment, then you know what to do.

1» Estremo
HVS 5a // 16m // ✪✪
Set into the corner is an attractive wide crack in the left wall. Polish this off before whizzing up the corner to finish.

2» Plexity
HVS 5a // 22m // ✪✪✪
Great! A big route with sustained interest. The steep lower crack leads to a niche where the upper crack above the overhang is reached by heading right and then back left above the lip.

3» Remembrance Day
VS 4b // 20m // ✪
Jam the wide crack in the corner passing a ledge at two-thirds-height.

The Cioch

Around the corner from North Bay is a friendly bay with a selection of cracks. Well-pegged in their previous lives.

4» Supra Direct HVS 5b // 20m // ✪✪

The line up the Cioch was once heavily pegged – now providing space for fingers. Follow the crack to the ledge and finish more easily above.

5» The Hacker VS 4c // 20m // ✪

The smaller pegged crack to the right of the previous route curves to a ledge and corner. Follow this before climbing the upper arête, mainly on its right-hand side.

The Great Slab

Perhaps slightly out of place in an environment governed by the right angle, the Great Slab breaks the 90 degree rule, if only for 20 metres.

6» The Great Slab HS 4b // 28m // ✪✪

Follow the angled crack in the slab to a precarious move to reach the half-height change in angle. A wide crack from here leads to the top, where care is required due to occasional loose rock.

Twikker Area

The crag maintains stature, but the slabs disappear, proving that the previous area was simply a by-product of a pre-pubescent phase the crag was experiencing at the time.

7» Lyon's Corner House HVS 5a // 30m // ✪✪✪

Interstellar climbing up and around the left arête of the wall. Head up and into the prominent cave, before breaking left for a large ledge. Head left again and follow the arête in a fine position.

Bird Restrictions

Every spring, Millstone is a popular nesting spot for ravens. They tend to nest in the same areas, usually around the Twikker bay. Also, in spring 2007, a tawny owl nested in a route adjacent to Great North Road.

When birds are nesting and restrictions are in place, signs will be placed at the foot of buttresses/routes advising climbers of the situation and requesting that they do not climb in the area.

Great North Road (HVS 5a) | **photo** : Peter O'Donovan

Corners Area

The corners represent the first stretch of the most popular area of Millstone where both the crag and the quarry floor below it open up.

8» Scoop Crack
VS 4b // 32m // ✪✪

A good route, centred around the large multi-tiered wall in the centre of the Corners area. Climb a broken corner in the lower arête of the mid-height ledge, with the possibility of a belay stance on the ledge itself below the final crack up which the route finishes.

9» Great North Road
HVS 5a // 35m // ✪✪✪

A tremendous outing and a must for all HVS leaders. Climb the stepped corner crack system throughout, with a brief pause at half-height.

8
9

Embankment Wall

A slight slab is the initial centre of attention here, although the cracks and corners to the right are equally dominant, both visually and historically. The short arête at the left-hand side of the **Embankment** is also noteworthy. *Technical Master* is a testpiece boulder problem, rated at Font 6b (and English 6b).

10» Embankment Route 2 — VS 4c, 4b // 25m // ∞

1: The twin cracks lead to a belay on the big ledge.

2: Finish up the large corner set back in the upper tier.

E The tall striking crack in the centre of the wall is *Embankment Route 3*, a popular E1 5b with a continuation 5b pitch just left of the finishing pitch of the previous route.

11» Whitehall — HVS 5a // 25m // ∞

The prominent corner at the right-hand side of the *Embankment Wall*.

12» Covent Garden — VS 4b, 4b // 25m // ∞

Messy downstairs, tidy upstairs – like my house.

1: Easy ledges and cracks lead to a ledge to the right of another ledge.

2: From here, take off leftwards across a narrow gangway to join and follow the left arête in a great position.

13» Bond Street HVS 5a // 22m // ✪✪✪

A fine traditional hand-jamming crack, which will be a doddle if you possess this skill. I didn't the first time I did it, but I still made it up. I was trying very, very, very hard though…so think on.

14» Great Portland Street HVS 5b // 20m // ✪✪✪

The big, bottomless corner is reached by a low mantelshelf and then followed with excellent technical climbing. This place really spoils the HVS leader, you lucky buggers.

15» The Mall VS 4c // 22m // ✪✪✪

Route finding is no problemo on the big, open-book corner.

16» Lambeth Chimney HS 4b // 22m // ✪

The broken chimney in the arête is followed to a ledge on the right-hand side. From here, an exposed step around to the left leads to the upper groove, up which the route finishes.

Keyhole Cave

The final area of significance is actually the closest to the car. It's probably worth knocking one off here (a route, not the subject of popular innuendo) before retiring to the pub/café/home/5-star hotel. We'd recommend *Skywalk*, as the upper section is Class A bonkers.

17» Brixton Road VDiff // 20m // ✪

This route is actually on the crusty wall between Lambeth Chimney and Keyhole Cave. Follow the blocky crack to a ledge before heading left to finish with care on some loose scree.

18» Skywalk VS 4b // 25m // ✪✪

Start as for *Brixton Road*, but head right at the top of the initial crack towards the ledge on the arête. Locate your remaining bravado, making sure you don't spill any, and traverse around the arête and across the wall, heading diagonally up and right to finish several metres right of the arête.

19» Shaftesbury Avenue HVS 5a // 20m // ✪

Big country jamming up the blocky crack right of the main wall. Surmount the overlap and continue more easily.

20» Gimcrack VS 4b // 16m // ✪✪✪

Both halves, the initial jamming crack and the upper corner, are equally enjoyable. Care is required when topping out due to some loose rock on the platform.

Millstone : bouldering

There is lots of good bouldering in the Millstone area, including a number of good problems on the edge itself. The bouldering described here, however, is found above the quarry on the large solitary block of **Mother Cap**, and on the blocks surrounding the diminutive **Over Owler Tor**.

Mother Cap

The big blob next to the tourist track. Be prepared for some funny looks…

1» Ink Cap // 4
The juggy arête.

2» Milk Cap // 3+
The crack.

3» 6a
The wall left of the crack.

4» Conan the Librarian // 6b+
The centre of the wall past sloping breaks. Totally classic. Shuffle off right at the wide break/ledge.

5» Blue Cap // 4+
The back arête, taken on its right to a sloping top-out onto the shelf.

Andy Banks on Blue Cap (4+) **photo :** John Coefield

Millstone : bouldering

Over Owler Tor

A wonderful collection of problems, well suited to the low-to-mid grade boulderer.

6» 6b
The front face on poor holds.

7» 3
The arête on good holds.

8» 6a
The technical little wall.

9» 3+
The very positive short arête.

10» The Roof // 6b
A crag classic that struggles out over the roof using a flake, foot-jams, some 'no way' slopers on the lip and plenty of beans for the top-out. A variation also pulls out of the left side of the roof at a slightly easier grade.

11» The Other Roof // 6a
Much more approachable than its neighbour.

12» 3
The left arête of the set of towers.

13» 3+
The crack, using everything (but the crack).

14» 4
The short right arête.

15» 3+
A good one-move wonder using the slot left of the arête.

16» 6b+
A superb problem up the left arête and crack.

17» 4+
A great problem up the right arête, from sitting on the big flake.

18» 4+
Start as for the previous problem but swing right past the big pocket.

crack climbing 101

Like it or not, at some point while out climbing in the Peak or elsewhere, you'll have to use cracks. These will either be beautiful juggy affairs that you could barely describe as cracks, or they may be flanked by big jugs, meaning that only gear – not limbs – goes in the crack itself. However, at some point you'll have to get stuck in, maybe only for one move, maybe for many.

Cracks vary greatly in size, angle and depth. Depth makes more of a difference than you might think. The bottom and top of horizontal cracks can be used as handholds and undercuts respectively, and the sides of vertical cracks can be laybacked like sidepulls. The following gives an overview of some techniques, from little to large, that should certainly come in handy on those big and little splitters.

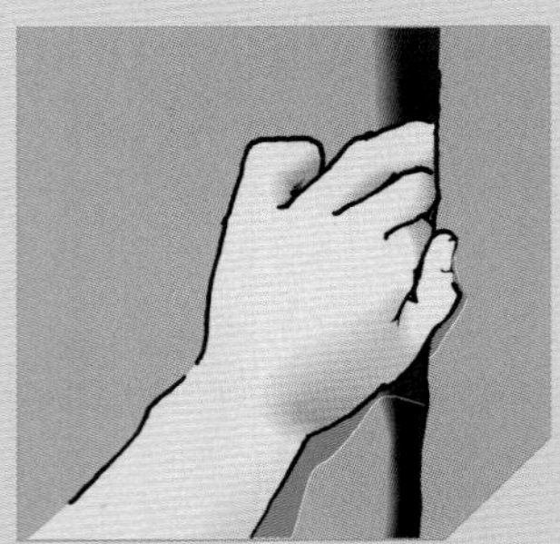

Finger-jamming: My favourite. For those dinky little cracks, particularly peg-scarred cracks such as those at Millstone, the fingers are usually inserted thumbs down. How far they go in will depend on the size of the crack. If there are natural constrictions, such as the bottom of a peg scar, then the fingers should naturally jam in place, otherwise they must be twisted in place.

Try: Camperdown Crawl, Birchen Edge

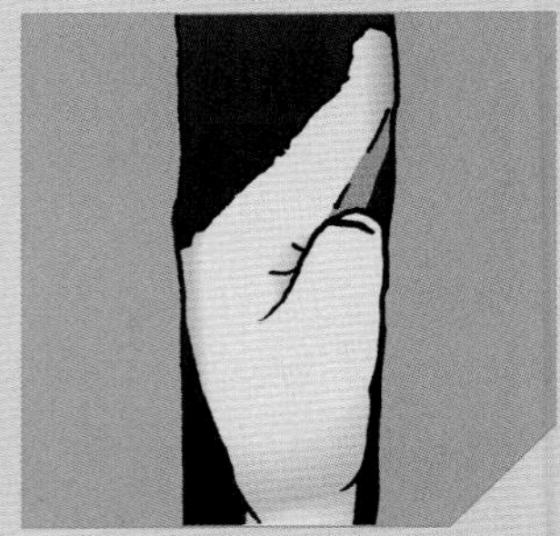

Hand-jamming: Depending on the width of the crack, the hand can be inserted with the thumb alongside the palm, or within the palm as the cracks widen. Hand jams can feel insecure until mastered and those that slip can be painful on the back of your hands. They should be persevered with, however as, in addition to being a good climbing technique, they can prove an excellent means of resting on strenuous routes, as they are less tiring than simply holding on.

Try: Crabbie's Crack, Third Cloud, The Roaches

Illustrations from ***Rock Climbing***, published by MLTUK

Fist-jamming: For slightly wider cracks. Again the hand is inserted widthways with the fingers squeezing to bulk out the hand.

Try: **Shaftesbury Avenue, Millstone**

When finger-jamming, hand-jamming or fist-jamming, the feet can also be cammed into the cracks to varying degrees providing improvised footholds.

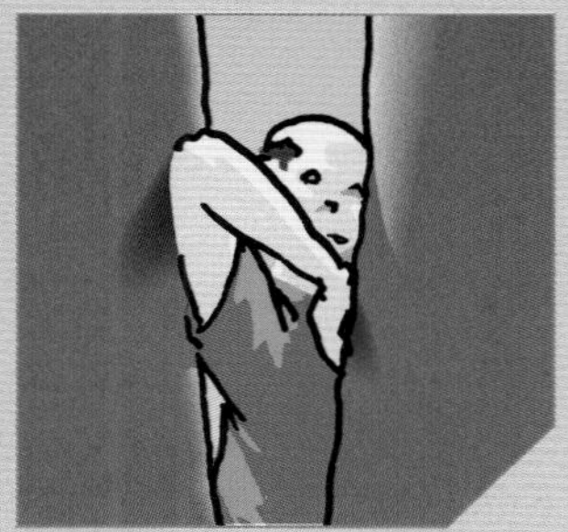

Off-widths: Probably the most awkward of the lot, off-widths are wider than fist cracks and narrower than chimneys, which means that neither fist-jamming nor traditional chimney techniques are remotely useful. Instead, combinations of various techniques, such as stacked jams (one hand jam and one fist jam) and cammed-in legs and arms must be used to aid upwards movement. Arms and legs can be inserted and 'locked in' – the aim being to generate opposing forces between the two sides of the crack.

Try: **David, Burbage South** *Laybacking it is missing the point (but obviously easier)*

Chimneys: When the width maxes out, but you can still reach both sides of the crack, traditional chimneying techniques must be employed. These typically involve inserting the entire person into the crack and again generating force between the opposing sides of the crack. One effective technique is 'back and footing': the back is pressed against one wall and the feet are walked up the other. The hands can be used to support bodyweight as the back is udged up. As the cracks widen to their maximum, up to the point when it would be silly to call it a crack anymore, it can be bridged, as you might a corner, with a hand and a foot on each wall.

Try: **Doctor's Chimney, Stanage North**

rivelin

Barely within the boundary of the Peak District National Park, Rivelin offers a friendly climbing experience along a compact and diminutive edge that peeks through the tree cover as though keeping lookout for its big brothers further down on the more famous eastern edges of Stanage, Burbage and Froggatt. A popular venue if time is short, as it falls within the Sheffield city limits. Indeed Steel City is clearly visible from the edge.

Although the tree cover can become quite dense during the summer months – and midges can be unbearable on still days – Rivelin is a popular sun-trap during the autumn and winter. It provides welcome shelter from the wind and can be miraculously dry while the rain pours at Stanage.

The rock is excellent, fine-grained gritstone and is generally very clean, suffering little vegetation on the more popular routes. The routes vary from bold excursions that require a steady head, to well-protected testpieces where the emphasis can be placed on technique and, occasionally, brute force!

The most notable feature, and arguably the major draw, is the Needle, one of the few free-standing pinnacles on gritstone. The two routes featured on it will reward leaders competent at VS/HVS.

Access

Parking is available in the car park across the dam. Cross over the A57 and the footpath, which meanders up the crag, is visible directly ahead through the wall. Follow this as it bends right, crossing a small stream, to a fork by a yellow waymarker. Head left and emerge at the Needle.

Please note that access is fragile here due to unauthorised tree felling in 2004. Therefore you are strongly advised to stick to marked paths and act responsibly in the woods below the edge. Furthermore, please note that **there is no agreed access to Rivelin for large organised groups, only for small parties.**

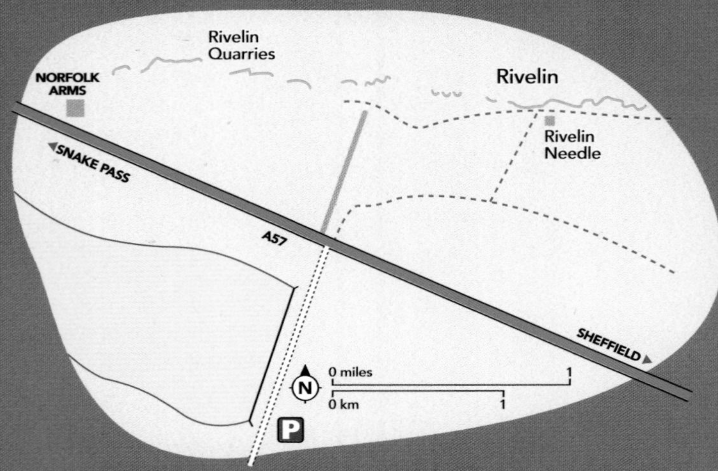

GR **SK279872**

Kim Leyland on Pitch 1 of The Spiral Route (VS 4c) **photo :** John Coefield

the **routes**

Scarlett's Bay

In a friendly and sheltered environment within the trees are these three climbs, with *Rivelin Slab* a potential first outdoor lead.

1» Kremlin Crack HVS 5a // 11m // ✪✪

A tiring route which will reward a confident approach. A splendid mix of jamming, laybacking and big gear are the keys to success.

2» Scarlett's Chimney HS 4b // 11m // ✪✪

Good, albeit perverted, fun up the wide crack to the right.

3» Rivelin Slab Mod // 10m

A good start to the day and a contender for a good first outdoor lead, if you need a confidence boost. Good holds and gear.

Blizzard Ridge Area

The area around the prominent arête yields two fine chimney climbs, in addition to its namesake route.

4» Blizzard Ridge HVS 5a // 12m // ✪✪✪
A bold and technical route that is one of Rivelin's 3 star outings. Gain the arête from the right and follow it on the left to a small nose of rock. Swing right and climb directly to the top.

5» Jonathan's Chimney HS 4b // 11m // ✪
One of the oldest routes at Rivelin has a tough start.

6» David's Chimney VDiff // 9m // ✪
A traditional route, requiring a three-dimensional approach.

7
7
8
7
8

David Norton on Croton Oil (HVS 5a) **photo :** John Coefield

The Rivelin Needle

The following two routes will reward confident and competent leaders. **Note:** Descent from the needle is via abseil from a bulky chain down the short, shady eastern face.

7» The Spiral Route VS 4c // 22m // ✪✪

The original free route on the needle is best enjoyed as a multi-pitch affair, starting from the very base of the needle within the trees (*see page 212 for helpful advice on multi-pitch climbing*). Pitch 2 on its own is also highly enjoyable, with no effect on the overall grade.

1: Climb a wide crack to a ledge and trend up and rightwards to a large platform and belay.

2: From the right-hand end of the platform, traverse rightwards along a horizontal break to a prominent notch. Finish up the hollow-sounding flake above.

8» Croton Oil HVS 5a // 20m // ✪✪✪

The must-do route at Rivelin is within your limit! Climb the previous route to the ledge, but rather than trending right to the platform, continue directly up the face to a short crack and balance leftwards to a flake (crux). Continue up this to the notch and finish as for *The Spiral Route*.

Roof Route Buttress

The following routes can be found approximately 150m further along the edge.

9» Renshaw's Remedy VDiff // 9m // ✪✪

A fun excursion up the large corner with plenty of protection.

10» Roof Route HVS 5b // 9m // ✪✪

The most difficult of the featured routes at Rivelin requires an appreciation of the finer points of hand-jamming (*see page* 104). Amble to the roof and place excellent cam protection in the crack. From here bridge outwards and believe in your jams. Many experienced climbers argue the route warrants E1, so give yourself a pat on the back if you are successful.

11» Root Route S 4b // 9m // ✪✪

A well-protected, yet tough challenge up the inviting corner crack.

Altar Crack Area

A fine clean wall with an impressive corner crack.

12» Altar Crack **VS 4c // 9m // ✪✪✪**

One of the best VS climbs in the Peak District, and a test of any climber's mettle. The corner cries out to be climbed and is well protected, but it won't give up easily. At the top, finish to the right.

13» Nonsuch **HVS 5b // 9m // ✪✪**

Found *Altar Crack* OK? This one should prove a tad trickier, particularly as shopping around for the best grade can earn you E1…

stanage

// North
// Plantation
// Popular End
// Apparent North

Stanage Popular End **photo :** John Paton

stanage

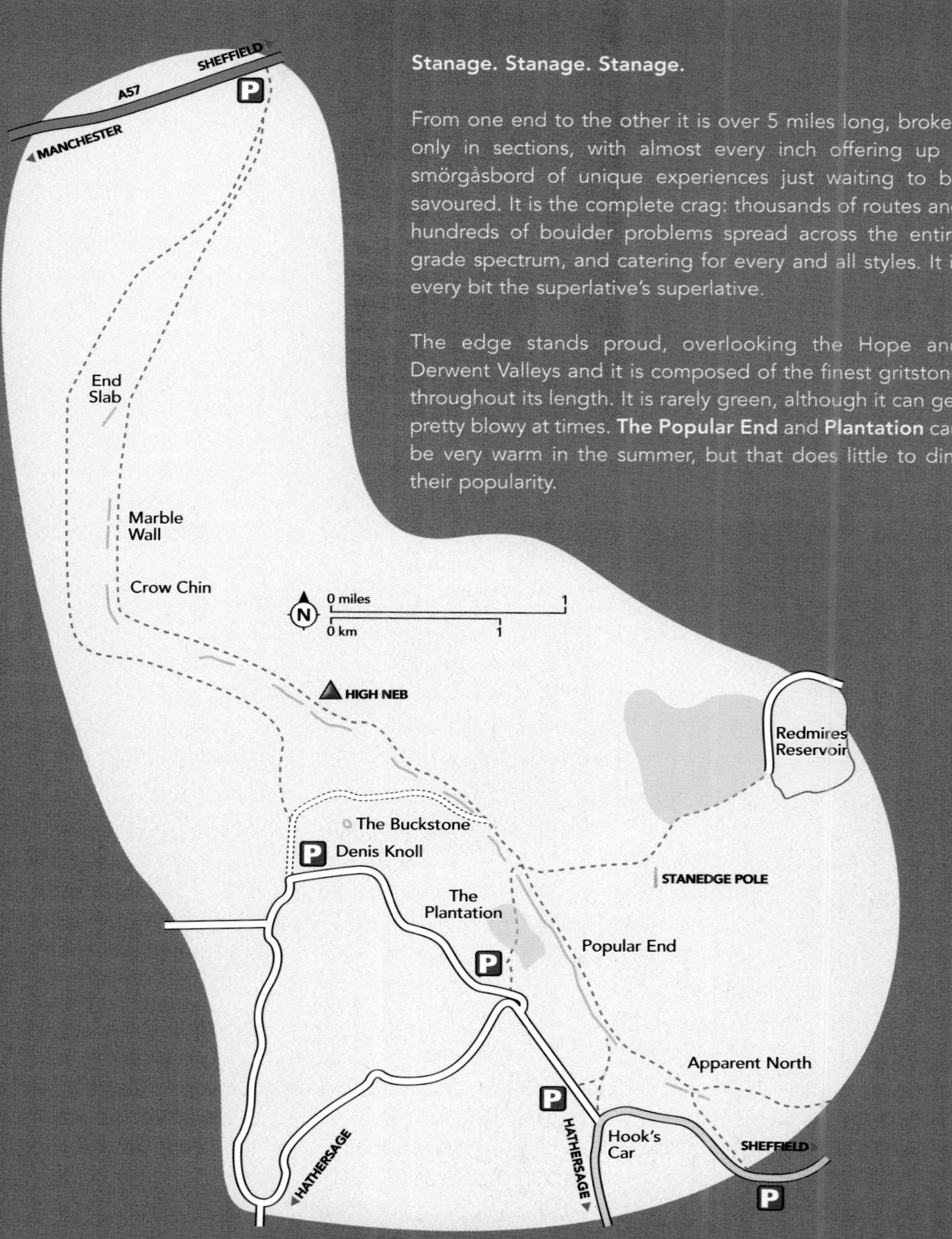

Stanage. Stanage. Stanage.

From one end to the other it is over 5 miles long, broken only in sections, with almost every inch offering up a smörgåsbord of unique experiences just waiting to be savoured. It is the complete crag: thousands of routes and hundreds of boulder problems spread across the entire grade spectrum, and catering for every and all styles. It is every bit the superlative's superlative.

The edge stands proud, overlooking the Hope and Derwent Valleys and it is composed of the finest gritstone throughout its length. It is rarely green, although it can get pretty blowy at times. **The Popular End** and **Plantation** can be very warm in the summer, but that does little to dint their popularity.

stanage **north**

Access

End Slab can be approached from either the small parking area on the A57 Moscar, or from the Denis Knoll/High Neb car park further south. It will take slightly longer from Denis Knoll, while Marble Wall and Crow Chin are approximately half way between the two parking spots. Whichever approach is used, it makes eminent sense to pay a visit to all three areas on the same day for maximum value (and of course come back for High Neb, clearly visible when approaching from the Denis Knoll car park).

In contrast to the crowds that gather at the aptly named Popular End, the northern stretch of Stanage can provide blissful solitude, tremendous views across the Derwent Valley out towards Kinder and Manchester and, of course, excellent rock climbing. Combined with a visit to End Slab, Marble Wall and Crow Chin will provide just the right dose of solitude, adventure and sumptuous rolling vistas – not your regular Stanage experience.

These buttresses are exposed and will tend to get any and all weather going. That said, the breeze may be welcome on a warm day; similarly, the sun may be a welcome sight on a chilly autumn/winter/spring day. The rock is good quality millstone grit and is rarely dirty, although **End Slab** can be green due to the direction it faces. **End Slab** offers pleasant slab climbs, while **Marble Wall**, big and brooding, is home to many classic testpieces. Don't fear, in and among the angles and fissures, there is also a fine selection of mid-grade routes for all abilities, of no less quality than their famous, more trying neighbours. In contrast, **Crow Chin** is a mecca for the mid-grade leader, with a great selection of approachable routes, particularly in the Diff to VS range.

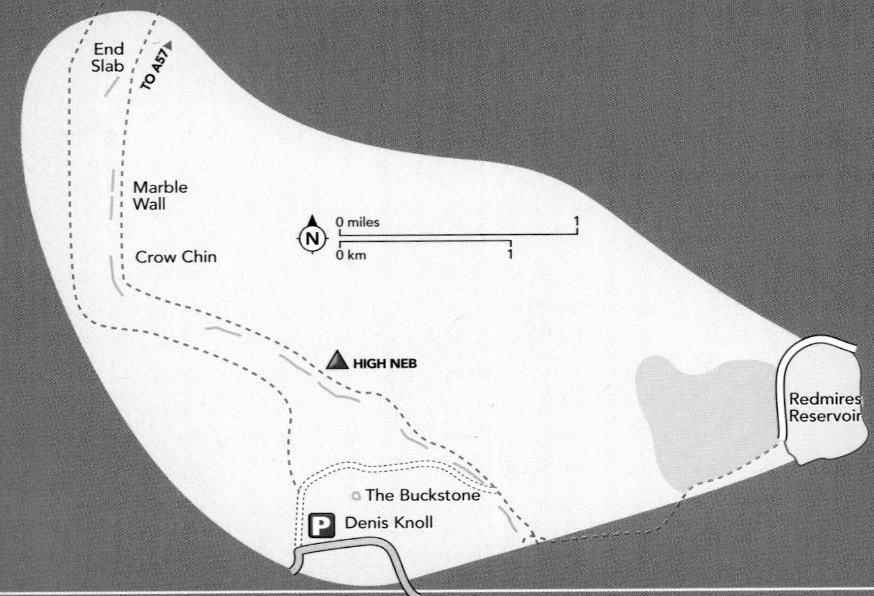

Jon Barton on October Crack (Diff) **photo** : John Coefield

the **routes**

End Slab

The area around the disembodied hanging block of **End Slab** offers a wonderful selection of low-grade routes, fantastic views out over the Derwent Valley and a peaceful environment in which to enjoy both.

1» The Pinion **VDiff // 12m // ∞**

Start just right of the arête and climb directly, before striding right past a hole and onto the bizarre small triangular ledge known as the *'Corbel'*. From here, head up to a break and move right for three metres, before heading up again to finish on the large ledge.

2» The Green Streak **HVS 4c // 14m // ∞**

Climb the slab directly, just left of the cutaway, with wonderful, delicate moves on small pockets.

The next two routes are on the cracked, slabby wall immediately behind **End Slab**.

3» Prospero's Climb **VDiff // 12m // ∞**

Start in the centre of the slab at a crack and follow this to the first ledge. Head left to gain the chunky flake line and romp up this in fine style.

4» The Crab Crawl **S // 11m // ✪✪**
Start below the left edge of an overlap at 3 metres. Climb up to and past it, continuing directly up the slab above.

Surgeon's Saunter Area

The next route is found on the large buttress 100m to the right.

5» Doctor's Chimney **S 4a // 18m // ✪✪**
Access the chimney by first conquering the three metre high pillar that guards entry to it. Once inside, continue directly.

6» Surgeon's Saunter **VS 4c // 20m // ✪✪**
The route after which the area is named. Start up the crack right of *Doctor's Chimney* and traverse the first horizontal break rightwards to access the foot of the upper twin cracks. Jam up these and finish via the left-hand crack.

E *Surgeon's Saunter Direct* (HVS 5b) is a three star alternative that approaches the twin cracks with difficulty from directly below.

7
8
7 8
9

Marble Wall

The angles of **Marble Wall** almost feel out of place on this quiet, moorland stretch of Stanage, but that's not to say we aren't glad they're here. Without them we wouldn't have the jamming testpiece of *Terrazza Crack*.

7» Marble Tower Flake **S 4c // 11m // ✪**
Gain the ledge on the arête (jump?) and traverse left. Exit via the huge flake.

8» Marble Arête **VS 4c // 11m // ✪✪**
Start as for the previous route, but continue directly up the arête with satisfying exposure.

9» Terrazza Crack **HVS 5b // 11m // ✪✪✪**
A jamming testpiece straight up the crack in the centre of the wall.

The next series of climbs is on the right-hand buttresses, over the jumble of boulders.

10» Left-Hand Tower **VS 4c // 18m // ✪**
Ascend the crack on the left of the wall to the tip of the large boulder on the left. Traverse the wide break rightwards around the right arête to finish up the gully wall.

11» Right-Hand Tower **HVS 5a // 16m // ✪✪✪**
The mind boggles. Not a good introduction to grit, as there is nothing here that resembles what might traditionally be defined as a 'hold'. Start at a short crack on the left-hand side of the arête and continue directly up the left-hand wall, before traversing the last break right around the arête to a final tricky sequence.

12» First Sister **VS 4c // 12m // ✪✪**
The thin crack in the sidewall widens as you near the top, and permits good jams.

Jon Barton on October Slab (HS 4b) **photo**: John Coefield

Crow Chin

A great wall when it comes to ticking off a bunch of low-grade climbs in a friendly and peaceful environment.

13» Perforation HVS 5b // 9m // ✪
From a flat block pull through the centre of an overlap and make difficult moves to gain a standing position in the horizontal break. The wall and slab above are much easier.

14» Feathered Friends VS 4b // 10m // ✪
From the blunt rib, veer left before teetering straight up the slab past a thought-provoking flake at half height.

15» Kelly's Crack VDiff // 10m // ✪✪
The well-protected gash dishes out a side salad of crux at half height, but it's low calorie so shouldn't be an issue. The upper crack is still digesting the loose chockstone, which has resisted years of attempted regurgitations.

16» Kelly's Eliminate HS 4a // 10m // ✪✪
A direct line up the centre of the wall to the right. Initially steep, the route eases in angle in the upper half.

17» October Crack Diff // 10m // ✪✪
The wide crack in the centre of the buttress is an excellent introductory route, with good climbing, good gear and sustained interest.

18» October Slab HS 4b // 10m // ✪✪
Climb the right arête of the cutaway before continuing directly up a thin seam in the slab to pass the overlap at its right-hand side.

19» Bent Crack VDiff // 10m // ✪
To the right is a left-facing corner crack. Climb this and the upper groove before trending left around the small overhang to finish.

stanage **plantation**

The second most frequented stretch of Stanage after the Popular End, the Plantation owes its popularity, certainly in recent years, to the boom in bouldering. Indeed, it is home to classic boulder problems of all grades – including some of the best and most famous in the country.

This is also great news for the novice climber, as much of the best bouldering can be found in the lower grades. For those in search of more traditional challenges, there is a fine selection of routes spread across the **Plantation** buttresses, from the charming *Paradise Crack*, to the stern test of *Goliath's Groove*.

It is rarely not in condition; it can be swelteringly hot in summer and midges can make it unbearable – but this is the case for all of the eastern edges. Its exposed aspect means that it dries quickly after rain and is a fair option on a nice spring or autumn day.

Access

Access is easy from the large Pay & Display car park at the foot of the plantation. From here, head up the wide track to the plantation itself. Once through, head left for the *Goliath's Groove* and *Tower Face* areas and right towards *Paradise Wall* and *The Unconquerables*.

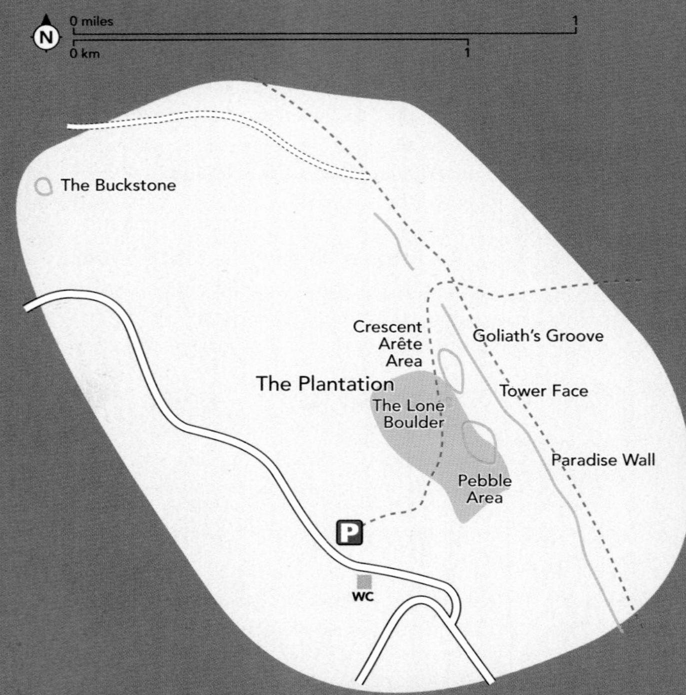

Adam Long on Crescent Arête (5+) **photo** : John Coefield

the **routes**

Goliath's Groove Area

Wallop, we're smacking you on the chin with yet more classics. The area's namesake is the sought-after tick, but the **Hollybush** routes should be at the top of the list too.

1» The Coign **VS 4b // 16m // ✪✪**
A good route, which follows the left arête of the buttress from a start up the crack and arête.

2» Wall End Flake Crack
VS 4c // 20m // ✪✪
Climb a short corner crack and head right to the base of the twin flake cracks. This route follows the left-hand one of these.

3» Helfenstein's Struggle
VDiff // 16m // ✪✪
Climb the large corner to an obstructive boulder. Exit through the hole, or around it at HS 4a.

4» Goliath's Groove HVS 5a // 22m // ✪✪✪
Gritstone at it's best – a subtle blend of thuggy, traditional thrutching on the lower groove, and elegant laybacking and bridging on the upper portion. All well protected.

5» Hollybush Gully Left
HS 4b // 20m // ✪✪
Follow the large corner, using the left-hand crack to gain the easier upper section.

6» Hollybush Gully Right
VDiff // 20m // ✪✪
Access the upper gully by traversing in from the blocks on the right.

Not To Be Taken Away (6c)
photo : Pete O'Donovan

Crescent Arête Area : bouldering

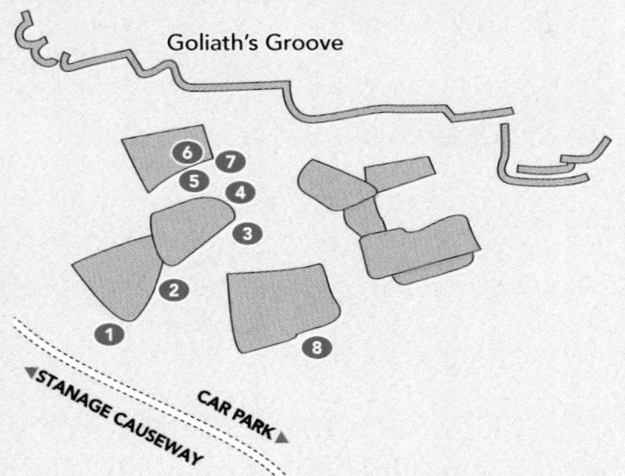

An impressive area, characterised by big, uncompromising lines. Thankfully, there's plenty of stuff closer to the floor too.

1» Crescent Arête // 5+
The classic highball arête taken on its left. Referred to as E1 5b in some quarters… because it is!

2» 5+
Mantel onto the sloping ledge.

3» 5+
The arête on its left. Much easier on the right.

4» 4+
Step onto the short wall from a block.

5» 6a
Climb the groove with a span to a pocket.

6» 4+
The scooped wall just to the right.

7» 4
The shallow angled arête taken on its left.

8» Not To Be Taken Away // 6c
On the large cuboid boulder down below is this classic rising rampline. The start is the crux if you are feeling strong.

Tower Face

The tall main wall is the focus of interest here, with two HVS routes of contrasting style.

7» Tower Crack HVS 5a // 24m // ✪✪

In the sidewall, left of a large hanging chimney (*Tower Chimney*, E1 5b) you will find this stern test of hand-jamming ability. An initial easy crack leads to a small ledge before the meat of the route. Once through the crack, step right onto a ledge and head right into a corner, up to an overhang, around the arête and finish on the ledge above the finish of the next route.

8» Tower Face HVS 5a // 26m // ✪✪✪

A classic wall climb with a delicate and sparsely protected first half and a wonderful, well-protected upper section. Start in the centre of the face and climb to a standing position in the second horizontal break. Tiptoe rightwards to a friable flake just before the arête. Climb this and pull up to reach a traverse line back left to join the excellent finishing flake.

The Lone Boulder : bouldering

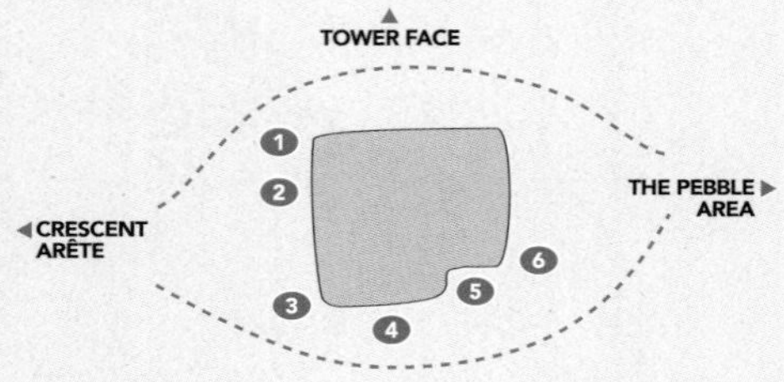

A lovely little boulder on the path between the two bouldering areas at the Plantation.

1» The Lone Slab // 5+

A hard step onto the slab just right of the arête.

2» 5+

The vague groove just to the right.

3» 3+

The arête on the left.

4» 4+

From ledges to the top, reachy.

5» 6a

An awkward groove in the arête.

6» 6a

Mantel over the nose. The wall facing the crag can be climbed at 4.

Pebble Area : bouldering

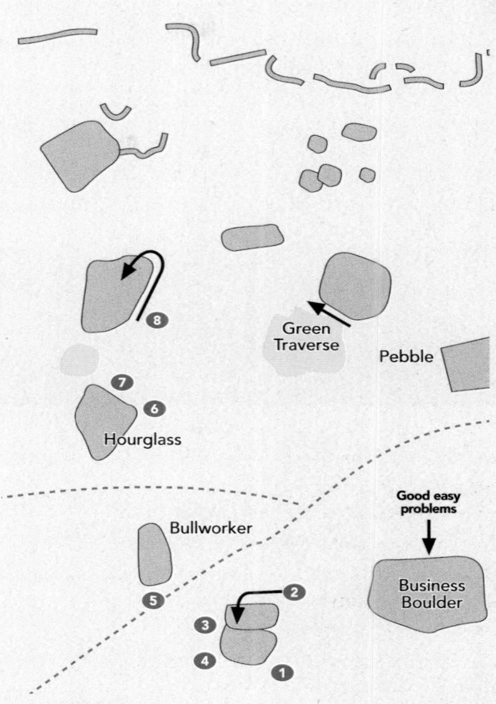

The next jumble of boulders is the main plantation area. The back of the **Business Boulder** provides a pleasant group of problems up to 4+: good for warming up and bolstering your gritstone 'feel'. The groove around to the right is also a pleasant 4 and the slab to the right again can be climbed from sitting at 6a+.

Left of the **Business Boulder** there are two boulders leaning against one another.

1» 5
The crozzly slab on rough holds.

2» 5+
Traverse the low lip from left to right and mantel out. Requires effort.

3» 6a+
The awkward wall right of the groove.

4» 6a
The arête taken on the left with a pop to the sloper.

Just across the path is:

5» The Bullworker // 6b
Hug the double arêtes.

6» Hourglass // 5+
The arête on the right started on the right. 6a+ on the left throughout.

7» 5+
The lovely wall to the right taken on pockets.

8» 6c
A classic traverse starting on the shelf, taking edges and slopes to finish up and around the arête.

Across the way is one of the Peak District's most famous boulder problems: *The Green Traverse*. Some may disagree, but it's also one to try as a first 7a, since all the moves are accessible and hard work does eventually pay off.

The Pebble : bouldering

The large boulder that dominates this area. Descent is by reversing either Problem 9 or 15.

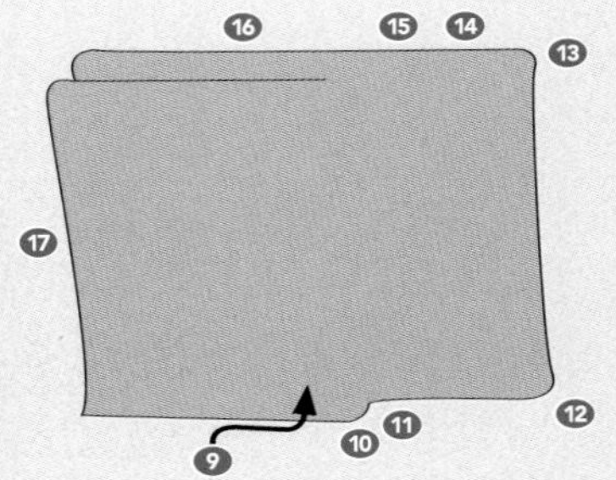

9» Pebble Face // 3+
Gain the ramp from the left.

10» Pebble Flakes // 4+
Gain the ramp from flakes on the right.

11» 6b
Squeeze up the slab just right avoiding the flakes and any ramp.

12» Pebble Arête // 5+
Totally classic. Start on the right and swing around the left or go all the way on the right. All the way on the left is 6a+. The centre of the concave wall is the world famous jump problem, *Deliverance* (7b+).

13» 6a+
The arête taken on its left from a sit down start. 5+ from standing, but it is one of those rare problems that is logical to start from your arse.

14» 4+
The wall just right of the arête.

15» 4
Slightly larger holds just right.

16» 5
The flakes in the centre of the wall. The back wall can be traversed from down and right along the slopey shelves to finish near the left arête at 6b+.

17» 6b
The tall end wall starting up the groove. Highball and excellent.

Paradise Wall

A good clean wall up and right of the main Plantation bouldering area is home to the following two routes, with the nationally significant *The Right Unconquerable* only slightly further along.

9» Paradise Wall **VS 4c // 14m // ✪✪✪**
Climb the twin cracks on the left-hand side of the buttress until they merge and follow the left-hand one to the top.

10» Paradise Crack **VDiff // 14m // ✪✪**
The wide crack in the right-hand side of the buttress.

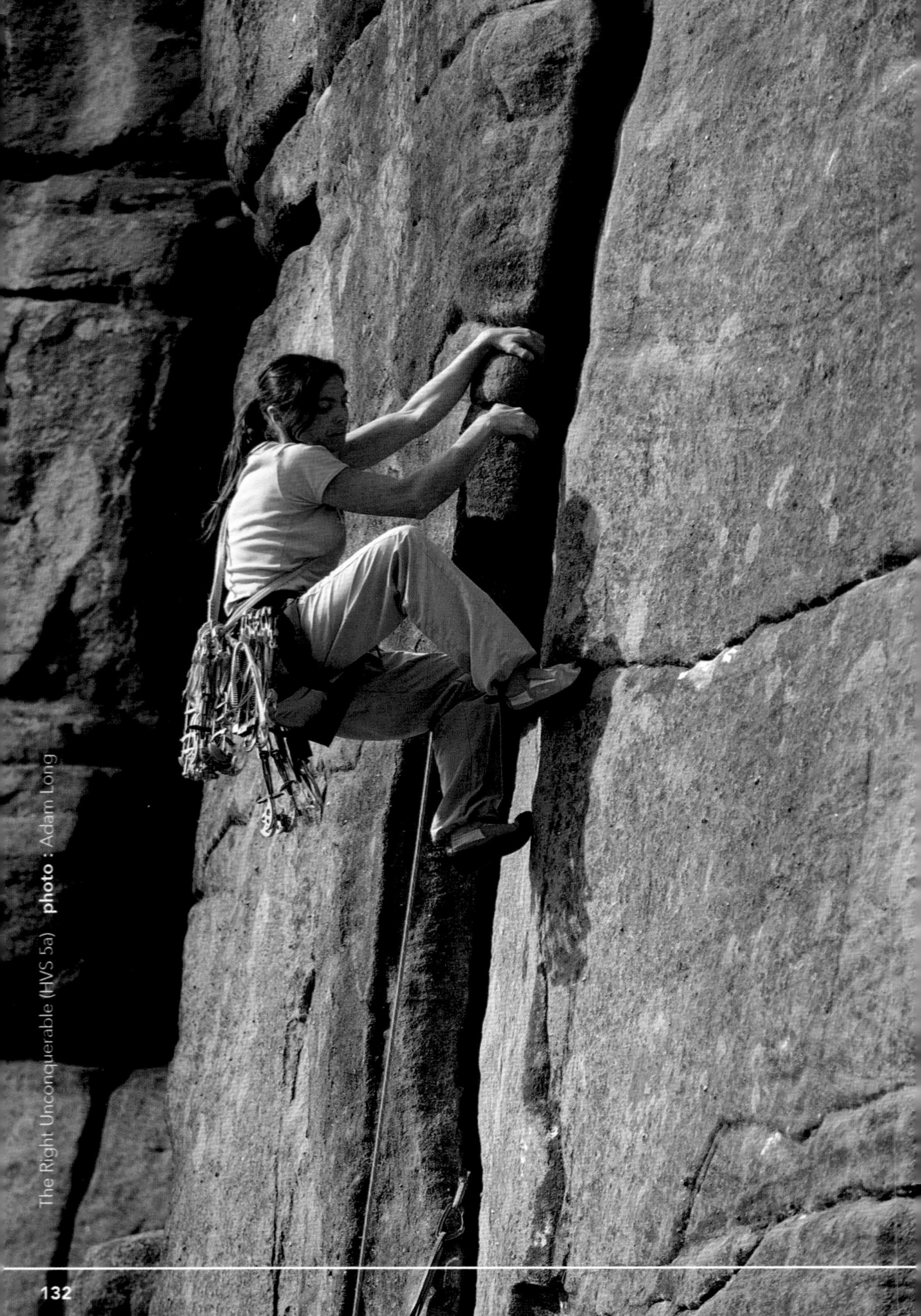

The Right Unconquerable (HVS 5a) **photo :** Adam Long

A short walk leads to:

11» The Right Unconquerable HVS 5a // 17m // ✪✪✪

From the slippery crack in the centre of the face, traverse right to the obvious flake line. Climb this with a clear idea of the shapes you're throwing for the masses below. The crux is passing the nose, although the approved finish straight over the top will have many grazing their stomachs and reaching for the Savlon. An alternative finish heads left to a short crack.

E Continuing up the flake line directly above the starting crack is *The Left Unconquerable* (E1 5b), a steep route, but with plenty of holds and gear.

stanage **popular end**

Access

The Popular End is easily approached from the large parking area at Hook's Car.

Aptly named and justifiably popular, this prominent stretch of "God's own rock", from south of The Plantation to Hook's Car, offers some of the best rock climbing in the Peak District, and indeed the country.

Housing many national treasures, including *Flying Buttress, Hargreaves' Original Route* and *Congo Corner*, the Popular End will never fail to satisfy. To the delight of the mid-grade climber, the majority of the climbing is contained within this grade bracket, with many gems in the VDiff to VS range.

The aspect is open with excellent views and belaying from the top of the crag on a spring or autumn day is bliss. Be warned, the midges do rage here in summer, particularly later in the day, and the wind seemingly has to reach gale force to encourage them to leave Homo sapiens in peace.

The quality of rock here is excellent: hard, clean, well featured and full of life.

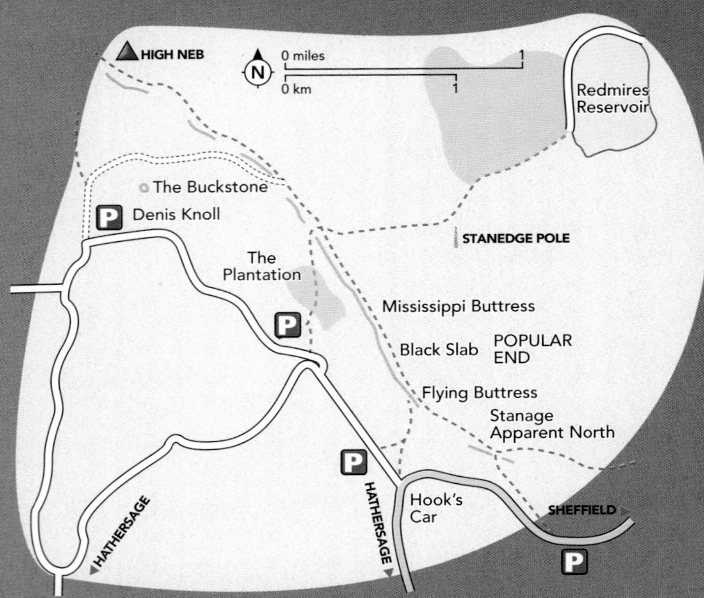

Mississippi Buttress Direct (VS 4c) **photo:** Pete O'Donovan

Katherine Schirrmacher on Congo Corner (HVS 5b) **photo** : Keith Sharples

Mississippi Buttress

The Pearly Gates and the fiery gates of Hell sit hand-in-hand here, playing good cop/bad cop on unsuspecting leaders.

1» Hell Crack **VS 4b // 14m // ✪✪✪**
Bad cop. The bulging crack system in the centre of the wall is climbed directly with the difficulties concentrated around the initial low roof. Jam through this with good protection and enjoy easier climbing above.

2» Heaven Crack **VDiff // 10m // ✪✪✪**
Good cop. Layback the left-facing juggy flakes, savouring every move, every hold. Bliss.

3» Mississippi Chimney **VDiff // 18m // ✪✪**
The large chimney shaft is entered via a short tricky crack. A good first lead.

4» Congo Corner **HVS 5b // 24m // ✪✪✪**
Start up the thin crack directly below the overhangs and climb to a rest beneath them. Traverse left until it is possible to step up and reach a traverse line back right above the overlaps to the arête. Make a crucial high step to a ledge and a final precarious move to a 'horn' and a superb finish.

E *The Link* (E1 5b) is a superb direct variation on *Congo Corner*. Where the previous route traverses left, instead continue through the overhangs on thin flakes, eventually moving back left to rejoin the previous route for the finishing sequence.

5» Mississippi Buttress Direct
VS 4c // 22m // ✪✪✪
The left facing flake line in the centre of the buttress is one of Stanage's classic VSs. Start in the overhanging corner and bridge this to a rest before powering over the bulges and into the delicious upper flake line.

6» Amazon Crack **S 4a // 12m // ✪✪**
The undercut crack has a tricky start, after which the difficulties soon ease.

Twin Chimneys Buttress

A good buttress with a selection of crack climbs, including two particularly good VDiffs.

7» Agony Crack HVS 5a // 12m // ✪✪

The low thin crack in the arête is merely a starter for the main course of jamming through the upper overhang. Well named but often tamed.

8» Crack and Cave VDiff // 18m // ✪✪

Climb the wide crack to the right-hand side of a prominent cave and then step right to finish up the face.

9» Twin Chimneys Buttress HVS 5a // 18m // ✪✪✪

Start just left of the arête and trend rightwards to it on slippery holds. A difficult move from the detached block gains the easier upper section.

10» Left Twin Chimney Mod // 14m // ✪✪

The left-hand fork of the large Y chimney system.

11» Right Twin Chimney VDiff // 14m // ✪✪

Good climbing up the rib right of the chimney leads into the chimney itself at half height.

Robin Hood's Cave Area

A home to climbers for generations, the large roofed terrace of **Robin Hood's Cave** is still an occasional stopover for the more adventurous. If you do spend the night here be sure to treat it with respect and take your rubbish away with you.

12» Cave Gully Wall HVS 5a // 14m // ✪

From jumbled boulders in the gully, climb the concave wall to the left-hand cave, before stepping right to continue up the narrow rib and groove above.

13» Robin Hood's Cave Innominate VS 4c // 14m // ✪

Reach the hanging crack by a thin traverse from the left. Follow this to *Balcony Cave* and head up and right to an easy finish.

E To add a little bit of spice to the previous route, try *Harding's Super Direct Finish* (HVS 5a). From the balcony step left and pull around the roof in spectacular fashion. Finish straight up the wall.

14» Cave Arête HVS 5a // 16m // ✪✪

An excellent route up the left arête of the wide, green gash. Gain the ledge beneath the overhang and make a series of long reaches to better holds and an easing in angle and intent. Climb carefully to the cave. From here, shimmy off right across the top of the wide chimney or through the cave system.

John Daly on Inverted V (VS 4b) **photo** : David Simmonite

Inverted V Area

A collection of excellent routes for the VS leader.

15» Ellis' Eliminate VS 4c // 20m // ✪✪✪

A good route, which will feel loads easier if you're any good at hand-jamming in horizontal breaks. From the left, jam the break out to the arête and climb this on big holds in a great position.

16» Inverted V VS 4b // 22m // ✪✪✪

A superb line, tackling the unmistakable crack and groove. When you arrive at the capping roof (good thread runners) head right and finish up the exposed finishing crack.

17» Robin Hood's Right-Hand Buttress Direct HS 4a // 22m // ✪✪✪

Tackle the initial flake to reach the overhang. Traverse right to enter the sumptuous wide crack and jam blissfully up this. Big gear will come in handy on the upper crack.

18» Bishop's Route S 4a // 26m // ✪✪✪

A good outing that meanders, albeit with great intent, up the right-hand side of the buttress. From the base of the huge leaning flake crack (*Zigzag Flake Crack*) climb left to reach the large ledge. Continue up the corner crack right of the holly to another ledge before a tricky sequence gives access to flakes and a finish directly over the buttress.

19» Zigzag Flake Crack VS 4b // 20m // ✪✪

Bold but never bonkers, the huge leaning flake system is climbed with limited elegance to a ledge where a sprint up the short wall behind provides means of exit.

Hargreaves' Original Route (VS 4c) **photo :** Pete O'Donovan

Black Slab

If you only visit one section of Stanage then **Black Slab**, and **Trinity Buttress** just to the right, will give you as good a taster as any of the classic gritstone climbing hereabouts. Depending on when you visit, you could opt to join the small crowd that meet on 25 December each year for a traditional ascent of *Christmas Crack*.

20» Hargreaves' Original Route VS 4c // 18m // ✪✪✪

A Stanage classic featuring gritstone climbing on large sloping breaks. From a boulder below the face, pull awkwardly up and left to gain the foot of the slab. Move up and right to a ledge in the centre of the face and continue directly trending ever-so-slightly rightwards with height to a steeper finish.

21» April Crack HS 4b // 15m // ✪✪✪

The deep, leaning corner crack gives excellent bridging with excellent protection.

Trinity Buttress

22» Christmas Crack HS 4b // 15m // ✪✪✪

Yule love this one. Direct all the way, climb the groove to access the crack and finish up the awkward leaning corner.

23» Central Trinity VS 4c // 15m // ✪✪✪

Climb the leaning crack to its end and traverse left to the foot of the continuation crack. Slippery jamming and/or laybacking from here leads to an easier finish up the blocky corner.

24» Right-Hand Trinity S 4a // 13m // ✪✪

The sunken crack in the right-hand side of the buttress, with a crux sequence at the overhang at two-thirds height.

Hollybush Crack

25» Hollybush Crack VDiff // 14m // ✪✪✪
The steep corner crack gives excellent bridging and plenty of jugs for the steeper upper section.

26» Queersville HVS 5a // 16m // ✪✪✪
The concave wall gives excellent wall climbing with just enough protection. Start up the projecting arête before trending left up a series of flat ledges. Head back right towards a right-facing flake and make a span for the large ledge above. Finish more easily up the wall above.

27» Leaning Buttress Crack VDiff // ✪✪
The long angled corner crack is climbed in its entirety with good protection throughout.

Flying Buttress

A super classic VDiff with an approachable and exciting relative.

28» Flying Buttress VDiff // 24m // ✪✪✪
Climb the unprotected 'question mark' at the left-hand side of the slab below the overlaps and move left to a ledge before the upper groove system. The bottomless groove is difficult but not desperate to enter. Once in, climb the exposed slab rightwards to finish on whopping jugs.

E *Flying Buttress Direct* (E1 5b) tackles the stacked overlaps in the centre of the roof after the initial slab. Lean out right, before trending back left using heel hooks and bravado, again to finish on whopping jugs.

Manchester Buttress and Heather Wall

The final featured section of the **Popular End**.

29» Castle Crack **HS 4b // 18m // ✪✪**

The slippery corner crack can be bridged, jammed or laybacked – it will likely feel a little awkward regardless of the approach taken. Finish direct or trend right to sustain the interest.

30» Manchester Buttress **HS 4b // 16m // ✪✪✪**

Follow the crack in the arête to a traverse line left, below the overhang. Once left of the overhang, climb up to the next horizontal break before heading back right, around the arête to finish directly above a ledge.

31» Crack and Corner **S 4b // 15m // ✪✪**

Follow the groove in the arête on polished holds to a difficult move left around the overlap into the continuation groove.

32» Heather Wall **VS 4c // 12m // ✪✪**

Steep wall climbing using a selection of horizontal and vertical cracks. Once at the ledge, trend right up the scoop to finish.

the next step

Phil Robins on Embankment Route 4 (E1 5b) **photo :** Pete O'Donovan

E1

Stepping across the void from HVS to E1

A selection of E1s to try if you're quickly becoming the master of the HVS art.

01 » Long Tall Sally **E1 5b** // *Burbage North*
A confident and cool head are required for this delicate friction puzzle which has just enough protection.

02 » Dead Banana Crack **E1 5c** // *Stoney Middleton*
The first few moves are as tough as the proverbial old boots, but get past them and it should be plain sailing above.

03 » Liquid Courage **E1 5c** // *Staden*
Pumpy, but with big holds and good gear.

04 » Embankment Route 4* **E1 5b** // *Millstone*
(*or **3** for that matter...)
Take your finger-jamming to the next level.

05 » Safety Net **E1 5b** // *The Roaches Skyline*
Three star climbing on the Skyline's **Trio Buttress**

06 » The Left Unconquerable
E1 5b // *Stanage Plantation*
If you find the *Right* one OK then go for it!
It's tiring but it's well protected too.

07 » Great Peter **E1 5b** // *Lawrencefield*
A pumpy finger crack, yet not desperate.

08 » Flying Buttress Direct
E1 5b // *Stanage Popular End*
It's all there, there's a safe fall-out zone (not that you'll need it) and it's crying out to be done (heel hooks at the ready).

09 » Round Table **E1 5a** // *The Roaches*
A sensational finishing pitch to a choice of lower routes – *Roscoe's Wall* being the natural link-up.

10 » Easter Rib **E1 5b** // *Stanage Popular End*
Delicate padding up the blunt rib right of *April Crack* with the requisite 'just enough' gear.

stanage **apparent north**

Access

So-called because it *appears* to be the northern end of Stanage – in fact it is the southernmost edge – Apparent North offers a range of good bouldering split between boulders and buttresses. All styles are catered for and it can provide a welcome break from the crowds at the Plantation on a busy day, even though it is only a 5-minute walk from the car.

Apparent North is a good bet on a summer day when seeking shade and wind, and it is fairly quick-drying after wet weather thanks to its exposed aspect.

Follow the road up from the Hook's Car parking at Stanage and park in the lay-bys on the right. The edge is clearly visible and is no more than a 5-minute walk from the car.

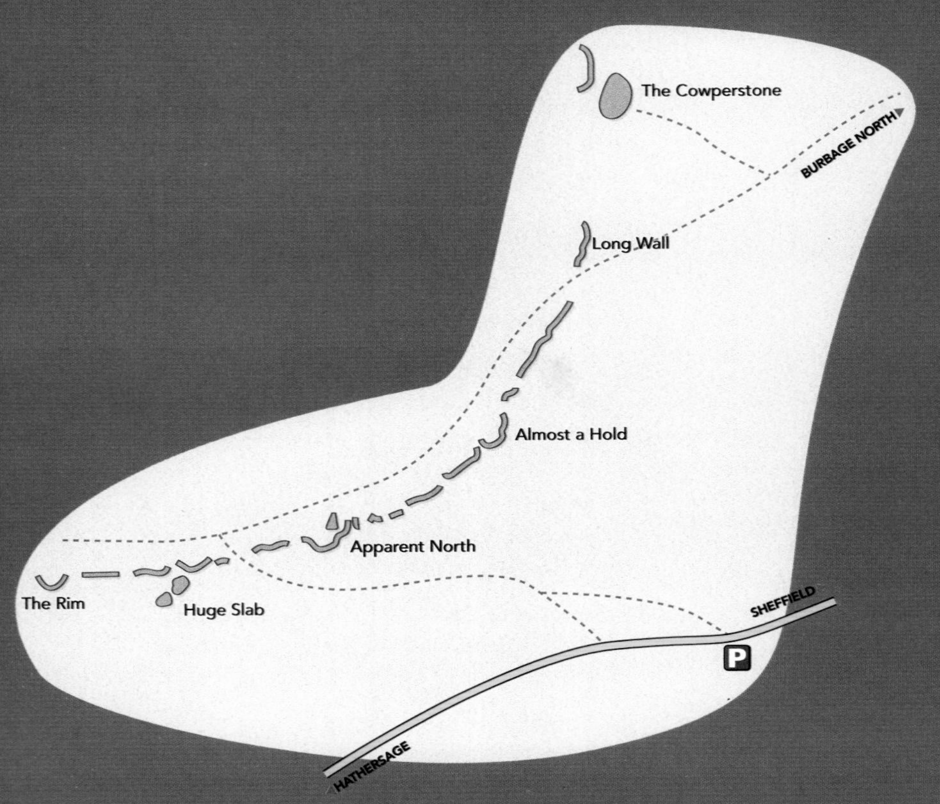

Lucinda Hughes on Problem 15 (6a) **photo :** David Simmonite

the **bouldering**

1» The Rim // 6a
About 70m left of the first set of problems is this excellent low roof, plonked at the northernmost end of Apparent North. Shuffle left to right along the break and slap for the top at a vague arête. Bingo.

Steps Wall

2» Front Flake // 3+
The blocky crack in the front of the buttress.

3» Quick Wall Traverse // 6b
A tough little traverse on slots with little for the feet.

4» Tweedle Dee // 3+
The left-hand side of the almost-high wall.

5» Steps // 3+
The superb flakey-ramp in the centre of the face.

6» Tweedle Dum // 3+
The right-hand side of the wall.

Huge Slab Area

7» 4+
The left-hand side of the wall is tricky to start but soon eases.

8» 5
The centre of the wall, above a poor landing, is climbed with the aid of big sidepulls.

9» 6c
The undercut arête from a sit start. Harder for the tall. (You don't often hear that!)

10» 5
The wall to the right using a beautiful seam and pebble hold.

Off down to the Huge Slab we go:

11» 4
Mantel onto the right-hand edge of the slab and continue up or escape off right.

12» The High Road // 4
Mantel onto the scoop by a chip on the lip, foot traverse right to the arête and finish as for the previous problem.

13» 5+
From slots in the low break to the top.

14» 5
The centre of the wall from the break.

15» 6a
The wall left of the arête with a tricky top-out.

Sam Whittaker on Problem 8 (5) **photo** : David Simmonite

Hamper's Hang (7a)
photo : Alex Messenger

Apparent North Area

The buttress after which the area is named. Home to a good 7a to try – *Hamper's Hang*.

16» 6a+
The right arête of the short wall up and left of the main buttress.

17» 5
Climb the wall opposite from slots in a low break past a flake and a wobble stone.

E *Hamper's Hang* (7a) traverses the break in the front of the **Apparent North** buttress from left to right and then shuffles along the sloping shelf to finish in the corner (the start of Problems 18 & 19).

18» 4+
At the right-hand side of the main buttress, traverse the upper crack line from the shelf to finish at the block in the gully.

19» 6b
The low traverse is more of a challenge. Finish up the next problem.

20» Magnetic North Start // 5
A short problem up the arête. Jump off.

Grand Theft Area

21» 6c
Climb the left-hand side of the wall past the sloping pod. Slink off left at the shelf.

22» 6b
Sit start and climb the right-hand side of the wall. The traverse from the arête on the left, finishing up this problem, is a fingery 7a.

23» Almost a Hold // 6c+
Traverse the bottom of the wall from the arête with a big reach crux. Finish up the next problem.

24» 4+
From a pod, swing right to climb good breaks up the right-hand side of the wall.

There are numerous short walls, arêtes and roofs to the right, all of which give fantastic problems, including:

25» 4
The left arête of the buttress (i.e. the right-hand side of the crack).

26» 5+
The centre of the face from a low start takes some figuring out.

27» 5+
Climb the right arête on the left hand side from a sit start. Awkward.

28» 5
The same arête on the right hand side from sitting is much more pleasant.

Long Wall

Some 50m further right is this pleasant wall.

29» Fig Roll // 5+
Climb the overlaps passing a pocket.

30» Double Flake // 4
Romp up the juggy flakes.

31» Crimpy Roof Problem // 6b
Span from the back to painful crimps on the lip and continue straight up past slopes and a crack. Tough.

32» The Medicine Ball // 5
Rounded holds on the arête.

Chippy Buttress

The final stop on our magical mystery tour, just behind the large cowpat-esque block of the **Cowperstone**.

33» Pudding // 5
The wall left of the arête, heading towards a crack.

34» Chips // 5+
The arête taken on its left.

35» Peas // 6c
Again, almost a route. Mantel over the bulge with no shortage of difficulty.

western crags

// Castle Naze
// Hen Cloud
// Kinder
// The Roaches
// Wimberry
// Windgather

Valkyrie (VS 4b, 4c), The Roaches **photo :** Adam Long

castle naze

Access

Castle Naze is located close to the village of Combs. From the village, follow the steep road towards the crag, which is clearly visible on the moorland to the east. There are two lay-bys below the crag with space for about 6 cars. If these are full please go somewhere else, as passing farm traffic tends to bash wing mirrors.

Think of Castle Naze as Windgather's big brother. The routes here are taller, steeper in places and extend further into the higher grades. Like Windgather it is a good beginner's crag, but in reality offers something for everyone.

The vast majority of the crag consists of natural rock; we have chosen not to include the quarried sections at the far end of the edge.

Like **Windgather**, it is a wonderful spot on a spring or summer evening. As it faces west, the crag dries quickly after rain.

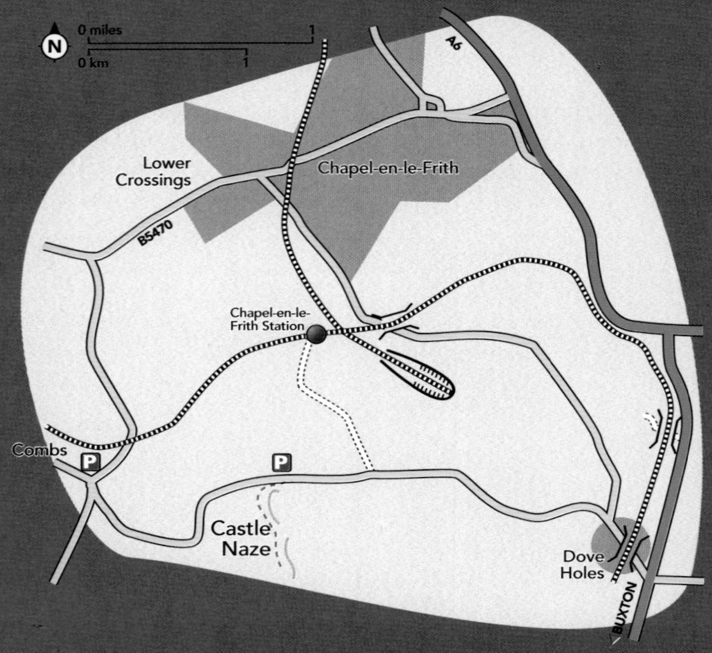

Adam Long on Scoop Face (HVS 5a) ◊ **photo** : John Coefield

the **routes**

Left-Hand Section

Castle Naze is a relatively compact crag and the various buttresses are spaced very closely together. The first routes can be found around 50m in from the start of the edge.

1» The Nose **HS 4b // 12m**
Bold bridging leads to the sentry box. Head back out and right to finish.

2» The Fly Walk **S // 10m**
The worn crack right of the corner, itself a traditional battle (*Main Corner*, S).

3» The Niche **S // 10m // ✪✪**
Good jamming up to and past the niche.

4» Niche Arête **VS 4c // 10m // ✪✪**
Bold, but not desperate climbing up the arête.

5» Studio **HS 4b // 9m // ✪**
The crack leaves nothing to the imagination.

6» Nursery Arête **HVS 5b // 10m // ✪**
The steep, hanging arête, started from the block, gives a good independent route.

7» Pilgrim's Progress **HS 4a // 11m // ✪**
The right-hand crack on the large wall.

E The central crack is *Pod Crack* (E1 5c), probably not a good first extreme...

8» Keep Corner **HVD // 11m // ✪**
The large corner left of the large scoop-shaped slab.

The Scoop

One of **Castle Naze's** big draws is this attractive scooped slab. The main event is a classic HVS.

9» Keep Arête **VS 4b // 11m // ✪**
Climb the arête of the buttress as closely as possible.

10» Scoop Face **HVS 5a // 13m // ✪✪**
Climb into the scoop from 3m right of the arête (polished holds will direct the way). Traverse tentatively rightwards to gain a useful pocket and crack. Trend up and left to finish. Classic.

E A direct start to *Scoop Face* is possible at E1 5c. If you found the original easy, why not give it a go?

Nicki Wood-Turner on Keep Corner (HVD) **photo :** David Simmonite

The Crack Area

Home to several classics, including the mouthwatering line of *The Crack* and the three star *Nozag*.

11» The Crack **VS 4b // 14m // ✪✪**
Climb into the sentry box and exit directly up the crack through the overhang.

12» Nozag **VS 4b // 14m // ✪✪✪**
Essentially a direct line up the face right of *The Crack*. Climb a crack until it curves right. Step left onto the face and climb this boldly, using a thin crack.

13» Zigzag Crack **HS 4b // 16m // ✪**
Start as for the previous route but keep following the curving crack to another crack and finish up this.

14» Central Tower **VDiff // 16m // ✪**
Climb the corner to the large ledge on the left. Step back right and climb the left-hand groove to finish.

15» Atropine **HS 4b // 16m // ✪**
Climb a flake right of the previous route into a recess and follow the ramp to a ledge at the foot of the groove. From here, climb up to the crack to finish.

hen cloud

Access

Although in reality vertical, the foreboding walls of Hen Cloud appear to lean forward with menace like Michael Jackson in the *Thriller* video. All that's missing is a gritstone shoulder shuffle and a red synthetic suit with outrageously short trousers.

Back to reality – the climbs here are good indicators of ability, being pretty much bang-on for the grade. It is an excellent venue to practice your crack art, and again another venue to string together multiple pitches and share leads with your partner.

The crag is exposed and can be a bit much on a cold and/or windy day. During prolonged wet weather, it becomes quite green. However, like the Roaches it is splendid on a spring/summer/autumn evening, sharing the same rolling views as its near neighbour. The rock is generally hard and good quality, with good protection and a decent smattering of holds, which more than compensates for the steepness.

As with The Roaches, park in the lay-bys on the road beneath the crag, being mindful to park in established bays. Approach the crag through a gate on the road and follow the track as it heads north towards the crag. At the kink back to the right, a track heads up to the Central Area, or alternatively a little further along the main track, another track leads up to the middle of the crag. A steep walk, but no more than 10 minutes.

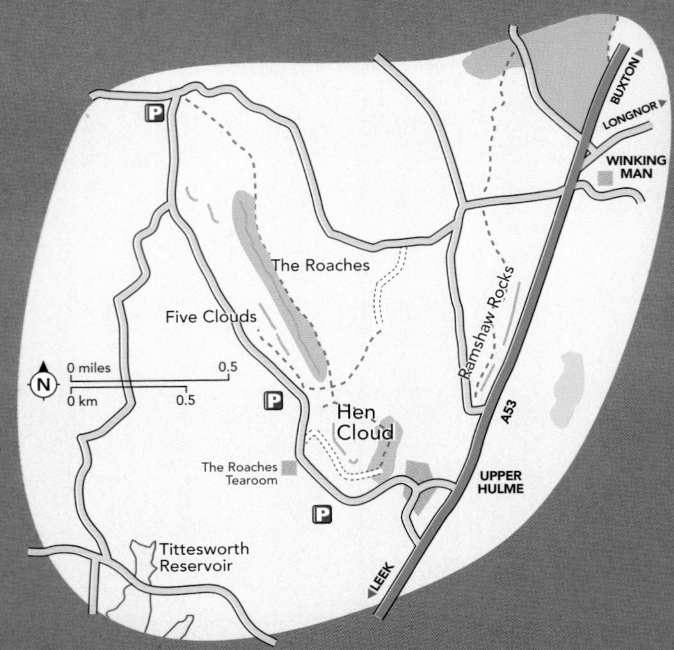

Mark Sharratt on Delstree (HVS 5a) **photo** : David Simmonite

the **routes**

Delstree Area

Although there is a significant body of climbing left of here, this area marks the point at which the crag grows in stature – which is why you came here in the first place. The first few routes start on the grassy ledge, which can be reached from the left.

1» En Rappel **HVS 4c // 12m // ✪✪**

From the ledge make a number of mantelshelf moves to reach the rampline. Follow this, bearing left to pull directly over the top of the crag.

2» Main Crack **VS 5a // 12m // ✪✪**

Do not let this route know you are afraid of it or it will gobble you up and spit you out. Mean at the start and awkwardly wide at the top, it does settle down in the middle.

3» Delstree **HVS 5a // 20m // ✪✪✪**

Super-classic bridging and jamming up the fine corner crack. Start below the low overhang.

Central Area

The largest stretch of rock on **Hen Cloud**, with three classic routes chosen for your deliberation, two of which are multi-pitch affairs.

4» Central Climb VS 4c, 4b, 4a // 32m // ✪✪✪

Three pitches of equal length and consistent quality provide a historically significant route.

1: Follow the crack to the first of two excellent belays.

2: Directly above the ledge, follow the corner before pulling onto another fine belay.

3: With little deviation, follow the crack system above the belay.

5» K2 S 4a, 4b // 8,611m† // ✪✪

*(† Just kidding – it's actually about **30m**)*

1: A fine corner to the right gives access to a ledge.

2: From the belay, take on the steep crack system, which gives access to the summit ridge.

6» The Arête HVD 4a // 30m // ✪✪✪

The exposed ridge of the buttress is climbed throughout, with a crux step at half-height.

Bachelor's Area

An excellent wall of compact gritstone, notable for its challenging cracks and technical extreme excursions. Be sure to use full-length ropes, as the crag top belays are difficult to reach in places.

7» Hedgehog Crack VS 4b // 11m // ★★

The tall crack widens at the top, and there lies the crux.

E If you're after a similar challenge at a harder grade, the shorter crack to the left is *Slimline* (E1 5b).

8» Hen Cloud Eliminate HVS 5b // 18m // ★★★

A series of crack lines on the lower wall lead to the crux sequence, into and through the upper groove.

9» Rib Chimney S 4b // 20m // ★★

Superb, pure chimney climbing.

10» Bachelor's Left-Hand HVS 5b // 25m // ★★★

An outstanding route that makes the most of the large wall at the right of the buttress. Gain the crack at the left-hand side of the buttress with difficulty and follow this before swinging right to reach a flake in the centre of the face. Follow this to a ramp line and finally the upper crack, at which point the difficulties have come to an end.

11» Bachelor's Climb VS 4c // 27m // ✪✪✪
Follow the large crack with a choice of finishes. Continue to finish up Great Chimney, or (even better) traverse left at half-height to join the finish of the previous route. The latter finish is still VS, but at the top of the grade.

12» Great Chimney S 4a // 18m // ✪✪✪
A traditional climb that tackles the crack system in the large corner.

13» Rainbow Crack VS 5a // 18m // ✪✪
Access the fine upper flake crack from a choice of starts to the left or right. Excellent jamming follows in a fine position.

14» Left Twin Crack HS 4b // 9m // ✪
Route finding shouldn't be a problem here. Layback or jam the left-hand of the two cracks.

15» Right Twin Crack VS 4c // 9m // ✪
The right-hand crack is slightly more challenging.

Bachelor's Left-Hand (HVS 5b) **photo :** Pete O'Donovan

kinder

Mark Hundleby on Moneylender's Crack (VS 5a) **photo**: Keith Sharples

kinder

In the middle of the Peak, there is a peak, and in the middle of that peak, there is a lot of mud (work with me on this – you'll only get lost if you go looking yourself) on the edge of the mud, a few million years of concentration and effort by the powers that be has left a fringe of buttresses, boulders, blocks and the odd bog.

We can split these crags into three main areas, which are best approached on separate trips from separate access points: **Kinder North**, **Kinder South** and a third area, **Kinder Downfall**, which is not described here, but covered in detail in other guidebooks. While the walk ins are epic, the climbing experience is not to be forgotten. The rock is sound and there are plenty of good routes available spread around the plateau.

Moving from buttress to buttress on Kinder is quick and easy thanks to the path that runs along the edge of the escarpment.

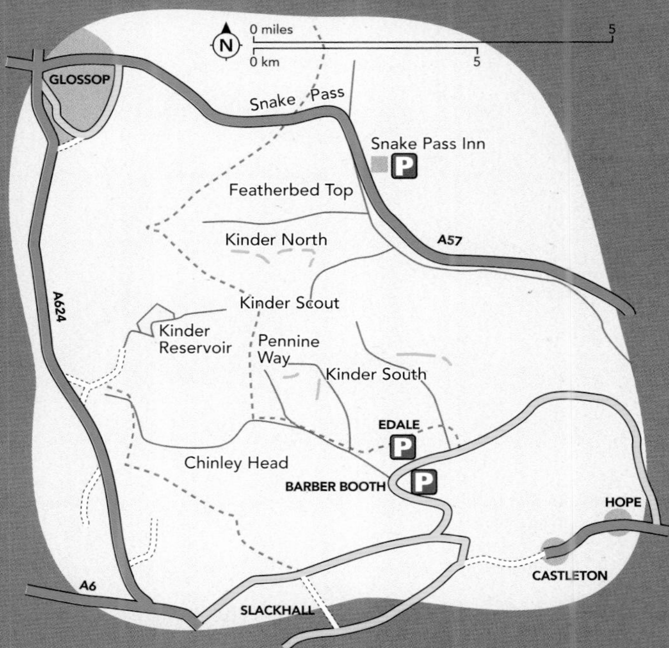

kinder north

Access

Kinder North is shady and often sheltered from prevailing winds. The climbing is on very good compact rock, the area is isolated and has a special feel about it and there are some quality routes, surrounded by what counts as wilderness in the Peak.

Kinder North is also known as **Ashop Edge**. This area offers some of the finest climbing on Kinder Scout. The routes receive a good deal of winter conditions – throughout the year – but are in great condition come the sunshine months. Well worth the walk-in! After rain, the routes are green and many are a little gritty, but after a few dry days they tend to clean up a lot. It is a good place for a summer's day, when much of the rest of the Peak's grit will be out of condition.

There are no special restrictions for access to Kinder, but please respect the Countryside Code, and always keep dogs on a lead, particularly during the nesting season

There is plenty of roadside parking in lay-bys below the Snake Inn. Take one of the paths down into the woods, head down to the footbridge, cross this, heading downstream for a few metres, then take the path up Fair Brook. Follow this path up to the plateau rim from where all the routes can be accessed. Allow upwards of an hour from car to route. The return trip straight down from the last route to the Snake Path, running along Ashop Clough, and following this back to the Snake Inn also makes this a good circular walk.

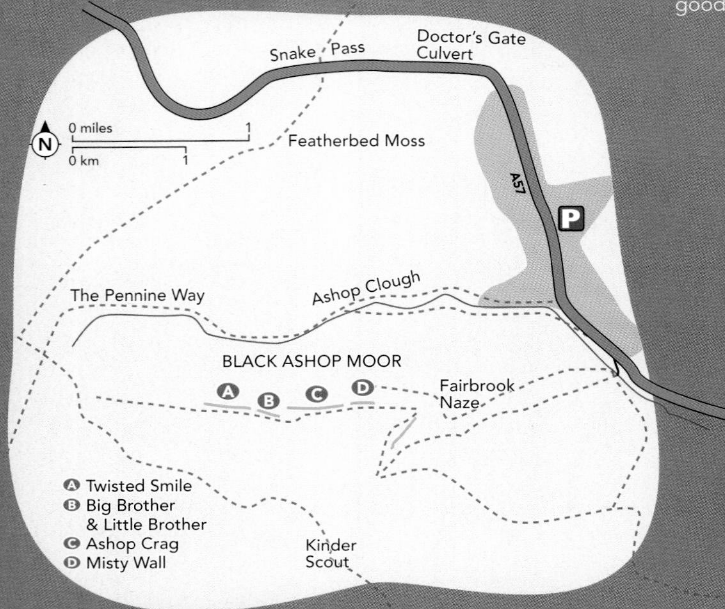

Fairbrook Naze and Kinder North **photo** : Adam Long

the **routes**

Misty Wall (SK095896)

1» Misty Wall **VS 4b // 12m // ✪✪✪**
A moorland classic and one of the best VS climbs in the region. Steep and exposed climbing up the widening crack. Not hard, and well-protected for the grade.

2» Wind Wall **VS 4c // 12m // ✪**
Start as for Misty Wall, but swing right above the overhang, around the arête and climb the centre of the wall above. A fine E2 – *Zyphyr* – climbs the wall direct.

3» Fixation **Diff // 12m // ✪**
A chimney, all very amenable, leads to the thrutchy groove in the back of the bay, which should allow safe passage to the summit.

E The next buttress contains a huge roof, split by a crack: *Trojan* (E1 5b) is that struggle.

On the right-hand side of the last buttress is:

4» Dependence Arête **VS 4c // 10m // ✪**
Starting on the left, head out to the obvious arête and climb this steeply through the overhangs.

Ashop Crag (SK092898)

Ashop Crag is perhaps the jewel in the crown of the Northern Edges, if not all of Kinder. That is not to say the routes are easy – they are certainly harder than a lonely guidebook checker first thought! A certain amount of experience will help the aspiring mountaineer.

5» Roman Roads **VS 4c // 14m // ✪✪**
From the corner, cross the right wall above the overhang to swing around onto and finish up the front face.

6» Ashop Crack **VS 4c // 15m // ✪✪✪**
Follow the crack to its wide continuation, splitting the headwall. Hard but well protected.

7» Ashop Climb **HVD // 15m // ✪✪**
Start up the wide crack, but at the roof, head right to a difficult squirm, which fortunately soon eases to the summit.

8» Eureka **VS 4c // 15m // ✪✪✪**
Another brilliant route. Climb the wall and groove to the overhang, swing right and finish up the headwall, taking the line of least resistance through each bulge. A Kinder classic.

9» Trial Balance **HVS 5b // 12m // ✪**
Scramble up a ramp to a platform beneath the overhangs. Climb steeply from here to a ledge, and then head right via a thin crack to a slopey finish. A great pumpy climb which demands a confident approach.

E *Britt's Cleavage* (E1 5b) starts as for *Trial Balance* but heads out left from the ledge across the roof via a break to finish out left – pumpy.

Big Brother Buttress (SK088897)

10» Legacy **HVS 5a // 20m // ✪✪✪**
Super classic. Climb the prominent rightward-slanting break to finish up the arête. Easy for the grade – or at least well protected.

11» Brother's Eliminate
HVS 5a // 18m // ✪✪
Start at the base of the buttress under the arête, climb up to the overhang, and then traverse the big slanting break rightwards to a niche. Exit left, finishing up the wall and crack.

Little Brother Buttress

12» Razor Crack **S 4a // 10m // ✪**
Climb the steep crack in the right wall of the chimney.

13» Dunsinane **VS 4b // 15m // ✪✪**
Climb the groove/crack right of the left arête. At the break, traverse right to the flake, take this, trending rightwards to a finish up the arête.

Twisted Smile Buttress (SK083897)

14» The Slice **HS 4b // 10m // ✪**
Climb the tricky wall to the slanting crack and an easy finish

15» Exodus **VS 4c // 15m // ✪✪**
Climb out of the cave and up and left to a layback around the roof into the corner. Climb over the left-hand end of the second overhang and continue up the crack to finish through the middle of the slab.

16» Jester Cracks **VS 4c // 12m // ✪✪✪**
A brilliant route. Climb the lower slab to a ledge and poor rest below the roof. Swing out and climb the obvious crack with fantastic jams leading to the top.

17» Lobster Crack **VS 5a // 11m // ✪**
Climb the left-hand crack, past a loose block to finish up the leftward sloping crack.

18» Crab Crack **HVS 5b // 11m // ✪**
The right-hand crack, hard to start.

19» Twisted Smile **HVS 5a // 16m // ✪✪✪**
Three metres further right, climb the crack direct via the breaks. Another mega Kinder classic.

20» Woe is Me **S 4a // 12m**
Climb the wide crack – remember those jamming lessons!

kinder south

Access

A varied collection of crags perched high above the village of Edale, Kinder South is the most accessible of the Kinder edges. The cliffs are sunny and clean, and the climbing varied, while the routes are in condition all year round. Starred routes up here are well worth the walk. Of course, what constitutes a sunny still day outside the pub in Edale can be a very different proposition on the plateau.

Many of the climbs on the southern rim of Kinder Scout have big features and need big gear to protect them: **Nether Tor** routes are quite long, while **Upper Tor** routes are quite twisty – so both need good-sized racks.

Take a helmet, particularly for **Nether Tor**. The top is loose, but fortunately the climbing is a lot better than first impressions would suggest. **Upper Tor** is perhaps the most obvious choice for those looking for their first Kinder experience: it's a compact area, with delightful user-friendly routes. **The Pagoda** and **Crowden Clough Face** can be a little gritty, particularly the less travelled routes.

There are no special restrictions for access to Kinder, but please respect the Countryside Code, and always keep dogs on a lead, particularly during the nesting season

The most accessible of the Kinder Edges. From Edale and its large Pay and Display car-park, walk up through the village and take the footpath across the stream. Take the first right fork from the path, heading up to a gated stile. Follow the zigzag path up to 'The Nab'. Take the left fork, traversing under the prow of Ringing Roger to emerge on the rim at Golden Clough. Romp around the rim to your chosen crag.

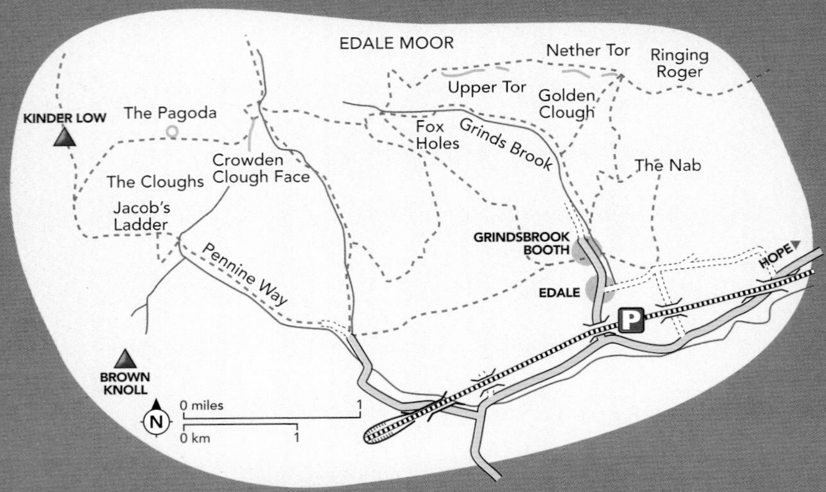

Andy Kirkpatrick on Upper Tor Wall (HS 4b) **photo :** Ian Parnell

the **routes**

photo : Keith Sharples

The Pagoda (SK092871)

1» Morrison's Route S // 15m // ✪

A good route on the left of the buttress. Jump up onto the shelf then bridge up the groove.

2» Hartley's Route HVS 5b // 18m // ✪

The steep awkward crack is climbed to a ledge. Move right then up the wall via some hard moves to another ledge. Finish direct or, as the author did, out left. Don't expect much change from E1.

3» Herford's Route HVS 5a // 18m // ✪✪✪

A brilliant climb up the centre of the buttress by one of Kinder's pioneers, Siegfried Herford in 1910. There is a difficult mantle to exit the wall, and an awkward finish. Well worth HVS.

Crowden Clough Face (SK094872)

4» Central Route VS 4c // 15m // ✪✪

A cracking little climb up the cracks, overhangs and the odd bit of wildlife.

5» Middle Chimney Diff // 15m // ✪

If you like chimneys – you'll like this one.

6» Chimney and Slab Variations VDiff // 12m // ✪

Climb the crack and make your choice of exits.

4
5
6

Upper Tor (SK115876)

7» Upper Tor Wall HS 4b // 15m // ✪✪✪
A Peak classic. One of the best Severes in the District and brilliant on every count. Start on the right-hand edge of the buttress, pull up and then move onto the front face, passing a thread and some hollow holds. Head upwards, via good flakes, to a ledge, stepping right to finish.

8» Hitch Hiker VS 4b // 10m // ✪
A good little pitch, heading out from the chimney of *Hiker's Gully Right* (S) to climb the rightward-slanting big flake. Awkward but well protected.

9» Grunter VS 4b // 12m // ✪
If you really wanted, you could belay in the niche and give your mate the pleasure of the final grunt! Pleasant climbing leads to the typical **Upper Tor** 'big finish'.

10» The Ivory Tower HVS 5b // 17m // ✪✪✪
A big climb taking in some big features with good protection. Climb up to a ledge, up the crack, and then make a tough move out left along the traverse line. Follow a crack to a finale up the beautifully wrinkled head wall.

Nether Tor Left (SK122876)

11» Artillery Chimney HS 4b // 10m // ✪
Climb the crack to the protruding gun barrel of rock, taken on its right. An overhang is all that remains between you and the summit.

E For the tough nuts, two brilliant extremes take on cracking challenges, traditionally given E1 and E2. The E1 is considerably harder than the E2, and perhaps E1 is a better grade for them both. *Brutality* gives steady climbing to a nasty jamming finish, while *Robert* is a much more amenable proposition, despite its steepness.

12» Moneylender's Crack VS 5a // 18m // ✪✪✪
A superb climb, much better than it looks. Starting on the left, make your way into the crack, which can be climbed either as a crack, the way nature intended, or by using the lovely variety of face holds that liberally sprinkle the buttress. A great natural line.

13» Mortgage Wall HVS 5b // 16m // ✪
A burly route in the fine tradition of the HVS grade. Climb cracks to the heather ledge, and then keep going up the steep wall on the left, all the way to the pumpy finish.

Jon Barton on Flash Wall (VS 4c) **photo** : Keith Sharples

Nether Tor Right

14» Snooker Route VS 5a // 25m // ✪✪

A long route, starting at the lowest part of the crag, climbing up the pocketed wall, past the holly forest to the ledge, before traversing several metres to the left to finish up a groove.

15» Hot Flush Crack HVS 5c // 26m // ✪✪

After a difficult start, follow the short crack to the holly, step right to the crack to the roof, and jam up and over to the top.

16» Flash Wall VS 4c // 20m // ✪✪✪

A big excursion on a big crag. Steep moves, always on good holds, give sustained 4c climbing in an exposed position. Start up the obvious crack, moving right around the flake to pull onto the wall. Climb the wall (crux), stepping right near the top to finish up the wide crack. Very good but take care to find a safe belay at the top.

the roaches

photo : Ian Parnell

Access

Park in the extensive lay-bys along the road below the crag. Be sure to park in the marked bays, as police monitor the area and show little leniency with on-the-spot fines.

From here, follow the main track that heads up towards the crag and branch off left at the walled garden outside the Memorial Hut below the lower tier. To reach the Upper Tier, seek out the stone steps to the left of Raven Rock. A path left of the Upper Tier leads to the Skyline.

Of all the gritstone edges in the west of the Peak District, The Roaches is by far the most popular, and rightly so. Offering three major tiers of differing styles, there is much to do here – an excellent place to practice your art.

Uncompromising cracks, sweeping arêtes and technical grooves and corners, The Roaches has it all. Descend into the abyss on routes such as *Raven Rock Gully*, showboat on the acclaimed *The Sloth*, or seek out solitude along the *Skyline*.

In common with the Eastern Edges, there is plenty of tree cover around the crags, although by way of a pleasant contrast with the Eastern Edges, the cover here is coniferous. The rock is also subtly different, but we'll let you discover that for yourself.

If you're a member of a club then you could consider staying at the Don Whillans Memorial Hut, built into the Lower Tier landscape. The waiting list at the time of writing is measured in geological time (well not quite – but you get the idea!). Contact the BMC for further information.

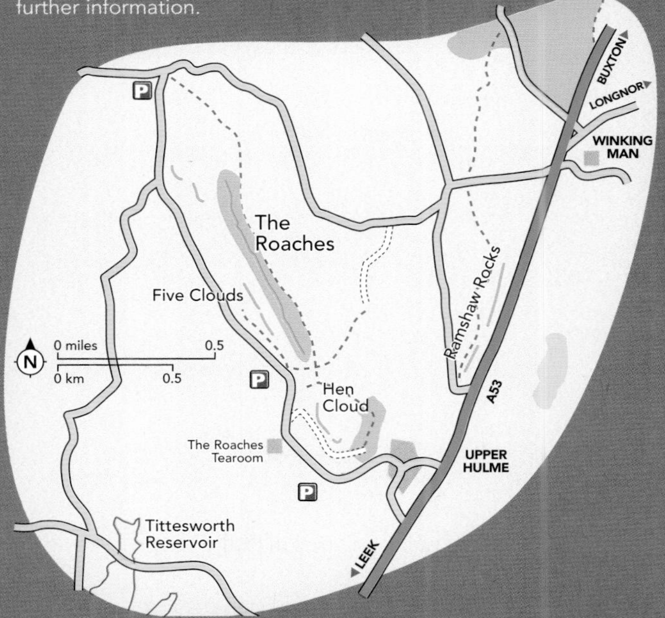

the roaches **lower tier**

Classic grit, the lower tier of The Roaches is home to the second of the Peak's two *Valkyries*. This one is slightly easier at VS and offers an experience that contrasts to its cousin at Froggatt, being larger in stature and featuring a *down-climbing* crux.

That's not all, though. There are plenty of routes here for all abilities, with *Raven Rock Gully* recommended at the lower end and the brutality of *The Mincer* at the upper end.

The bouldering hereabouts is excellent and in a wonderful setting. Low-grade boulderers are well catered for and there are a few sterner problems to try for those willing to test their mettle.

Access

See page 189.

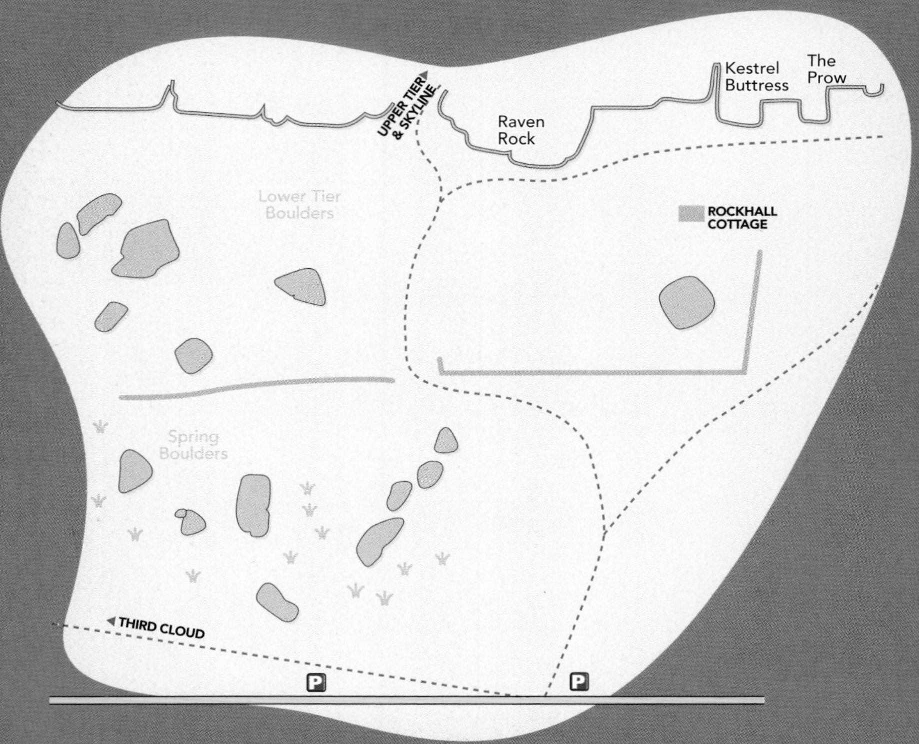

Jon Barton on Prow Corner (VDiff) **photo :** John Coefield

the **routes**

Raven Rock

The imposing fortress of **Raven Rock** looms large over the coniferous plantation and scattered boulders below the Lower Tier. In places steep and brooding, it allows safe passage for climbers on routes surprisingly located in the lower grades.

1» Raven Rock Gully Diff // 20m // ✪

The first route to be climbed at The Roaches, and therefore an essential tick. Climb flakes in the right-hand side of the gully before returning to daylight through the manhole.

2» Via Dolorosa VS 4b, 4a, 4c // 33m // ✪✪

Tick this and *Valkyrie* in a day for full VS certification.

1: Climb a narrow polished slab before moving up and left, through the holly, to a ledge.

2: Traverse left to a rib and climb a short crack. Follow a slab to the left and belay at a block by the arête.

3: Bold moves lead to a flake. Climb this and swing right around the arête and climb to the top just right of the arête.

3» Valkyrie Direct HVS 5b // 25m // ✪✪

Follow the first pitch of *Via Dolorosa*, but shortly before the ledge, detour steeply in the direction of the prominent *Valkyrie* flake to a rest just below it. Tackle the crack and join the finish of the original route.

Valkyrie (VS 4b, 4c) **photo :** Pete O'Donovan

4» Matinee HVS 5a, 5b // 23m // ✪✪✪

Plenty of jam in this sandwich.

1: Climb the lower crack with glee to a thread belay on the ledge.

2: Confiture up the ever-widening crack to the final bulge, which is surmounted with interest/ease† (†delete as appropriate).

5» Valkyrie VS 4b, 4c // 38m // ✪✪✪

Simply one of the best. Careful ropework is essential, as is blue-sky thinking on the rollercoaster second pitch.

1: Plough up the corner and traverse left to belay at the thread belay on the ledge.

2: With a sling draped over it for protection, climb up and over the huge flake, allowing your brain time to adjust to the fact that you are *down-climbing*. Keep going, before somehow stepping down and left to swing around the arête and finish up much easier climbing on the front of the buttress.

The Swan Wall

The next series of routes is centred around the attractive steep wall to the right.

6» Pebbledash HVS 5a, 4b // 21m // ✪

1: Climb the crack system until the wedge disappears. Move left to a belay in the corner.

2: Follow the wide corner crack and then the flake on the left to finish.

7» The Mincer HVS 5b // 20m // ✪✪✪

Where boys become men. Climb the crack in the stepped overhangs. Traversing right around the prominent overhang is the crux, with all four limbs within a space of about 1 square foot. Once around the nose, jam up to and past a ledge.

8» Pincer VS 5a // 20m // ✪

Climb the low groove and trend up and right to the vegetated crack. Head left to reach the bottomless crack in the slab and finish up this.

Kestrel Buttress

There is another prominent fortress further along, although not quite on the scale of **Raven Rock**. This, and the slabs and corners either side of it, are home to a selection of excellent routes, including several enjoyable VDiffs and a corker of an HS.

9» Kestrel Crack **HS 4b // 20m // ✪✪✪**

The stubborn crack that splits the centre of the buttress is best approached from the left.

E A good E1 (*Hawkwing*, E1 5b), takes a wandering line up the front of the buttress with adequate protection. Start around to the left near the chimney and follow the curving crack rightwards onto the front face to join *Kestrel Crack*. Follow this for 2m before swinging onto parallel cracks which lead diagonally left up to the arête.

10» Rhodren **HVS 5b // ✪✪**

There is an attractive stepped corner around to the right. Similar to The Mincer, although not quite as character building.

11» Flake Chimney **Diff // 14m // ✪✪**

Layback the edge of the fallen flake before heading right into the corner and finishing up the chimney.

The Prow

12» Prow Corner **VDiff // 12m // ✪**
Good, clean fun up the slabby corner crack. Best finished on the left-hand upper cracks.

13» Prow Cracks **Diff // 10m // ✪**
Twin cracks split the right-hand side of the slab. A good first lead, they can be either bridged or jammed.

14» Rocking Stone Gully **VDiff // 8m**
The blocky corner crack isn't pretty but it does the job. Beware its namesake.

15» Sifta's Quid **HS 4c // 9m // ✪✪**
Climb up to the ledge and either over the bulge (cop out) or through the tunnel. Not one to try immediately after a big dinner.

David Norton on Stretch and Mantel (6c) **photo** : John Coefield

Lower Tier : bouldering

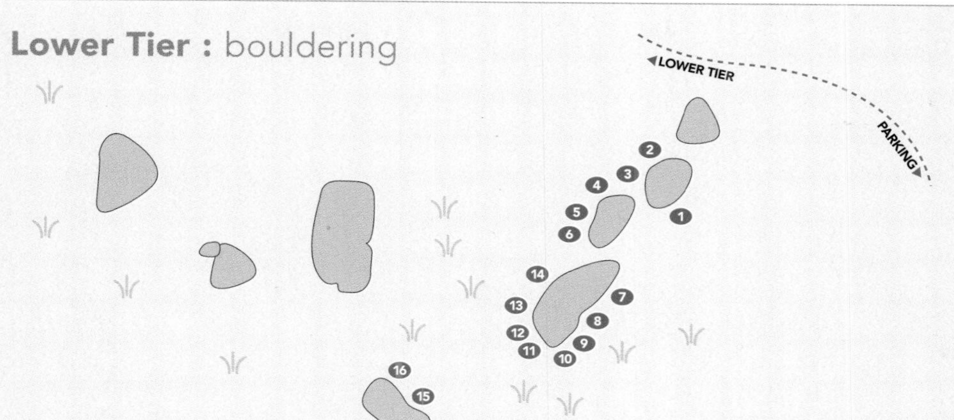

Spring Boulders

An excellent selection of mid-to-low grade problems, spoiled only slightly by the semi-permanent bog which masquerades as the floor.

1» Spring Roll // 4+
The right-hand side of the arête.

2» Slabby Seam // 3

3» 3
The blunt arête.

The slab to the left is home to a collection of smearing testpieces, mostly 7a and above.

4» Easy Wall // 3

5» 5
Climb the flake from sitting.

6» 4+
The arête on its left-hand side.

7» Scoops // 5+

8» Pebbles and Seam // 6a

9» 6c
Hard pebble pulling above the splodge.

10» 6b
The arête on the right.

11» 3+
The left side of the arête and scoops.

12» 3+
The wall from undercuts.

13» 4
Big holds left of the arête.

14» 3+
The scooped slab. The slabs left again are also 3+.

15» 5+
The scoop.

16» 6a
The top via the hole.

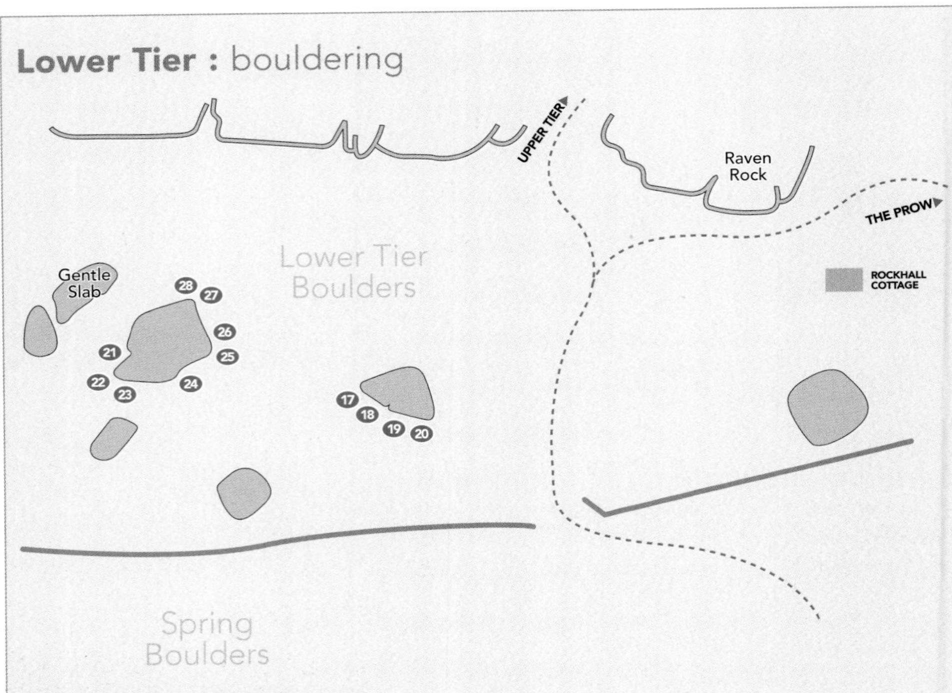

Lower Tier Boulders

The next collection of boulders is found within the walled area of the lower tier. The first boulder is a pleasant easy-angled slab with a crack running up the centre.

17» 4

The slab.

18» 3

The cracking crack.

19» 4+

The slab right of the crack provides good smearing practice.

20» 3+

Up the chips. The flake around the back of the boulder is a 4.

In the centre of the lower tier, there is a large green boulder. Behind this is a gentle slab, which is good for beginners and can be climbed on almost anywhere at around 3 – 4+. The best problems are the short left arête (3), the short slab left of centre past flakes (3+), the rounded feature just right of centre (4+) and the easy block and crack (3).

21» 4

The short slab.

photo : Keith Sharples

Lower Tier : bouldering

22» 5
The right-hand side of the arête.

23» Three Pocket Slab // 6a
A classic testpiece with just enough holds. Link the pockets to an exhilarating final rockover at the top.

24» 3
The big flakes are the easiest way up the boulder.

25» Flake Crack // 4

26» Stretch and Mantel // 6c
Another classic. Streeeeetch to the boss on the slabby top and mantel out. One of the two moves is much harder than the other, this will be all too apparent soon enough. An ingenious problem name, no?

27» Stretch Left // 6a+
From the arête, stretch left to the boss on the left wall and mantel out.

28» Classic Arête // 4+
Big holds up the arête.

the roaches **upper tier**

Access

See page 189.

Generally speaking, the Upper Tier is larger than its neighbour downstairs and the routes also offer a bigger experience, many charting a course through the roofs and steep rock that abound across much of the crag.

Another venue to offer multi-pitch outings, a day out here can be truly memorable, with views possible to Wales on perfectly clear days! If you're after the definitive Roaches experience, be sure to get on *Black and Tans*, *Pedestal Route* or *The Sloth*. Whatever you choose you're sure to get on with it.

The bouldering is again excellent, and can be found on a collection of freestanding blocks below the main walls. It is a good bet after wet weather, as it dries rather quickly.

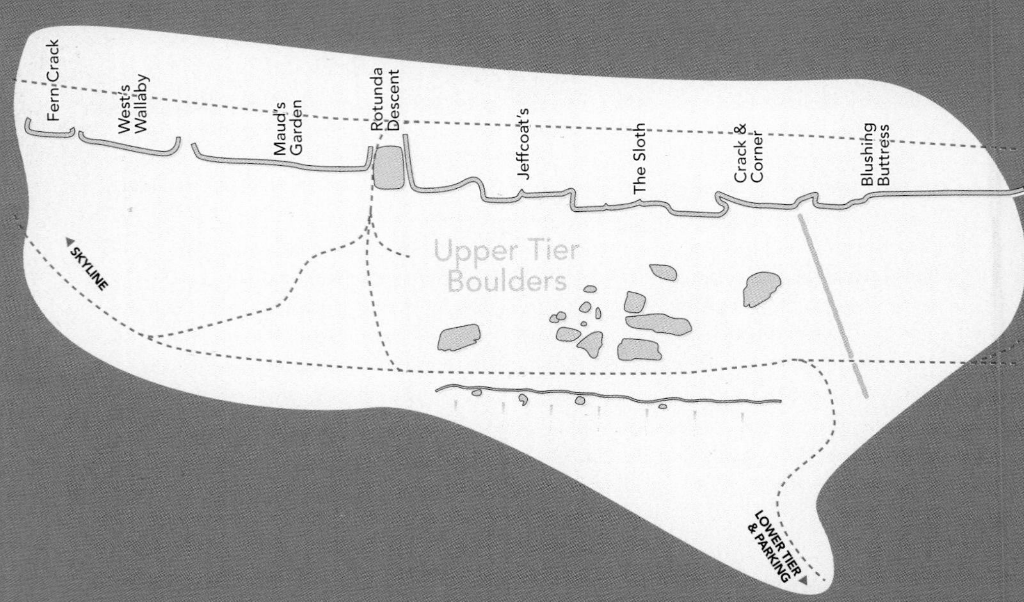

Sam Doyle on The Sloth (HVS 5a) **photo :** Adam Long

the **routes**

Left-Hand Section

The left-hand section of the **Upper Tier** lacks the stature of the central walls and roofs, but still provides a selection of good routes up to VS.

1» Fern Crack **HVD 4b // 18m // ∞**

A difficult start (hence the 4b tech grade) gives access to the crack and flake. Climb past a thread and move left to a ledge. A mantelshelf leads to another ledge and a possible belay. Walk left and around the corner to finish up the right wall of the recess.

2» Inverted Staircase **Diff // 21m // ∞**

A good climb that takes a line up the groove right of the large overhang. Start to the left at the lowest point and climb the groove to a huge ledge and possible belay. From here, finish by squeezing between the small gap in the boulders.

West's Wallaby

Another area dominated by roofs and overhangs, but again in the relative tranquillity of the tree cover.

3» West's Wallaby **VS 4c** // **23m** // ✪✪

Climb up to the block at the right-hand side of the roof. Traverse rightwards into the gully and climb this briefly before finishing back on the left on slabby rock. A better quality direct finish heads straight up from the traverse line at VS 5a, avoiding the gully.

Maud's Garden

The overhangs of the previous two buttresses disappear and the angle relents. Good climbing is found in the lower grades and the area doesn't get as busy as the main areas slightly further along.

4» Beckermet Slab **VDiff** // **15m** // ✪

Bridge the gully to gain the horizontal break on the left wall. Access this with difficulty before moving up and left to the arête. Once at the ledge above, finish up the groove and the left-hand side of the slabby arête.

5» Maud's Garden **VDiff // 21m // ✪✪**
A good route for the beginner, with a tricky start and interesting climbing throughout.

1: Climb the centre of the slab to a crack and protection. Keep going and belay in the alcove below the overlap.

2: Head right and up the chimney. Where it ends, step onto the left wall and finish up this on good holds in an exhilarating position.

6» Runner Route **S 4a // 11m // ✪**
Climb diagonally rightwards across the slab from the corner. Mantelshelf the break and head back left to the holly and follow the crack behind it.

7» Damascus Crack **HS 4a // 12m // ✪✪**
Great gear and good climbing up the crack with a finish up flakes to the left.

Black and Tans Area

Moving further right, the edge begins to grow in size, leaving the tree cover behind.

8» Bachelor's Buttress VS 4b // 18m // ✪

A bold route with exciting climbing. Climb the low slab to the left-hand side of the overhang. Move up and traverse out right across the sidewall, above the overlaps, to the arête and a finish up the short crack.

9» Saul's Crack HVS 5a // 18m // ✪✪✪

A direct line that storms straight up the wall and through the overlaps. Climb the crack and battle through the corner above to finish over the overhang.

10» Jeffcoat's Chimney VDiff // 24m // ✪✪

A classic multi-pitch excursion.

1: Climb the chimney, passing the holly tree on your left to a belay ledge above the cave.

2: From the left-hand side of the ledge, avoid the overlaps by heading right and then back left to finish.

11» Jeffcoat's Buttress HS 4c, 4a // 27m // ✪✪✪

An excellent route that somehow finds safe passage through the steep terrain right of the previous route.

1: Climb the fingery scoop to bigger holds and the corner above. Follow this before

David Smith on Saul's Crack (HVS 5a) **photo :** Keith Sharples

traversing out right above the roof to belay below twin cracks.

2: Climb the twin cracks above the belay to finish.

12» Black and Tans S 4a, 3c // 30m // ✪✪✪

An **Upper Tier** classic, with technical and exciting climbing on both pitches.

1: Climb the gully and head left to a hanging corner. Follow this to a ledge, before heading up and left to belay in a second corner.

2: Climb the corner above the stance and traverse a good break left onto the projecting nose. Continue directly with a series of mantelshelves to finish.

13» Black Velvet HVD 4a // 27m // ✪✪

Climb to the first hanging corner as for *Black and Tans*. Climb directly out of this onto the wall above, passing the roof on its right.

The Great Slab

The huge central section of the **Upper Tier** is home to three star routes of all grades.

14» Hollybush Crack S 4a // 26m // ✪

The crack line up the left-hand side of the huge roof system is excellent throughout.

15» The Neb Finish VS 4b // 25m // ✪✪

Once past the overhang on *Hollybush Crack* arrange a runner. Step down and traverse out right on pockets with feet just above the lip to finish near the arête.

16» Technical Slab HS 4a // 23m // ✪✪

A bold route with technical climbing at the grade. Climb the slab right of *Hollybush Crack* to the roof. *The Neb Finish* provides the most suitable exit and makes for an exciting combo.

17» Pedestal Route **HVD 4a, 3c // 27m // ✪✪✪**

1: Climb the flake crack up either side of the pedestal to a belay on the top.

2: Teeter off the left-hand edge of the pedestal and traverse up and left to the corner of the roof. Finish more easily up the crack.

18» The Sloth **HVS 5a // 24m // ✪✪✪**

An outrageous route through the crack that splits the overhang. Climb to the top of the pedestal, arrange runners, and blast out across the roof on big flakes to the lip and wide finishing crack.

19» Central Route **VS 4b // 15m // ✪✪**

Climb boldly up the slab on shiny holds and traverse right under the overhang to a belay on a large ledge. Finish up the second pitch of the next route.

20» Right Route **VDiff // 24m // ✪✪**

A popular route, although this is beginning to show in the form of polish.

1: Climb pockets to reach the slanting overlap. Move tentatively left and up to a large ledge.

2: Head diagonally left over the overlap to reach and finish up a crack.

21» Kelly's Shelf **S 4a // 17m // ✪**

Climb up to the shelf and step onto it with as much grace as you can muster. Follow it to a crack and finish.

Roscoe's Wall

The edge again eases in height following the excitement of **The Great Slab**.

22» Jelly Roll VS 4b, 4b // 23m // ✪

1: Climb a thin crack to belay on a ledge.

2: The wall above is followed boldly to a hanging groove and a finish up the crack and corner.

23» Roscoe's Wall HVS 5b // 11m // ✪✪

Good wall climbing with a hard start and a great finish onto the ledge.

E *Round Table* (E1 5a) is a good continuation pitch for the previous route, taking the steep crack through impressive terrain in the tallest section of the buttress.

Blushing Buttress

Good rock and steep, testing crack climbs.

24» Crack and Corner

S 4c, –, 4a // 35m // ✪✪✪

A long and thoroughly enjoyable outing that makes the most of the buttress.

1: Thrutch up the undercut crack with no shortage of difficulty to a belay on the ledge.

2: Saunter along the ledge to the foot of the continuation corner.

3: Climb the wall to a ledge and continue up the groove to the foot of the overhang. Surmount this with plenty of gusto on massive holds.

25» Left-Hand Route HVD 4a // 13m // ✪

A steep start past the hanging flake leads to delicate climbing above.

26» Right-Hand Route S 4b // 13m

A good companion to the previous route with a difficult start on shiny footholds, and a steady finish up the upper groove past the overlap.

Upper Tier : bouldering

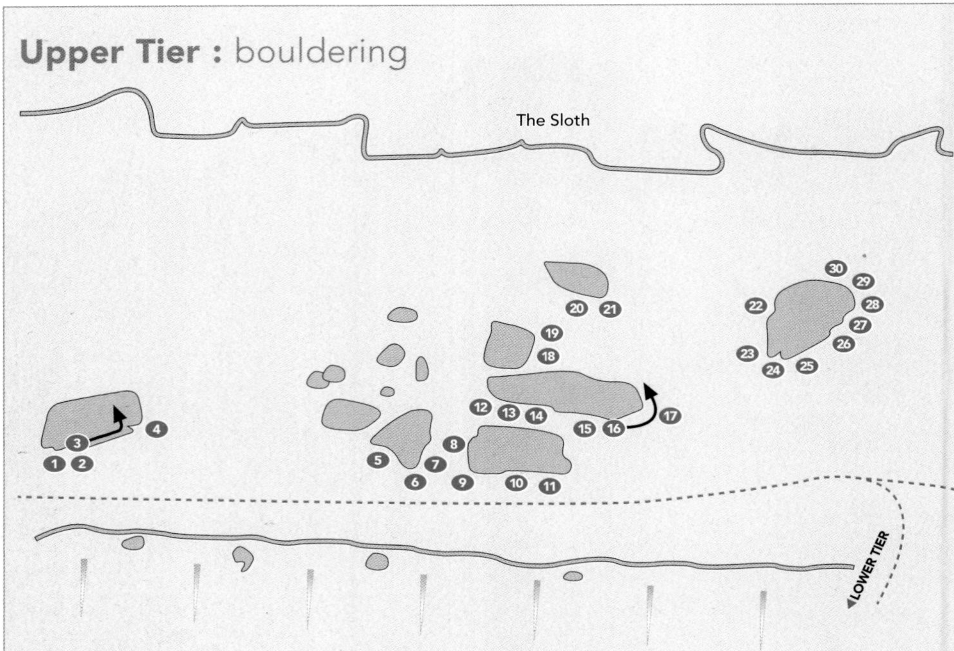

A good selection of boulders on fine-grained rock. They are more exposed than the **Lower Tier** boulders and are a better bet following wet weather.

1» 4
The left arête.

2» 6a+
Rock up leftwards on a round hold.

3» 6a
A rising left-to-right traverse above the lip.

4» 5
The arête.

5» 4
The wall left of the arête.

6» 5+
The slab and arête are most entertaining.

7» 6a
Mantel onto the hanging slab from a low start.

8» 3+
The big holes in the sidewall.

9» Joe's Arête // 5+
Super classic, as the polish testifies. Balance up the arête and, more often than not, pop for the top.

10» 4
The big flakes in the centre of the face.

11» Joe's Portholes // 3+
Big holes on the right-hand side.

Upper Tier : bouldering

12» 4
The juggy arête starting low.

13» Glued Up // 5+
Start low on the glued jug and climb the wall.

14» 5
The flake in the centre of the wall.

15» The Staircase // 4+
From sitting.

16» Cooper's Traverse // 6b
Start right of The Staircase and traverse the lip rightwards until it gets easy.

17» 6b+
Sit start under the bulge and snatch your way to the top.

18» Don's Crack // 4+
The crack, really. Superb.

19» Don's Arête // 3+
The arête, of course.

20» 5
The wall past breaks.

21» 6a+
Climb the undercut nose from a hanging start.

22» 5
The slippery groove.

23» 5
The arête on its left-hand side.

Joe's Arête (5+) **photo : David Simmonite**

24» 3+
The easy groove.

25» Flakes and Chips // 4+
Polished chips lead up to the high flake.

26» Left Groove // 6b
The classic right-facing groove.

27» Right Groove // 6a
The groove to the right.

28» 5
The arête is barely that.

29» The Nose // 6b+
Start hanging on the low break.

30» 5
Jugs up the groove.

multi-pitch climbing

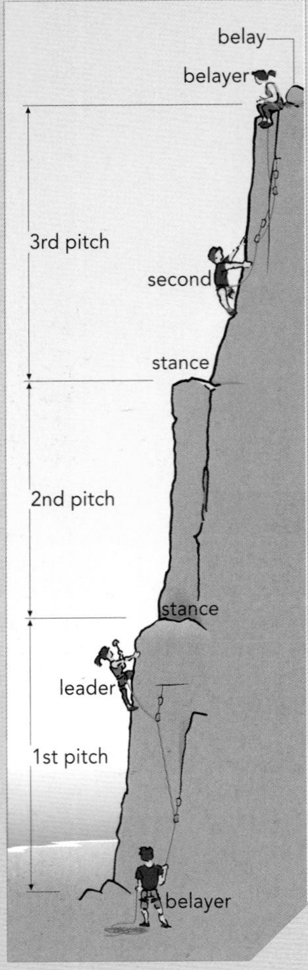

Although there are far fewer of them in the Peak District than in the more mountainous climbing areas of the UK, the supply of multi-pitch routes in the Peak still provides a good introduction to longer routes where multiple pitches are linked together.

It is no surprise that most of the multi-pitch routes are on the bigger, taller crags, such as **Millstone**, **Stoney Middleton** and **Hen Cloud**, but good multi-pitch climbs can also be found at traditional single-pitch venues, such as **Froggatt** and **Curbar**.

Multi-pitch routes bring with them a whole new experience, as both climbers must play a central role in the route. Mid-climb belays are taken, thought must be given to careful ropework and protection, and route-finding is important to ensure you don't stray off-route.

If you or your partner are new to multi-pitch routes, it is worth considering dropping your grade a little and perhaps picking a route with comfortable ledges where it is possible to belay and organise yourselves safely. A good route to try as a first multi-pitch is *Maud's Garden* at **The Roaches**.

Belaying

In addition to traditional belays at the bottom and top of the crag, on multi-pitch routes belays are taken at additional mid-climb points, either because the length of the route dictates it, or the route may follow a devious line that it is simply not practical to climb and protect in a single-pitch. These belays might be very large ledges, not really any different to crag-top belays, or they might be cramped ledges where a stance must be arranged in a confined space with care. There are several important things to consider with multi-pitch belays:

Making yourself safe

As is the case when completing single-pitch routes, it is important to make yourself safe when reaching a belay stance on multi-pitch routes. Multiple pieces of gear should be placed that provide a solid stance and that will not pull the belayer off-line, or unbalance him/her, should the second fall while following the pitch. Thought must also be given to whether the second will lead

Illustrations from ***Rock Climbing***, published by MLTUK

through onto the next pitch, or whether the second will take over belay duty and the original leader continue. If the second will take over belaying, the belay should be set up with the anchor points equalised to a central point, which the second can clip into and the leader can unclip from, when ready to lead on.

Restricted stance:
Top: The rock is preventing correct braking.
Above: Stance improved by standing and twisting sideways

Which way does the route continue from the belay?

An essential part of route finding (*see overleaf*) is being aware of where the next pitch departs the belay stance. This is important because if the second is to continue past and lead the next pitch, he or she will have to pass the belayer and collect the remaining gear from the original leader to protect the pitch. It is even more important if the next pitch departs in a different direction and the belayer must be sure the belay is versatile enough to handle forces from another direction.

Standing or sitting?

Sometimes the location of the anchors will mean it is more sensible to belaying sitting down, and sometimes standing will be more appropriate. Give consideration to what might happen in the event of a fall. If the second falls and his or her weight must be held from above, would a standing position make this more or less easy to hold? Alternatively, would a sitting position on a small stance be quite constricted, limiting the range of movement possible by the belayer? It is worth considering this before establishing the belay and before the second begins climbing, as after this it is not possible to adjust since the focus must be placed on safely belaying the second climber.

The next pitch: runners

The first runner when starting the next pitch is very important and should be placed early on in the pitch. A leader-fall straight onto the belay can generate a large force – this can be difficult for the belayer to hold, and is not good for the life of the ropes. If there are no runners immediately available, one of the solid belay runners can be clipped to begin with before departing the belay. This can then be unclipped if necessary by the belayer once additional runners have been placed.

multi-pitch climbing

Mark Stevenson and Rich Mayfield on Pitch 2 of Valkyrie (HVS 5a, 5a), Froggatt **photo :** Keith Sharples

Route finding

Stand back and take a good look at the route, committing the line and important features to memory. This is important even if you carry a guidebook up with you, as the route will appear a whole lot different when you're up close and peering out from corners or leaning around arêtes, looking for that overlap that was so clear from below.

Look for the stances, make a mental note about which way you'll approach them from and in which direction the leader of the following pitch will depart.

Finally, make a note of any particular descent notes for the climb. A good example is the descent from the *Rivelin Needle* and the *Froggatt Pinnacle*, both of which are by abseil, so be sure of how to get off once you've finished the route.

Communicating with your partner

Clear communication with a partner is essential, as very often you may not be able to see him or her. As with single-pitch climbing, keep calls short, sharp and simple: "*safe*" once you have reached and set up a belay, followed by "*off belay*" by the belayer as he or she removes the leader from belay and prepares to climb. "*Climb when ready*" informs the climber that he or she can begin, and "*climbing*" from the climber informs the belayer that he or she is climbing. While climbing, "*slack*" or "*take in*" informs the belayer either to pay out or take in rope. If you are in any doubt as to whether your call has been heard, repeat the call. Likewise, if you are in doubt as to your partner's call. Never use phrases such as "*take in the slack*", since on a windy day the only bit the belayer may hear is "*slack*".

Gear for multi-pitch routes

Although the core gear remains the same for longer multi-pitch routes, it is worth considering adding a few additional pieces and using double ropes if you're confident with your ropework.

Extra gear

Multi-pitch routes are likely to be longer, so take a few extra quickdraws to extend your runners. Take along a few extra wires, slings and screwgates, if possible, as those in your standard rack may be used in the set up of mid-route belays. As most of the multi-pitch routes featured in this book are still relatively short, it is not usually necessary to take additional gear, such as a rucksack with spare jackets for belays, food and drink or shelters. Be aware, though, that a two-pitch route will often take at least as long to climb as two normal routes.

Double ropes

Using double ropes on both single and multi-pitch routes can significantly reduce rope drag and allow the route to be protected more comprehensively. Double ropes can also be tied together to allow for longer abseil descents, although it is not necessary for any of the routes in this book.

When using double ropes the climber and second tie into both ropes, with one clearly on each side (left and right) of the climber. The belayer then ensures that the left rope and right rope go through the left and right sides of the belay plate.

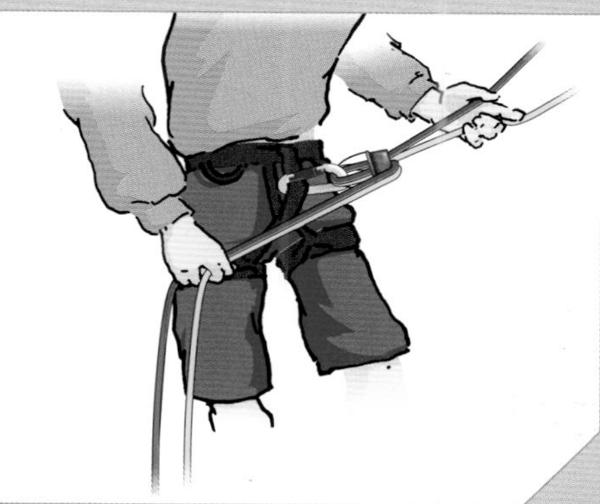

Above: Belaying with double ropes

For straight pitches, the ropes are clipped into gear alternately, while for meandering routes, the ropes are clipped into gear on either side as appropriate to ensure they run smoothly. When reaching belays, the ropes can be clipped into anchors independently and both attached to the harness.

Belaying on double ropes does require practice and it is important to feel confident with the technique since the ropes must be managed independently when taking in and paying out slack. Practice is the key and this can be done on easier routes when the leader can climb slowly and confidently, allowing the belayer time to concentrate on what he or she is doing.

the roaches **skyline**

If you're after a little bit of peace and quiet, you could do worse than bypass the Lower and Upper Tiers and seek out the more diminutive buttresses along the Skyline. The routes tend to be shorter, but there is certainly no reduction in quality, with many of the finer routes at The Roaches tucked away along this series of intermittent buttresses.

At the very far end, the edge becomes significantly more broken and is home to a number of harder routes (mid-extremes) that are on some of the finest rock in the Peak District. Routes along this section are included to allow you to sample the geological delights further along.

The **Skyline** is exposed, being the highest point on the Roaches, but it also offers jaw-dropping views on a clear day. Spend an autumn day up here and all your earthly woes will fade away.

Access

See page 189.

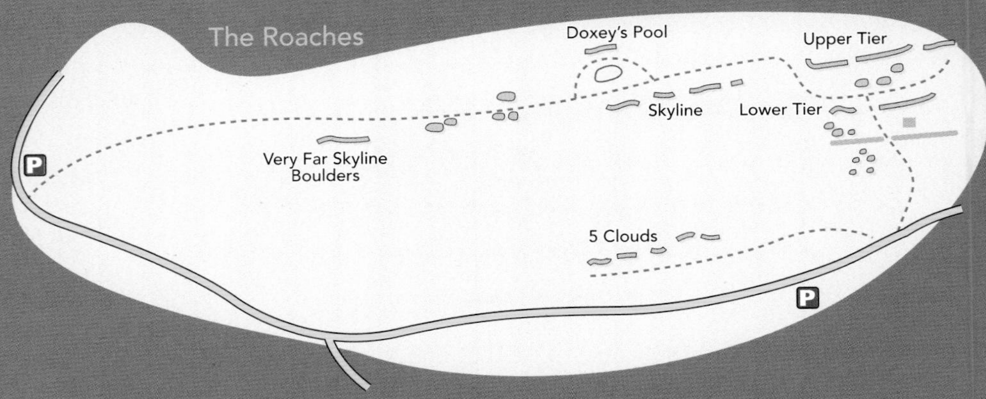

John Coefield on Condor Slab (VS 4b) **photo** : Adam Long

the **routes**

Condor Buttress

The first significant collection of buttresses on the **Skyline**, only a 5-minute walk from the **Upper Tier**.

1» Bruno Flake **VS 4b // 7m // ✪**

The corner leads to a steep sequence through the flaky roof.

2» Tobacco Road **VS 4c // 8m // ✪**

Climb the centre of the wall passing some interesting, large 'crozzly' holds.

3» Condor Chimney **VDiff // 8m // ✪✪**

The large chimney requires little chimney technique and instead gives good bridging.

4» Condor Slab **VS 4b // 12m // ✪✪**

A bold route, the best hereabouts. Start up a short crack and climb to a hole. Move up from this with difficulty, before stepping right to finish, left of the blunt arête.

Tower Buttress

A tall buttress dominates in an area with a selection of routes across the lower grades.

5» The Black Pig **VS 4c // 8m // ✪✪**
Use the chimney to gain access to the attractive, rightward-slanting crack in the wall.

6» Ogden Arête **HS 4b // 8m // ✪✪**
The left-hand side of the steep arête is pleasingly technical.

7» Thrug **VS 4c // 10m // ✪✪**
The first route on the **Tower** proper tackles the steep crack in the sidewall.

8» Perched Block Arête **VDiff // 15m // ✪**
A fine route up the right-hand side of the arête. Once over the perched block and below the final wall, head off left to finish up the chimney. The direct finish is VS 4b.

9» Tower Chimney **Diff // 18m // ✪**
The gaping chimney in the front of the buttress pulls no punches.

10» Tower Eliminate **HVS 5b // 15m // ✪**
Steep cracks in the left-hand side of the **Tower** lead past a poor rest in a niche.

Skyline Buttress

The largest of the **Skyline** buttresses, with several classic outings.

11» Slab and Arête HS 4a // 18m // ✪✪✪
Move in from the left, go up a little and traverse the half-height break all the way to the arête, up which the route finishes with no shortage of exposure.

12» Karabiner Cracks Mod // 12m // ✪
A pleasant, if a little vegetated, excursion up the blocky cracks and groove left of the main slab.

13» Karabiner Chimney VDiff // 12m // ✪
The enjoyable chimney formed by the leaning outer slab.

14» Mantelshelf Slab VS 4a // 10m // ✪
Beware the grade – this is a bold climb. Tackle the centre of the slab, trending left, which becomes bolder but easier with height.

15» Pinnacle Arête VS 4c // 6m // ✪
Down and left of the main walls there is a leaning pillar. Climb the right arête.

Alpha Buttress

A compact buttress, the routes here require focus and will punish a lazy leader.

16» Right-Hand Route **S 4a // 12m // ✪**

Climb the chimney until it is possible to traverse out left and finish up the first of two large flakes.

17» Wallaby Wall **S 4a // 10m // ✪**

Gain the left-hand of the two flakes from an awkward start.

18» Mantis **HVS 5b // 8m // ✪✪**

A steep, bold start on the right leads to the half-height break. Swing around onto the left-hand side and finish more easily. The arête can also be climbed entirely on its left-hand side at E1 5c.

19» Breakfast Problem **VDiff // 8m // ✪**

The close, twin cracks are a good first lead.

Doxey's Pool : bouldering

Above and set back from the Skyline area, there is a cracking set of boulders next to a miniature tarn – **Doxey's Pool**, named after the daughter of the occupant of Rock Hall, who was tragically raped and drowned here. The rock is good but the outer crust is thin in places, so care should be taken when brushing holds and after wet weather.

1» 6c
The left arête behind the roof.

2» Soggy Bottom Crack // 6a
The crack above the puddle.

3» 6a+
Jump to the ledge and mantel.

4» The Staffordshire Flyer // 6b
The superb overhang is possible at the grade, proving looks can be deceptive. Span left from the thin rail to slopey jugs on the lip and glory above. Poor swimmers may wish to wear armbands.

5» The Arête // 6c

6» Groovy Crack // 4
Climb into the hanging crack.

7» 3+
The chipped wall.

8» 4+
The flake line on the right.

9» 6a+
The arête on its left-hand side. On the right it's 5+.

10» 5+
Climb the flake, no arête.

11» 6c+
Start in the corner and trend up and right to a pocket. Finish direct.

Doxey's Pool : bouldering

12» 6c
Start below the arch and climb up and left to the same pocket.

13» 6a+
Start as for the previous problem but continue along the arch.

14» 6a+
Climb directly into the flake at the end of the arch.

15» 6b+
The arête from low undercuts.

16» 3+
The terrific jamming crack.

17» 3+
The arête.

18» Pancake // 4
A great problem in and out of the big dish.

James Parrott on The Staffordshire Flyer (6b) **photo :** Dave Parry

Very Far Skyline : bouldering

A good circuit of low-grade problems on good rock with one particularly excellent slab. Definitely worth the walk. These boulders are below the path. The boulders above the path are very soft and climbing damages them, so you are asked not to climb on them.

1» Rounded Arête // 3
The delicate arête.

2» Open Groove // 5
Smear up the faint groove.

3» Two Pocket Slab // 5
As the name suggests, climb up the twin pockets.

4» Lazy Trout // 5
The tallest section of the slab.

5» 4+
Climb directly to the upper arête.

6» 5+
The steep arête.

7» 5+
The right-hand side of the arête.

8» 5
The corner crack.

9» Pinkies to Perkies // 3
The excellent thin crack.

10» 3
Walk up the slab.

11» Inner Tube // 6a+
With hands in the hole, launch for the top.

Very Far Skyline : bouldering

12» 3
The gentle wall.

13» 3
The left-hand crack.

14» 3
The right-hand crack.

15» 3
The vague ramp line.

16» Flight Exam // 4+
The excellent slab with 99.9% of the climbing revolving around the mid-height pocket. Smearing up and right from the pocket is a good 5.

17» 6b+
The thin seams up the rib to the right.

18» 6b
The right arête.

James Parrott on Problem 5 (4+)
photo : Dave Parry

the roaches **third cloud**

There are five Clouds in total, of which the third is the largest. The other Clouds do offer routes, although many are short solos. There is also excellent bouldering along the clouds, albeit limited and in the harder grades.

Just like the **Skyline**, the **Third Cloud** is a good way to escape the hustle and bustle of the lower and upper tiers. There is a good selection of routes of all grades – *Crabbies Crack*, being one of the best VSs at the Roaches.

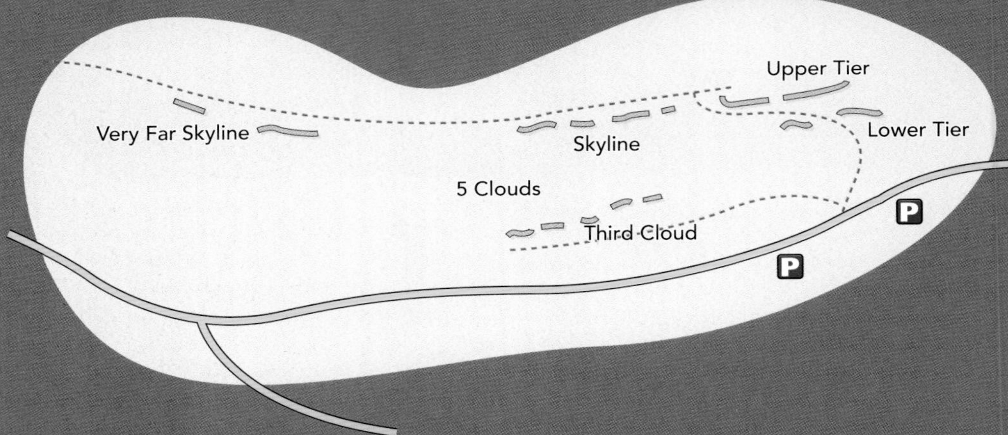

Access

Park as for the bulk of The Roaches in the extensive lay-bys below the crag; remember to park in the marked bays, as police monitor the area and show little leniency with on-the-spot fines. Once through the gate turn immediately left and follow a path uphill and almost parallel to the road. Where the path forks right towards a small quarry (and the **Upper Tier**) take the left-hand fork past a National Trust sign and follow the path parallel to a wall. A series of smaller outcrops can be seen up the hill (the **First** and **Second Clouds**) before the impressive buttress of the **Third Cloud** is reached. The **Fourth** and **Fifth Clouds** are a little further along if you're feeling adventurous...

Seasonal bird restrictions do apply from time to time but these will be clearly signposted. Please do not approach 'as the crow flies' from the road and keep the noise down. The nearby farm and cottages are inhabited and the owners will likely take a dim view of climbers if walls are knocked down and/or they are frequently disturbed.

Ian Parnell on Rubberneck (HVS 5a) - photo : John Coefield

Jon Winter on Crabbie's Crack (VS 4c)   photo : Ian Parnell

Third Cloud

An excellent buttress with full-length routes on peerless rock.

1» Rubberneck **HVS 5a // 15m // ✪✪✪**

A wonderfully technical challenge centred on the groove and crack system on the left-hand side of the wall. Shimmy up the groove with no shortage of difficulty and gain the crack (good gear). Romp up the crack and the final slab above.

2» Crabbie's Crack Left-Hand **HVS 4c // 16m // ✪✪**

Climb the crack for several metres, but head off left below a small overlap and boldly climb flakes to reach easier ground. A good alternative to the next route.

3» Crabbie's Crack **VS 4c // 15m // ✪✪✪**

An excellent crack climb that may well wear you out. Tackle the initial crack, arrive at a ledge and finish up a much easier crack in the upper wall.

4» The Bender **VS 4b // 7m // ✪**

Starting up on the right, follow thin curving cracks left of two flakes. If you're in the gully, you're in the… err, gully. Don't go in the gully.

wimberry

Two things will probably strike you as Wimberry first comes into view on your way from the car park: *"Wow, that's a big hill"*, and *"Wow, that looks like a scary crag"*.

But don't go home. The quality of climbing on offer, and the fact that Wimberry is often at its best on a summer day, make it a real asset in the Peak's gritstone inventory. It looks scary because, from below it looks so… so dark – but this is because it is likely in the shade, with the sun directly behind it. With the character-building walk in behind you, the crag opens up with a clutch of traditionally featured routes with no nasty surprises. There are good, solid belays up on top and tremendous views to be enjoyed out over Dovestone Reservoir and the Chew Valley.

The rock is tough, solid moorland grit, and despite the crag's north-facing aspect, it is only green after prolonged damp weather or in the depths of winter. If you're up here during the latter then you're a nutter.

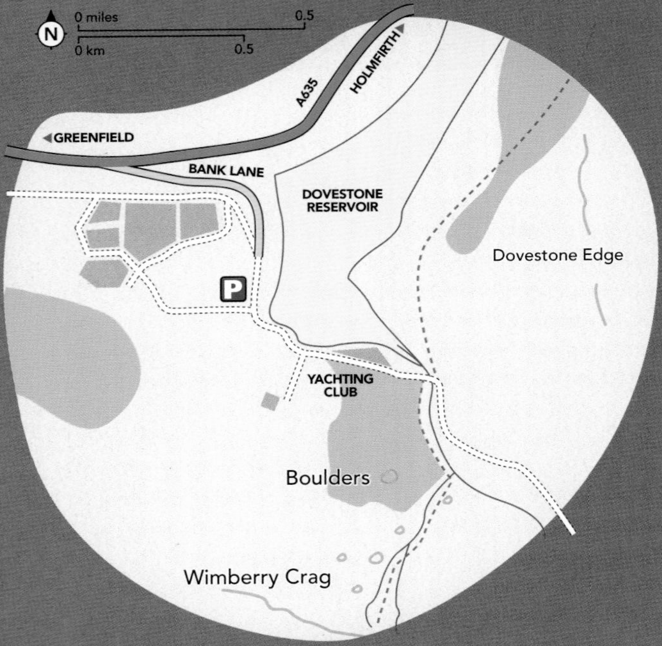

Access

A large Pay and Display car park can be found adjacent to Dovestone Reservoir just off the A635. Follow the road towards the crag and eventually break off right along footpaths that lead to a steep 'footpath' directly up to the crag at its left-hand side.

The **bouldering** can be located easily in the sloping meadow below the crag.

GR **SE016024**

Lucinda Hughes on Route II (VS 5a)   **photo :** David Simmonite

the **routes**

Surprise Area

The first series of climbs is found on the leftmost rocks as you reach the crag, although you may want to spend 10 minutes getting your breath back before climbing.

1» Thermometer Crack **VS 4b // 8m // ✪**

One of the first routes on the crag, the steep crack gives good jamming and laybacking.

2» Crack and Slab **S 4a // 8m // ✪**

From the short chimney, climb left to an awkward exit up the groove.

3» Ornithologist's Corner **VS 5a // 12m // ✪✪**

Climb the corner to a strenuous exit right around the overhang. Varied climbing with excellent protection.

4» Surprise Arête **HVS 4c // 12m // ✪**

Follow the arête on its right before finishing up the crack as for the previous route. The grade reflects the bold nature of the initial arête, which is harder for the vertically challenged.

5» Surprise **VS 4c // 14m // ✪✪**

The leftwards crack is climbed to a tricky move around the protruding block.

6» Overhanging Chimney **VDiff // 12m // ✪**

The chimney is awkward as far as the thread and then eases above. A tip? Face left.

E For an E1 challenge, the next crack to the right is *Freddie's Finale*, a Wimberry classic and also a classic at the grade. It's no pushover, though, and you will need to be familiar with the finer points of fist-jamming and in possession of a selection of large gear.

Hanging Groove Area

A right pair. Two, not too dissimilar, crack systems requiring plenty of effort.

7» Hanging Groove **VS 4c // 16m // ✪✪**

A steep and strenuous start on good holds gives access to the upper crack and groove, which thankfully eases somewhat.

8» Coffin Crack **VS 4c // 16m // ✪✪✪**

Gain the obvious, coffin-shaped niche at 3m and layback furiously from here to an easing of angle and effort above. Classic crack-climbing.

9» Bertie's Bugbear **S 4a // 18m // ✪✪✪**

The prominent central groove is well protected throughout. A superb route – the best on the crag below the extremes, many of which surround it.

Route I Area

Home to a classic pair of complementary routes, both in the shadow of Wimberry's famous prow.

10» Starvation Chimney HVD // 18m // ★

Believe it or not, this route has a powerful tractor beam which pulls climbers in and rarely lets them out. It's time we put a stop to this madness. Follow the crack to a blocked exit and move left to a narrow squeeze, which proves to be the crux.

11» Route I HS 4b // 18m // ★★★

The gently leaning groove is a crag classic with interesting climbing and good protection.

12» Route II VS 5a // 18m // ★★★

The tricky initial crack is the crux, but the interest is sustained above. From the crack, head right to the protruding rock boss. Tackle this and head up the left-hand crack to finish.

13» Twin Cracks S 4a // 8m // ★

From the ledge below the sidewall, climb the right-hand of the two cracks.

Herringbone Slab Area

The edge begins to tail off now, but does offer a few more classics, including the second of the following two routes.

14» Squirmer's Chimney S 4a // 12m // ✪

Sorry – another chimney. But they are bloody good fun aren't they!? Tackle the wide crack to the left of the tall, narrow buttress.

15» Herringbone Slab HVS 4c // 10m // ✪✪

A bold and serious route with a difficult move at two-thirds height to reach a sloping ledge.

Kim Leyland on Problem 1 (6a+) photo : John Coefield

Wimberry : bouldering

The bouldering is described **from low to high**, beginning with the first boulder reached from the car park: **The Sugar Loaf**.

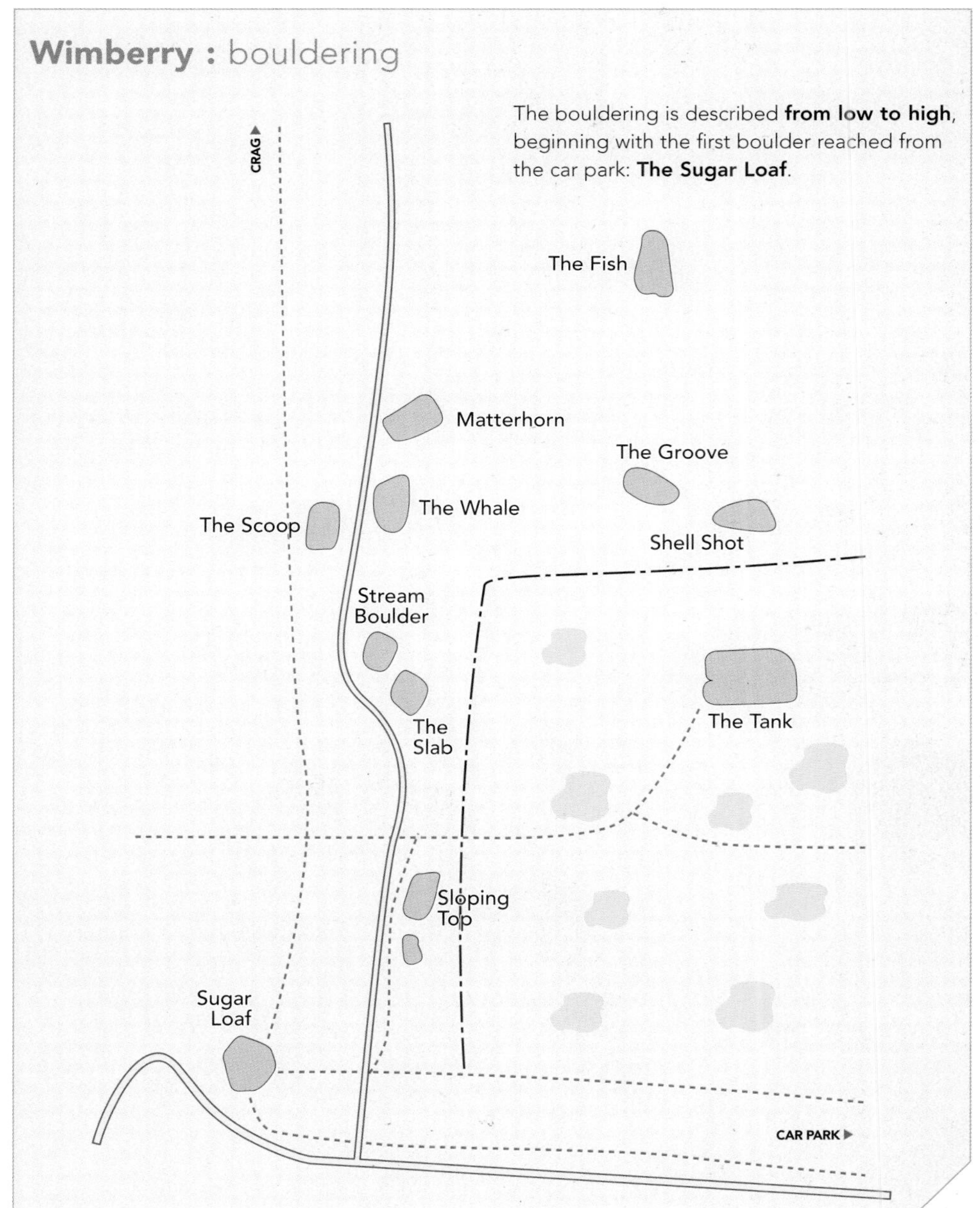

Wimberry : bouldering

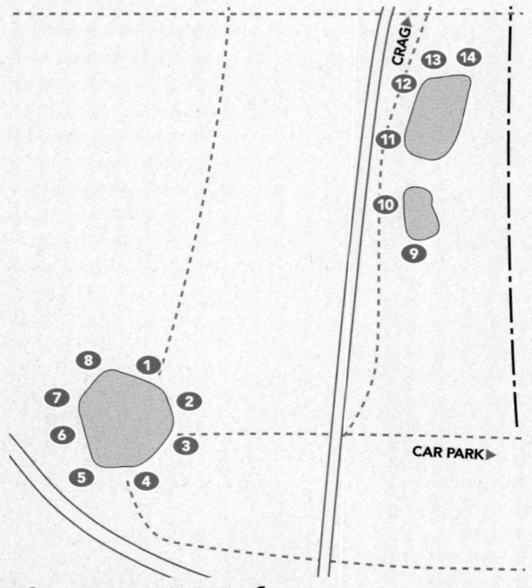

The Sugar Loaf

Don't be put off by the graffiti and old and not-so-old chips, **The Sugar Loaf** is a good spot to develop steely fingers.

1» 6a+
The blunt arête facing the hillside is started from the flake in the centre of the wall.

2» 3
The way down is also an easy up-problem.

3» 4+
Pockets, scoops and chips up the high wall.

4» Artificial Route // 4+
The short, hanging arête and wall above on chips.

5» Baxter's Wall Direct // 5+
The vague arête on yet more chips.

6» Local Hero // 6b+
The wall is a crimpy little meany.

7» 5+
The rib to the left on chips.

8» 4
The heavily chipped slabby wall to the left.

Sloping Top

The ingeniously named boulder, the second of two, located just uphill from **The Sugar Loaf**.

9» 6b
The undercut right arête from a sit start.

10» 4
Sadly chipped, the slab is quite easy.

11» Slap Happy // 6c
A classic of the genre – grovelling onto the top of a piece of gritstone. From the high right-hand hold, slap the top, match and start topping out. And then keep topping out.

12» Fat Slapper // 6b+
The featured arête to the left.

E The sit start is a good introduction to the 7a grade. Sit start with a flat hold for your right-hand, an undercut for your left and slap up and into the stand-up version.

13» The Slot // 5
Undercut the slot.

14» 5
The wall to the left with a left-hand sidepull.

Wimberry : bouldering

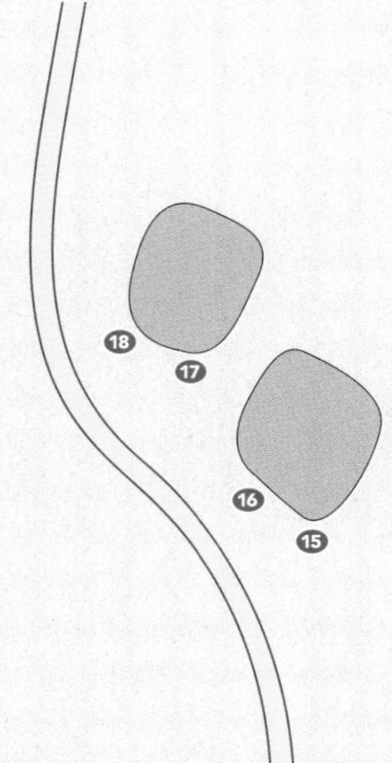

The Slab

15» The Slab // 4
The right arête of the slab.

16» 3+
The centre of the chipped slab.

Stream Boulder

17» 4+
The short arête on the downhill side.

18» 4
The wall to the left. The groove above the stream is 6a but must be done first go, as failure is not an option.

The Tank

The large boulder within the clearing inside the plantation has a classic mid-grade testpiece, *Think Tank*, in addition to several lovely, low-grade problems.

19» 6c
The wall to the right of the wide crack.

20» Elephant's Bum // 5
The rounded crack feature.

21» 6c
The slab to the left of the crack, starting with either your left or right hand on the big pebble.

22» 4
The wall with the flakes.

23» 4+
The large, leftwards slanting crack.

24» Think Tank // 6b+
The classic line of leftward-slanting flakes is climbed to a high top-out. A rite of passage at the grade.

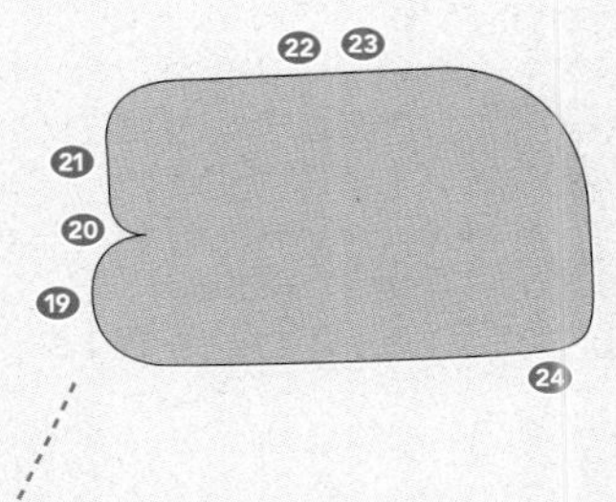

Wimberry : bouldering

Shell Shot

Located just up the hill from The Tank, outside the perimeter of the fence.

25» Shell Shot // 4
The downhill arête.

26» Shell Shock // 4
The slab.

27» The Cannon // 6a
A slight eliminate up the flakes to the right.

28» The Groove // 6b
On a small boulder, up and left of *Shell Shot*, there is a lovely little groove tackled from a sitting start.

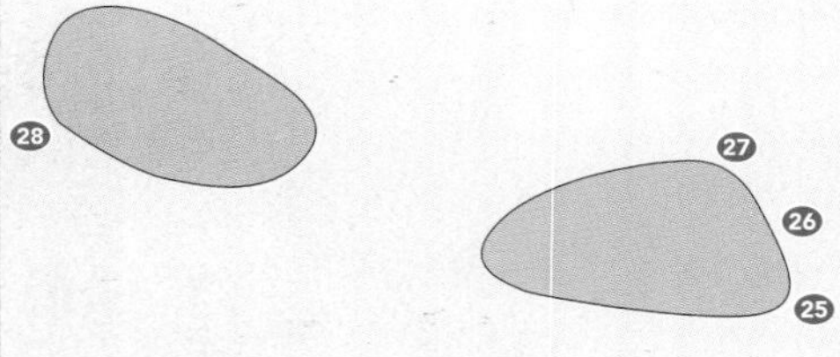

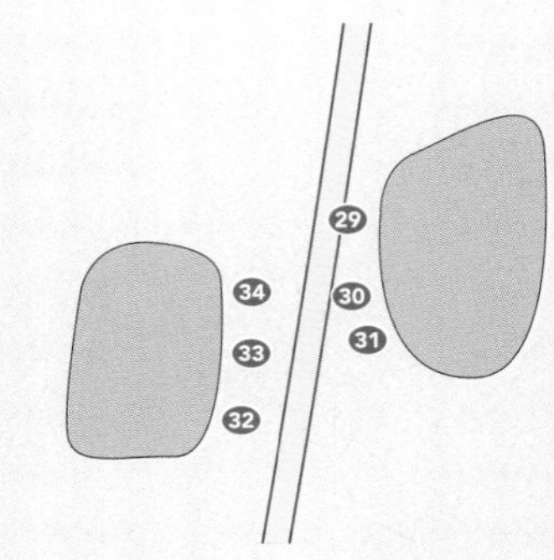

The Whale

29» 4+
The crack line facing the stream.

30» 6b+
The bulging wall, avoiding the crack with your feet.

31» 5+
The pockets and the wall.

The Scoop

The boulder over the stream from The Whale.

32» 5+
The left side of the scoop.

33» 5+
Direct up the wall above the scoop.

34» The Scoop // 4
The scoop, exiting right.

Wimberry : bouldering

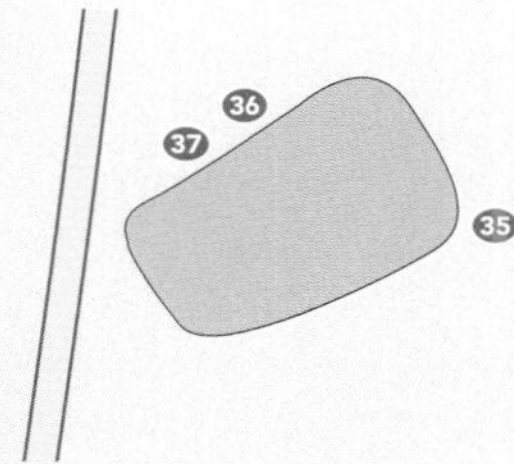

The Matterhorn

The large angular boulder just above is home to some tall classics, and several good easier problems.

35» 4+
Climb the arête on its right-hand side. Straight up the narrow wall to the right is the same grade.

36» 6a
An eliminate problem up the black slab.

37» 4
Chips up the centre of the wall. Various eliminates can also be concocted on this wall.

Jim Hilliard on Local Hero (6b+)
photo : David Simmonite

windgather

A wonderful introduction to climbing, Windgather features a large number of routes concentrated in the lower grades. It is a good place to learn to lead, with many of the climbs centred around cracks that feature good protection, although this can be sparse on some of the face climbs.

Beware! The crag is very popular with outdoor groups who tend to top rope many of the established routes. Fortunately there is plenty of crag and if one buttress is under siege, chances are you'll find something else to go at a little further along.

The rock is moorland gritstone of generally good quality. The strata lean gently in, providing both a slabby angle and a good supply of positive holds. Its aspect ensures that the crag stays clean. As it is exposed and west-facing, it can be a wonderful spot on a spring or summer evening.

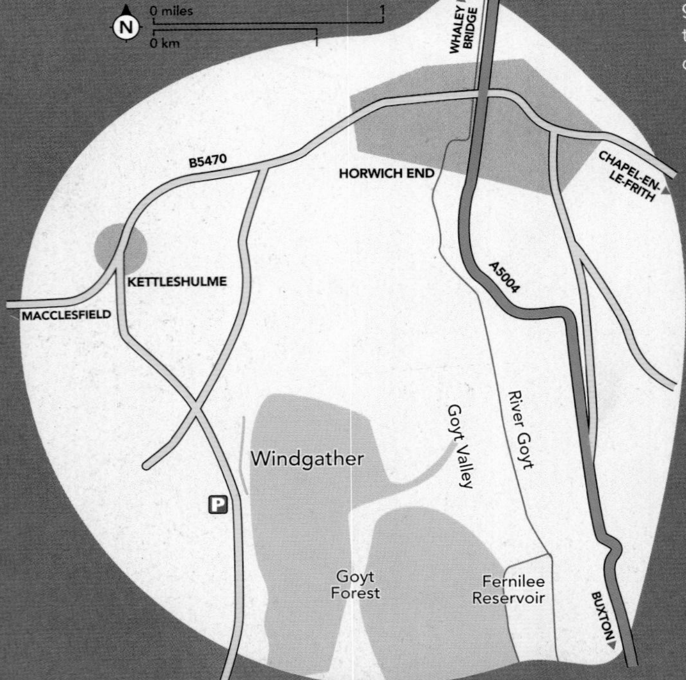

Access

The crag is best approached from Kettleshulme and is clearly visible from the road. Roadside parking is available for a dozen or so cars. If this is full there is additional parking back up the road near an old quarry.

Please note that the crag must only be approached from the lane via the two stiles and the fenced alley. Climbers also only have access to the area between the fences above and below the crag; please do not go beyond these or damage the walls which bound the crag at either end.

Simon Wilson on High Buttress Arête (Diff) – **photo** : Adam Long

the **routes**

North Buttress

The first prominent buttress on the left.

1» Staircase **Mod // 9m // ✪**

A good beginner's route up the well-featured, stepped corner.

2» Green Crack **S // 9m // ✪✪**

Steep, accessible climbing up the blocky groove and crack.

3» North Buttress Arête **VS 4c // 9m // ✪✪**

Big holds compensate for the sporting protection and steep angle of this crag classic.

4» Chimney and Crack **VDiff // 9m**

Scramble up to the ledge and tackle first the chimney and then the wide crack on the left wall.

Middle Buttress

The next major buttress along.

5» Portfolio **HVS 5b // 8m // ✪**
Avoiding holds on adjacent routes, climb the polished slab to the overhang. Pull over this with difficulty.

6» Central Route **HVD // 9m // ✪**
Follow the awkward, poorly-protected wall to finish up a thin crack in the upper wall.

7» Chockstone Chimney **Diff // 9m // ✪**
More of a crack really. Well-protected.

8» Mississippi Crack **S // 9m // ✪**
The excellent undercut crack gives a good introduction to the Severe grade.

9» Mississippi Crack Variant **VDiff // 9m // ✪✪**
Start up the bulges to the right (*The Medicine*, HS 4a) but traverse left under the overlap to finish up Mississippi Crack.

High Buttress

The next buttress, with a prominent arête. Popular.

10» Toe Nail **VDiff // 9m // ✪**

Climb up to and through the left-hand side (toes) of the mid-height sandy footprint. The route is bolder in the upper half.

11» Nose Direct **HVD // 9m // ✪✪**

Climb direct to the nose from just left of the arête. Climb over it, step left and finish directly.

12» High Buttress Arête **Diff // 9m // ✪✪**

Climb the arête almost entirely directly. One of the best at Windgather.

Buttress Two

Closest to the road, it's no surprise that this buttress is popular.

13» Buttress Two Gully **Mod // 9m // ✪**
Another good first lead up the leaning gully.

14» Squashed Finger **VDiff // 9m // ✪**
The recessed crack is well protected.

15» Corner Crack **VDiff // 9m // ✪**
The name says it all. A friendly route with good gear and enjoyable climbing.

16» Aged Crack **HS 4a // 9m // ✪**
Climb the low corner to the crack. Starting from the previous route lowers the grade to VDiff.

17» Traditional **HS 4a // 9m // ✪**
From the block, climb the centre of the face. A bold route with gear provided by small wires and cams.

18» The Broken Groove in the Arête **Diff // 9m**
Steep. Good gear. Good climbing. A contender for a good first lead.

John Coefield on Traditional (HS 4a) photo : Adam Long

South Buttress

A large undercut buttress at the right-hand end of the crag.

19» Route 2 **VS 4b // 9m // ✪**

The steep crack through the overhang is harder than it looks.

20» Route 1 **S // 9m // ✪✪**

Climb half-way up the next route and then traverse left around the arête onto a ledge above the cave. Climb directly to a blocky finish.

21» South Crack **Mod // 9m**

Get down deep and dirty in this 3D affair.

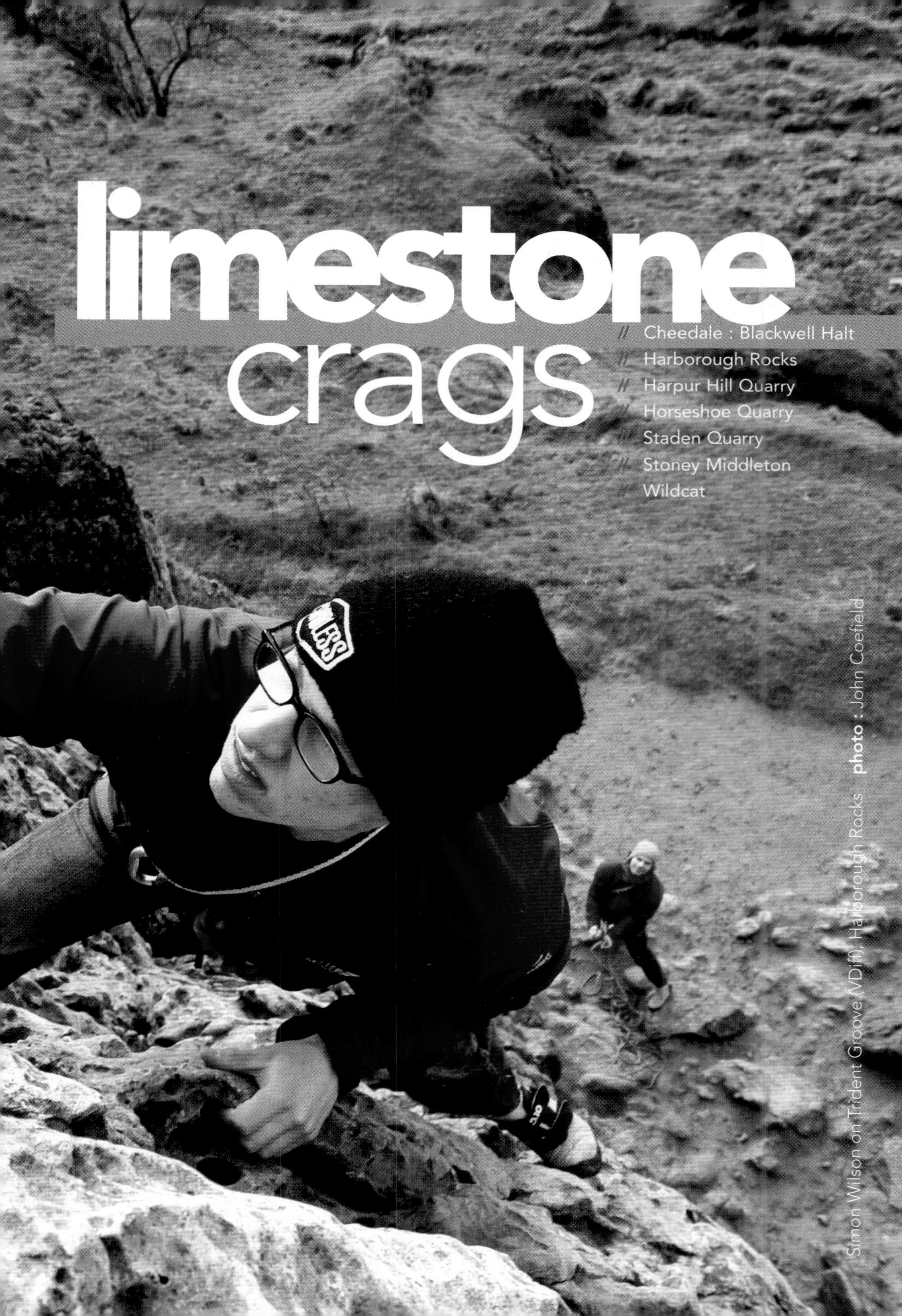

limestone crags

// Cheedale : Blackwell Halt
// Harborough Rocks
// Harpur Hill Quarry
// Horseshoe Quarry
// Staden Quarry
// Stoney Middleton
// Wildcat

Simon Wilson on Trident Groove (VDiff), Harborough Rocks **photo :** John Coefield

cheedale : blackwell halt

A compact little wall, featuring a number of routes that despite having that "done one, done them all" feel about them, each manage to maintain independence and quality. They are all of a similar length and grade, with similar holds, and all are situated on the same pleasant sunny little buttress. This is the tip of Cheedale, with another world of classic sport and trad climbing to be found further downstream.

Blackwell Halt is a sunny, south-facing compact buttress. Usually dry, but with some seepage low down, it is quite sheltered.

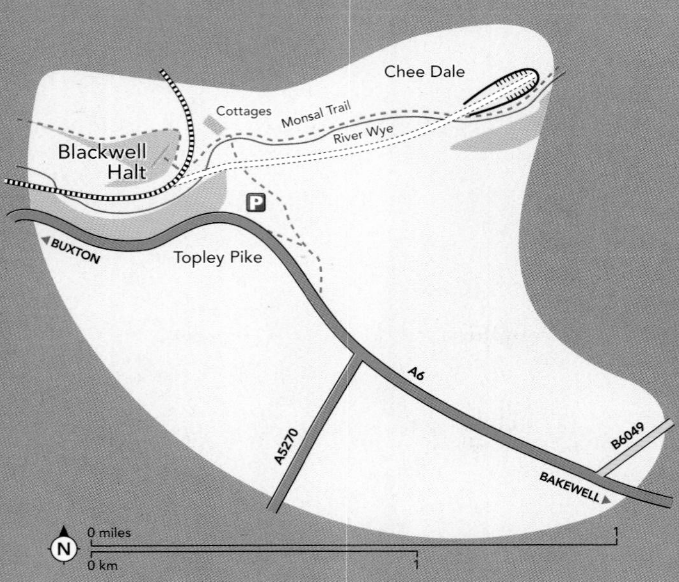

Access

Park at the large Topley Pike lay-by on the A6, on the summit of the hill before the road descends to the river and Buxton. There should be a convenient tea wagon if you are lucky. Go through the gate and follow the path downhill, joining a track that cuts back further downhill and crosses the disused railway line. (Turning right up the line accesses the main Cheedale crags.) Go down to the river, cross the footbridge, and turn left away from cottages following the line of the river. Go through a small tunnel under the live railway. After re-emerging, head up the hill and cross through/over the fence after a few metres. Rock steps lead up to the plateau on which the crag can be found.

GR **SK110726**

Kim Leyland on Windows 95 (F6a+) **photo :** Dave Parry

the **routes**

cheedale : blackwell halt

1» Micro-chip **F6c // 8m**
A short, hard route starting from the bank.

2» Modem **F6a // 8m**
Make sure you are warmed up, because this route has a couple of good pumpy moves.

3» The Arapahoe Connection **F6b // 15m // ✪**
A worthwhile route, the first to climb the full height of the wall.

4» Hard Drive **F6b+ // 15m // ✪**
Another long route, accepting the full challenge of the wall.

5» Megabyte **F6b // 15m // ✪**
Similar to the previous route, but a slightly easier upper wall warrants the lower grade.

6» Gopherspace **F6b // 15m // ✪**
The crux is saved for the top wall.

7» Windows 95 **F6a+ // 15m // ✪**
A little bit of steepness through the low roof, fortunately on good holds.

8» Falling Irons **F6b // 15m // ✪**
More good climbing past the right-hand side of the overlap.

9» She Got the Bosch, I Got the Drill **F6b // 14m // ✪**
Start on the slope up right, with more wall-climbing on flat holds.

10» Waste Bin **F6a+ // 12m // ✪**
If you're a master of the 6s, then this may provide a good warm up. Start a short distance up the bank.

harborough rocks

Access

Parking is available on the minor road that runs from Wirksworth to Brassington, just east of a large factory and works. A track leads through the works, over the High Peak Trail and up the left-hand end of the crag.

Limestone's answer to Windgather, Harborough is, quite rightly, a popular crag with a pleasant aspect and a fine selection of routes in the lower grades – excellent for beginners.

Although largely concentrated in the lower grades, the routes do tend to be steep and so provide solid challenges. Unfortunately, the crag's popularity over many years has seen it become polished but the rock is still of good quality and the aspect is very nice overlooking the High Peak Trail.

South facing, the crag catches any sun going, dries quickly and doesn't seep.

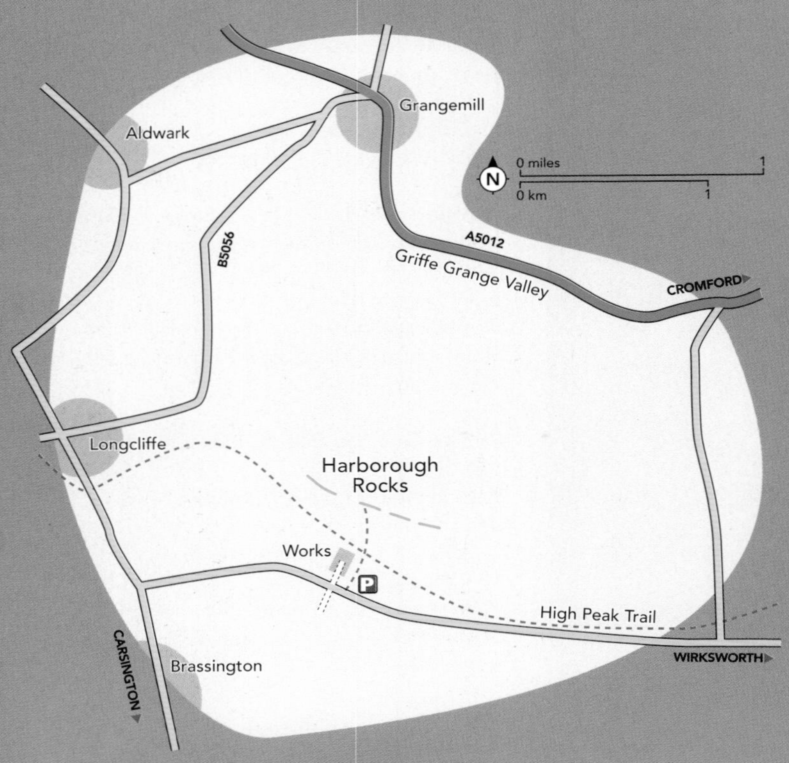

...ong on Steep Ridge (VDiff) **photo** : John Coefield

the **routes**

The Steeple

The first group of routes surrounds the prominent pinnacle of The Steeple.

1» Overhanging Wall Variant
VDiff // 10m // ✪

Climb the groove right of the cave to a ledge. Step out right and climb the wall above the overhang to finish.

2» Overhanging Chimney Direct
S 4a // 8m // ✪

The corner crack has awkward moves around the nid-height bulge.

3» Pedestal Crack **S 4a // 12m // ✪**

Slip and slide up the initial crack to a ledge before moving left to climb the shallow groove in the middle of *The Steeple*.

4» Concave Wall **HVD 4a // 6m // ✪**

Climb the wall to the ledge.

5» Steeple Arête **VDiff // 12m // ✪**

Climb the lower arête to the ledge and then the upper, exposed continuation.

6» Harborough Crack **HS 4c // 6m // ✪**
The slippery groove was first climbed in 1898 by James W Puttrell.

7» Little Arête **Diff // 6m**
The short arête right of the old ruined building.

Creased Wall

8» Thin Air **VS 4b // 10m // ✪**
Climb the twin cracks that slice down the left-hand side of the wall.

9» Creased Wall **HVS 5a // 10m // ✪**
The fingery crack in the centre of the wall is one of the toughest challenges at Harborough.

10» Crinkle Crack **VS 4c // 10m // ✪**
The crack right again leads to the upper groove. Care should be taken with protection as there isn't much available.

11» Steep Ridge **VDiff // 10m // ✪**
The right-hand arête of the wall.

12» Little Gully **Diff // 10m**
The gully, passing a half-height ledge.

Trident Buttress

13» Trident Face **VDiff // 12m // ✪**
Follow the prominent shallow groove to a ledge before moving left to finish swiftly up the steep groove above.

14» Trident Eliminate **HS 4b // 12m // ✪**
Climb the rib right of the previous route to the ledges, step left and pull over the overlap finishing on the right.

15» Trident Groove **VDiff // 12m // ✪**
The leaning groove just left of the arête.

16» Trident arête **VDiff // 12m // ✪**
Follow the arête throughout: tough at the start, airy at the finish.

The Arête

17» Overhanging Crack VS 5a // 6m // ✪
The steep, leaning crack.

18» The arête S 4a // 6m // ✪
Starting on the left hand side, weave up and right before moving back left to finish.

19» Blinkers VS 5a // 6m // ✪
The thin crack right of the arête.

20» Legs Over VS 4b // 6m // ✪
The centre of the wall to the right.

harpur hill quarry

In terms of their sport potential, the angular walls of Harpur Hill have only been developed relatively recently. There is a smattering of older trad routes here, and some of them are very good, but it is the breadth of mid-grade sport climbing which draws climbers in and, from F5, and particularly in the mid F6s, sport climbers are very well catered for.

On the main buttresses, the rock is good; the quarry sees plenty of traffic (climbers, not industrial), so the routes are fairly clean and much of the suspect rock has been removed. However, this is still a quarry so caution should always be exercised.

If it faced 180° the other way, then Harpur Hill would likely give Horseshoe a run for its money in the popularity stakes. As it happens, the combined north-west and north-east aspect means it sees the sun towards the extremes of the day, and hardly at all during the winter months. A good place to escape the sun on hot summer days, it can be cold and exposed when conditions are less than ideal. It doesn't suffer from seepage and tends not to stay wet too long after bad weather.

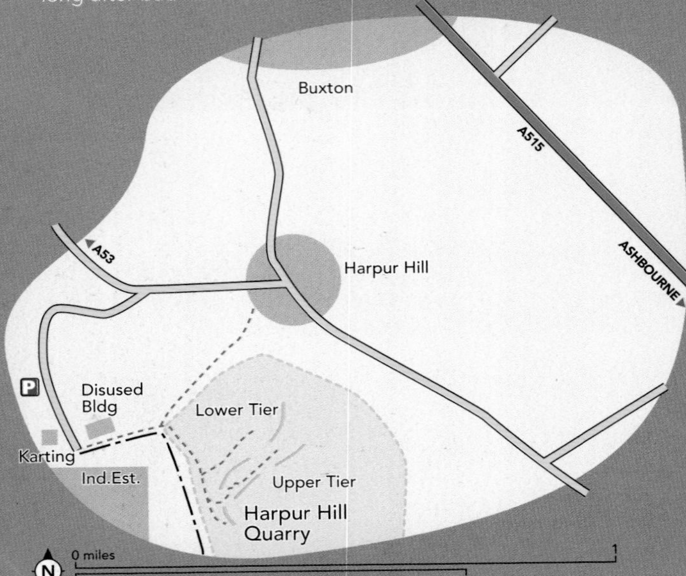

Access

Located south of Buxton, above the village of Harpur Hill, the village and the quarry can be accessed by either the A515 or the A53. West of the village a well signposted road leads off to an industrial estate. There is parking for 3 or so cars on the right in lay-bys. If these are full, or someone objects, then additional parking can be found in the village. From the lay-bys, head up the road towards the industrial estate and follow the signposted footpath left along the edge of a field towards the quarry. Pass through a gate and after a further 30m an obvious scramble can be made up a short wall to gain a wide track that leads into the quarry. The climbing listed here is all located or accessed from the right-hand side of the quarry. A zigzag path near the Cairn Area leads to the Upper Tier.

Note: There is no formal access agreement for the quarry so please leave if you asked to. Up-to-date information can be found on the BMC's Regional Access Database: **www.thebmc.co.uk/bmccrag**

Dementia Normale (F6a) **photo**: Ian Parnell

the **routes**

Upper Tier: Papacy Buttress

Tall and imposing, this double-fronted buttress is home to the best rock and most of the best climbing at Harpur Hill.

1» Strangled at Birth **F6b // 18m // ✪**

The short arête and thin wall above.

2» Coral Seas **F6a // 28m // ✪✪✪**

Super! Climb up and deviate left into the corner. Stretch out left onto the slab and press on to the break. Pull through the bulge and climb diagonally up and right to the lower off.

3» Avarice Allsorts **F6c+ // 24m // ✪**

A direct on the previous route through the roof above the corner.

4» Rocky Variations **F6b // 24m // ✪**

A meandering route right of the gully in the front of the buttress (*Lust*, VS 4c). Step off a block and climb the flat wall to a groove. Trend left out of this and up to a small roof. Step right around this into another groove and climb this leftwards to finish.

5» Apollo Creed **F6b // 24m // ✪✪**

Step off the block, as for the previous route, but head further across before commencing upward movement. Climb past the right-hand side of the roof and up to ledges. Step briefly right before heading straight up to finish.

6» Full Frontal F6c // 28m // ✪
One for the shirehorses. With blinkers on pursue a line directly up the narrow front of the buttress, starting from the right.

7» Dementia Normale F6a // 18m // ✪
An amenable line up cracks in the shorter right-hand side of the buttress.

Upper Tier: Prophecy Area

The largest stretch of walls and routes on the upper level, but the quality isn't quite up to that of Papacy Buttress.

8» Calci-Mauve F6b // 24m // ✪
Climb up the pillar and press on to the break. The upper wall is worth the effort.

9» Over the Hill F6c // 22m // ✪✪
A pumpy sucker up the cracks and through the roof right of the previous route.

10» Four Telling Tales F6c // 20m // ✪✪
A technical excursion up the crack to the left of the arête.

E The *Prophecy* is an F7a worth trying if your arms are jam-packed with stamina. Climb up to a roof 5m right of the previous route and pull rightwards over it to access the upper wall and arête.

11» Different Seasons **F6a+ // 20m // ✪**

The arête and crack. The lower off is at half height so don't keep climbing past it…

Lower Tier: Kamikaze Area

A good area to get in some mileage on the lower grades.

12» Geisha Grooves **F6a // 14m**

The main groove, with the emphasis on the left-hand side.

13» Saweno Gancho **F6c // 14m // ✪**

The exception in the area – a tough one, which is both technical and sustained. Climb the right wall of the groove.

14» Kamikaze Clone **F6a+ // 10m**

A short route up the left edge of the buttress.

15» The Rising Sun **F5 // 10m**

The centre of the same buttress. A good introduction to sport climbing.

16» Riding Shogun **F6a+ // 14m**

Climb the lower wall and bulges above.

Lower Tier: Cairn Area

The best route hereabouts is actually F7a, but it's worth a shot if you're going well.

17» Great White **F6a // 16m**

On the leaning sidewall climb around the roof on the right.

E Cairn is the F7a up the attractive wave on the left wall. A hard move gives access to it and further hard climbing allows an exit trending left before finishing straight up.

18» The Naked Spur **F5 // 20m**

The easiest line on the buttress up the structurally varied arête.

19» Senile Delinquents **F5+ // 24m // ✪**

The roof and flake on the right-hand side of the wall. Finish with care over the top roof.

20» Breakfast at Safeways **F6b // 12m // ✪**

The left-hand side of the final slab.

sport climbing

Bob Mort on Pale Rider (F6a), Horseshoe Quarry **photo :** Nick Smith

What is Sport Climbing?

Sport climbing is an imported style of climbing with *in-situ* bolts used as protection. It allows focus to be placed on the physical and technical difficulties, as the danger element is to a large degree removed. That is not to say all hazards are removed; accidents can still occur and it is important to ensure that care is still taken, particularly when communicating with your belayer and when lowering-off from a route.

The French grading scale is used for sport climbing. It runs from very low, as low as F4+ in this book, and currently peaks at over F9a+ in the UK and even higher abroad – very hard! In this book, though, we only go up to F6c+. Since it is possible to push oneself that little bit harder on sport routes, it is more difficult to make an exact comparison between French and British grades. As a guide, F4+ can span from HS up to low-end HVS – moves up to English 4c in difficulty, and English 5b/c moves can be found on sport routes of F5+ through to F6b+. We have included a number of routes above this grade, as, with a good standard of fitness and confidence, it is possible to progress through the grades fairly rapidly.For more information about grades, see *A Note About Grading* on page xx.

Clipping bolts

All you need are bolts (already in the rock) and quickdraws (hanging from your harness). Sounds easy, doesn't it? Well there are a few things to take into consideration when out clipping bolts.

About bolts

Expansion bolts are bolts with an expansion sleeve that are inserted into drilled holes in the rock. As the bolt is tightened, the sleeve expands to grip the drill hole. The actual hanger through which the quickdraw is clipped is screwed to the crag face by the bolt. It is not possible to lower-off with the rope through the bolt hanger.

Glued bolts tend to be a single piece of metal bent to create a 'U' shape that protrudes from the rock, often referred to as 'staples'. Again these are inserted into a drilled hole but are held in place by epoxy resin, which also serves to protect the steel of the bolt. The quickdraw is clipped directly into the eye of the bolt and it is possible to lower-off these bolts with the rope threaded through – very handy for retreating from routes.

Bolt disclaimer

Fixed gear comes with no guarantee. It has evolved over time with different bolts, staples and lower offs placed over different years by different people with different levels of expertise. What you use is ultimately for you to judge. The authors of this guidebook do not accept any liability for the death of, or injury to, any person involved in bolt-protected climbing arising from equipment failure or otherwise or to any person involved in placing bolts and against whom such a claim has been made. Like any other form of protection, a bolt is only as good as the rock it is placed in. Climbers must rely upon their own experience.

The BMC has carried out a great deal of work on both bolts and the placing of bolts (the **Better Bolts Campaign**). To find out more, and to download the BMC good practice documents, please visit **www.thebmc.co.uk**.

How do I reach the first bolt?

The first bolt on sport climbs is often located several metres from the floor, providing protection when climbing past or above it. This does mean, however, that clipping it can be a tall person's game, not to mention slightly spooky if the climbing to reach it is tricky. In sport climbing it is commonplace to use a **clipstick** to reach and pre-clip the first bolt. An extendible stick, the clipstick holds a quickdraw, with the upper gate held open to snap around the bolt and the rope threaded through the lower gate. Once the bolt is clipped, the rope is already safely through the first bolt. If you do not have a clipstick then most climbers at a crag will happily let you borrow theirs. Alternatively, the belayer can provide a spot, as in bouldering, to help protect the initial moves.

Where is the best place to clip from?

Ideally it is better to clip bolts when you are alongside them, as this minimises the amount of rope that is paid out by the belayer. However, this is not always possible if the section of climbing around a bolt is particularly difficult. Clipping bolts from below at full stretch is tempting, but you should avoid this, as double the amount of rope must be paid out, increasing the length of any potential fall should an accident occur. This method of clipping also takes more time, making it more tiring and so easier to fumble the rope.

Which way should the quickdraw face and how should it be clipped?

This is often a matter of personal preference. Ideally the gate needs to rest away from the rock, although many climbers prefer the gate facing towards them as they clip. In other words, if you clip with your left hand, the gate faces right, and vice versa. The most important point is that the rope should run **from inside** the krab **to outside**, thereby avoiding the potential kink that would cause it to unclip in a fall.

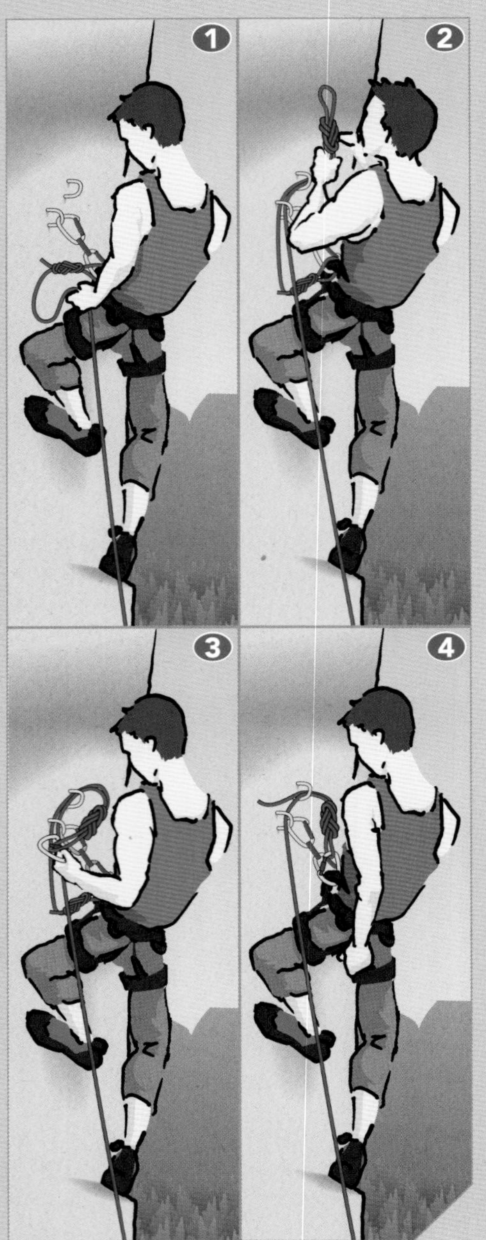

What should I do if I discover a damaged bolt?

If the bolt is at Horseshoe Quarry, contact the BMC, which owns the venue. You can also contact the Peak District Bolt Fund who will know the best people to contact if you're unsure.

Lowering-off

Upon reaching the lower-off, it is common practice to clip into part of it with a quickdraw or sling before setting up the lower-off. Initially clipping into the lower-off, with your belayer holding your weight, also gives you the chance to gather your thoughts, take a breath or de-pump following the climb.

As with the clipping of bolts, lowering-off is a relatively straightforward process, yet one that requires plenty of care to ensure it is done safely. Some recently-equipped sport routes come complete with double-snapgates or screwgates for the lower-off, allowing you simply to clip in and be lowered off. It is more common for routes to have double (or sometimes single) maillons or staples, which must be threaded with the rope before you can be lowered. Some even have snapgates/screwgates, the gates of which may have seized up. You must also thread these, which is slightly more complicated.

If the route is to be seconded or re-lead by the second climber, it would not be necessary to thread the lower-off. Instead, you could clip two quickdraws (assuming there are two bolt anchors for the belay) and pass the rope through these. Screwgates should be used if the route is to be top-roped. The second would then be responsible for threading the lower-off when the last climb is completed (ensuring they are clipped into multiple anchors prior to undertaking this process).

When preparing to thread the anchors to lower off, you must remain tied on and on belay. You should then clip into one or both anchors with quickdraws to take your weight (*see Part 1 of the diagram left*). You can then ask the belayer for slack rope which you can pull through. A bight of this should be passed through the staples/maillons/gates and tied into a figure of eight (*see Part 2 of the diagram left*). This can then be clipped into the belay loop using a screwgate karabiner (*see Part 3 of the diagram left*). The original knot to the harness, used for climbing, can now be untied and the loose end passed through the anchors (*see Part 4 of the diagram left*). You remain safely on belay throughout the entire process with the rope threaded from below through the anchors, ready for lowering off.

Your belayer then takes your weight again, allowing you to release the quickdraws and be lowered to the ground.

Stripping the route

Once the lower-off is threaded, you can lower-off and strip the quickdraws from the route, if your belayer does not intend to second the route, or you can lead the route with the quickdraws already in place. Sometimes you can strip the quickdraws to make subsequent top rope ascents of the route easier. If the route takes a wandering or traversing line, however, we recommend leaving some bolts clipped to minimise the swing taken by a falling second.

Very often the line of the route will be fairly direct, and many of the mid-grade sport routes found in the Peak District are vertical. This means you will typically lower straight down the line, making the retrieval of quickdraws quite easy. If the route takes a meandering line, however, and perhaps passes an overhang or a series of overhangs, stripping the route may be more difficult. To make this process easier, clip a spare quickdraw (perhaps the one clipped to the last bolt and therefore the first to be removed) and clip one end to the belay loop on your harness and the other end to the live end of the rope that leads up from your belayer. Your belayer will then pause each time you reach a bolt, allowing you to remove the quickdraw in control. This will ensure that as you are lowered, you are guided down the line of the route, making the whole process a lot easier.

Retreating from a sport route

If the sport route is equipped with staple bolts, through which the rope can be threaded, then the same procedure can be followed as for lowering off anchors. However, if the route is protected with expansion bolts and hangers this becomes more complicated. The simplest and safest method is to abandon an old krab.

Peak District Bolt Fund

Set up with the aim both of maintaining existing, popular routes and bringing new life to routes and crags that have slipped by the wayside, the Peak District Bolt Fund is a central source to fund new bolts, bolting equipment and the technical support necessary to equip sport routes. Several generous donations from local activists ensured that the bolt fund got off to a good start and it now invites contributions from climbers who regularly enjoy bolted climbing in the Peak District, in particular anyone who is able to volunteer their time to aid the bolting effort.

For more information visit:
www.peakboltfund.co.uk

horseshoe quarry

Horseshoe is undoubtedly the best of the limestone sport climbing quarries. The main wall in particular, offers excellent, well-equipped routes on sound rock. The crag is popular, easily accessible and, thanks to the efforts of the BMC, the once precarious access situation has been largely resolved.

These routes offer a great chance for fit, young climbers to transfer skills learnt on the indoor walls to 'real rock' – a sports apprenticeship here will often lead to success on some of the Peaks harder climbs. Alternately, the veteran ticker may just want a stress-free afternoon climbing fine walls and grooves, clipping bolts, lowering off, and enjoying the view, which is at best, unchallenging. The quick drying main walls are climbable all year round, the quarry is open and pleasant and so justifiably popular.

While climbs of varying quality exist on just about every square inch of rock, the best routes are concentrated on the compact, south facing main wall, and the walls either side.

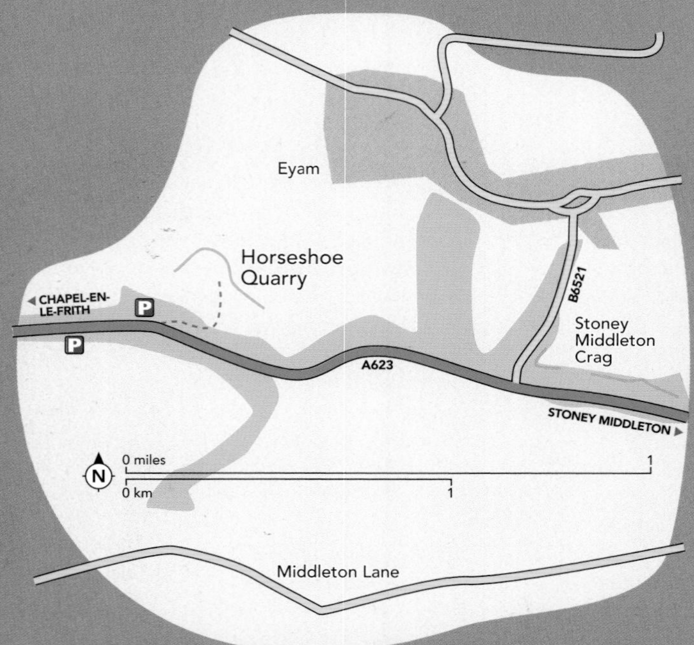

Access

Situated up the valley from Stoney Middleton, the crag is located just off the A623. Heading up the valley, look out for a track on the right-hand side. The best parking is at a large lay-by a little further up on the left. Follow the track a little way to enter the main quarry. The big compact wall facing you is the 'Main Wall'. The climbs are described from left to right.

Adrian Berry on Litany Against Fear (F6b+) **photo :** Matt Heason

the **routes**

Sunday Sport

A popular wall, although the rock lacks quality in some places.

1» Mail on Sunday **F6b // 18m // ✪**

With an obvious crux move, this route is perhaps the best on this part of the wall.

2» Due Care and Attention **F6a+ // 23m // ✪**

A good little groove, the name refers to the rock quality, which fortunately these days is only suspect at the very top.

3» Sunday Sport **F6b // 18m // ✪**

It seems like only yesterday that Mark Pretty ventured off the main wall to establish this new route and in so doing realised the potential of the whole quarry. A good groove climb, of historic importance!

4» Removal Man **F4+ // 20m**

An easy route that is surprisingly worthwhile.

5» Sag Ponir **F5 // 14m**

A short crack, actually marking the edge of the main wall.

Main Wall

The main event and home to the best routes hereabouts.

6» Pale Rider **F6a // 20m // ✪**
A great climb, sticking to the arête all the way.

7» Rain Dance **F6c // 20m // ✪✪**
Another great route, three metres right of the arête.

8» Rotund Rooley **F6b // 20m // ✪**
Pleasant wall climbing with an obvious crux move – enjoy.

9» Wall of Jericho **F6b // 20m // ✪**
Technical wall climbing with quite a few interesting moves.

10» Legal Action **F6c // 20m // ✪✪**
A brilliant route – the first to be put up on the main wall. After a hard start, the climbing is enjoyable all the way.

11» Run for Your Wife **F6c+ // 20m // ✪✪**
One of the harder routes on the wall, but like the rest, well-bolted on sound rock.

12» Private Prosecution F6c // 20m // ✪✪
Another great climb. Again, one of the original routes, if not the original line. It seems to have got easier over the years.

13» Litany Against Fear F6b+ // 20m // ✪✪
A popular route with a bold and precarious finish.

14» Megalithic Man F6b+ // 20m // ✪
Another Peak Limestone classic! Either finish direct at 6c+ or, at the groove, move left over the bulge to a big hold.

E There are two F7as to try before the next route. *Poisonality* is a direct start to a popular F6c (*An Ancient Rhythm*) and starts to the right of the 'No Climbing' paint. A hard, tricky low crux gives way to fine climbing above. *Demolition Man*, also F7a, climbs the wall left of the crack and groove (the next route) and may feel a little bold in places.

15» Shot Yer Bolt F6b+ // 20m // ✪
Another classic! I remember first doing this route in the late eighties, when the rock was dusty, the crag was deserted, except for the hippies who lived there and the man from Tarmac who kept calling the police to get you thrown out. Now the route has queues under it, the rock is approaching a fine, polished marble and the bolts have got bigger and closer. Still worth the entrance fee, though.

16» Lost Monolith F6b+ // 20m // ✪
Another Horseshoe sport route, survivor of at least six guidebooks, it is something of a veteran – who would have thought it? Follow the ramp to some better and slightly harder climbing higher up.

photo : John Coefield

Androids Area

Named after the large, open book trad corner in the centre of the wall. The routes here are popular, yet the rock is still a bit iffy in places.

17» Clean Your Mouth Out F6c+ // 18m
Climb the right-hand side of the rock scar.

18» The Director's Cut F6a+ // 16m
Climb the wall with the crux at mid height.

19» The Running Man F6a+ // 16m // ✪
Finishing at the lower off of the classic horseshoe trad line of *Do Androids Dream of Electric Sheep* (E1 5c), which takes the corner and wall rightwards. Climb up through the roofs.

20» Derailed F6a+ // 16m
From half way up the bank climb past the left-hand side of the cave at two-thirds height.

21» Latrine F5 // 16m
A good easy route.

the next step

Keefe Murphy on The Colostomy Finish (F7a) **photo :** Jerry O'Donnell

F7a

Climb F7a *plus vite!*

You've built up stamina, bouldering has bolstered your technical ability and you're ready to bridge into the French 7s.

01 » **Cairn** **F7a** // **Harpur Hill Quarry**
A three star classic following the attractive wave.

02 » **Demolition Man** **F7a** // **Horseshoe Quarry**
Solid at the grade. Start just left of *Shot Yer Bolt.*

03 » **The Colostomy Finish** **F7a** // **Horseshoe Quarry**
A left-hand finish to *Rain Dance*, breaking left at two-thirds height to climb through a small roof just right of the arête.

04 » **The Prophecy** **F7a** // **Harpur Hill Quarry**
Slightly eliminate, but a good long route for all.

05 » **Poisonality** **F7a** // **Horseshoe Quarry**
The crux may require advance beta – ask a local. A direct start to *An Ancient Rhythm.*

staden quarry

Tucked away in the White Peak between Bakewell and Buxton, there is a crag that meets virtually none of the Peak District limestone crag stereotypes, expect perhaps that it is quarried. The climbing is high-quality in a friendly environment, and what's more, you may often be the only party here.

Quarried it may be, but the rock lends itself to terrific features, including good cracks and intermittent sections of flowstone tufa. If you're going well, make sure you get on *Joint Effort* (HVS 5a) – you won't regret it!

The crag does face north, so bear in mind that it won't get any sun on cool days, but it will provide a good escape from a blazing sun.

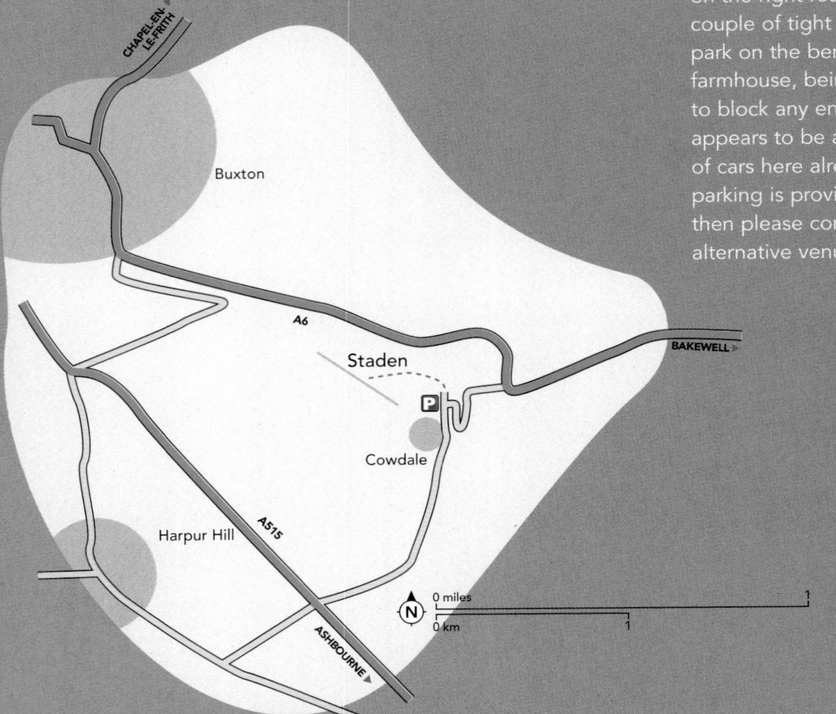

Access

The BMC have done a great deal of excellent work here in terms of access and so climbers are asked to park sensibly and abide by current access arrangements.

Approximately 3km east of Buxton, a minor road branches off right just before a bend to the left. If you pass an interesting and probably dirty overhanging limestone wall on your left, shortly after leaving the A6, then you're on the right road. After a couple of tight switchbacks, park on the bend by the farmhouse, being careful not to block any entrances. If there appears to be a large number of cars here already and parking is proving difficult, then please consider an alternative venue.

Dave Johnston on Joint Effort (HVS 5a) **photo** : Nick Smith

the **routes**

A Game of Chess Wall

A small, but worthwhile buttress before the main walls are reached. Descent is by abseil, or with care down the gully to the right.

1» Rupert Bear Goes Hiking VS 4c // 12m
Reach the left-hand crack from the ledges on the right. Finish direct.

2» Bimbo the Exploding Lorry Driver's Gulch HS 4b // 12m // ✪
The right-hand crack on the wall is solid, although care is advised on the top-out.

Joint Effort Wall

Excellent quality limestone on this large wall. Again, descent is by abseil or on foot via the gully as per the previous buttress.

3» Suscipiat VS 4c // 24m // ✪
The left-hand side of the wall, starting at some attractive flutings. From here, head left to the arête before moving back right to join the long crack in the right wall to finish.

4» The Nails HVS 5b // 28m // ✪✪
The crack several metres right of *Suscipiat*, leads to a finishing groove that needs clean technique and good footwork. Hard for the grade.

5» Joint Effort **HVS 5a // 28m // ✪✪✪**
A stonking line up the soaring crack line in the centre of the buttress. The start is technical but the climbing soon settles down and is thoroughly enjoyable.

6» Investal **HVS 5a // 26m // ✪**
As the bank starts to rise the visually disappointing crack does offer up sections of good climbing, although equal time may be spent navigating around the vegetation.

E There is also a good E1 to consider here if you are competent at HVS. *Liquid Courage* (E1 5c) at the extreme right-hand side of the wall (about 3m right of *Investal*) is pumpy, sustained and high in the grade. Climb a low scoop and pull rightwards over the bulges to a deep crack.

stoney middleton

Famous, infamous. Polished, full of life. There are many differing opinions of Stoney, and it has been unjustly slighted in years gone by. Yet the truth is that the climbs are good tests of ability with a definite adventurous feel. Treat it with respect and you will be rewarded – the climbs are certainly memorable.

There is a clutch of excellent low-to-mid grade outings, including the corner of *Froth*, the cracks of *Aurora* on **Windy Buttress** and the never-ending sideways shuffle of *Pendulum*.

The rock is limestone of varying quality. Where it's good, it's good; where it's not, it's not. It is polished in places, but this detracts little from the quality of the climbing. The entire crag dries quickly after rain and can be pleasantly sheltered when it is too cold to climb on the grit, catching much winter sun.

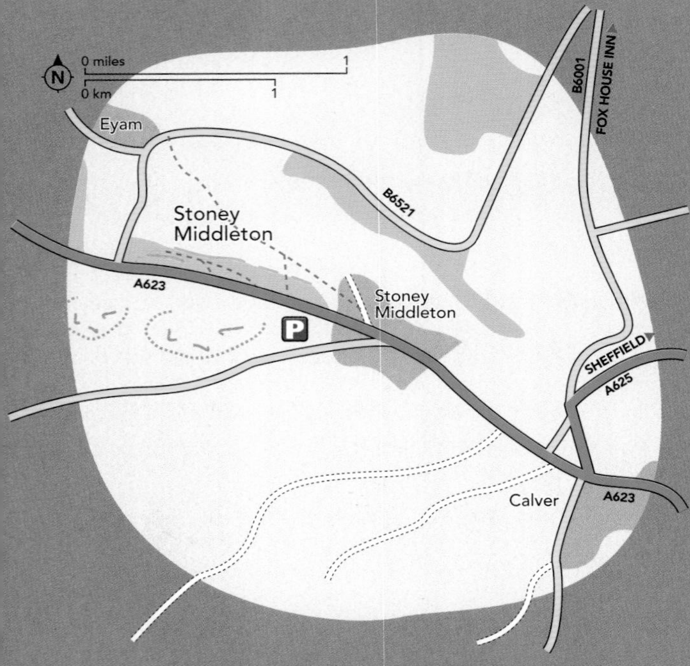

Access

Parking is available in a large lay-by opposite a garage, just before you leave the village heading west on the A623. Garage Buttress, visible up the road, is a short walk and the other areas aren't a great deal further. Please do not park in the mouths of the now-blocked tracks below the crag, nor outside the electricity substation close to the junction with the Eyam road – lest you get the plague!

Susan Hatchell on Aurora Arête (HVS 5a) **photo :** Ian Parnell

the **routes**

Mortuary Steps Area

Two excellent climbs, not quite as intimidating as the name would suggest.

1» Mortuary Steps
HVS 5b // 25m // ✪✪

An excellent, tough route, well protected, but with plenty of good climbing to maintain interest. Not as intimidating as it looks. Climb the obvious big groove.

2» Little Capucin
HVS 5a // 25m // ✪

Another great Stoney HVS, climbing the clean front of the buttress.

The Triglyph

The isolated tower of rock between **Mortuary Steps** and **Prayer Wheel Wall**.

3» How the Hell
VS 4c // 20m // ✪

A Joe Brown route from the 50s. Good climbing, starting below the central crack. Move left to the next crack and so the finish.

4» What the Hell
VS 4b // 20m // ✪

Excellent climbing up the central crack.

5» Morning Crack
S 4a // 24m // ✪

The wide right-hand crack is particularly pleasant.

Padme Area

Two good routes on the popular **Prayer Wheel Wall.**

6» Padme
HVS 5a // 12m // ✪

A great little climb following the shallow groove in the left wall of the bay. Finish on the ledge.

7» Asparagus
VS 4b // 15m

Climb the corner of the bay to its conclusion on the ledge.

Pearly Gates Bay

8» Gabriel/Pearly Gates

VS 4c, 4c // 33m // ✪

A brilliant combination, and one of the Peak's better limestone VSs.

1: Climb the corner to a ledge, and then make crux moves up and right around the bulge. Belay on the top.

2: Traverse out left to the arête and follow the groove to the top. The traverse is perhaps easier at the higher level, but looks easier at the lower, if this is of any help at all.

9» Parachute

VS 4b // 18m // ✪

A popular polished route – even more so than all of the other polished routes. Climb the corner around to the right of the previous route.

Minus Ten Bay

10» Minus Ten **HVS 5a // 18m // ✪**

Minus Ten wall is at times a haunt for the hard men of bouldering – women have more taste – once described by a visiting Australian climber as the only crag in the world to get the full Minus Ten points for quality. The bouldering is at best 'specialist', but don't be put off as the routes are rather good. *Minus Ten* itself climbs the steep crack on the left-hand side of the wall.

11» Cointreau **HVS 5a // 20m**

The crack left of the corner. The crack and wall to its left is *Double Scotch* at an amenable E2.

Wee Doris Bay

Home to some very good classic harder routes at Stoney, as well as the selection described below.

12» Medusa
HVS 5b // 18m // ✪✪

Right, it is well-protected, but it is also seriously pumpy, you will need refined jamming technique, and good stamina. *Gesemini* HVS 5a, takes the higher crack to the right, stepping out from Medusa at two-thirds height.

13» Frisco Bay
VS 4c // 30m

The corner is a little overgrown, but well worth the fight.

14» Golden Gate
HVS 5a, 4c // 32m // ✪

An excellent route.

1: Climb up the deep chimney to belay on the right at the tree.

2: Traverse left to the corner, then climb out to the arête. Climb this in a great position to the summit.

Lucy Creamer on Froth (VS 4b, 4c) **photo :** Keith Sharples

Bitterfingers Bay

15» Froth

VS 4b, 4c // 24m // ✪✪

1: Climb the big corner to the break/ledge. Belay.

2: Traverse the break rightwards and move up to finish through a groove, being mindful of a little loose rock on the last moves. Belay at, and abseil from, a tree.

E The crack in the wall to the right is *Dead Banana Crack* – an excellent, if polished, E1 fight.

16» Fe Fi Fo Fum

HVS 5a // 20m // ✪

Three metres to the left of the arête, climb the crack system to finish on the arête. Excellent climbing. Again, belay/abseil at a tree.

Tower of Babel

The routes are accessed via the easy chimney to the left of the tower.

17» Glory Road **VS 4b // 25m**

Climb the left-hand groove, polished but good.

18» Sin **VS 4c // 25m**

Climb the right-hand of the two grooves.

Descent: Quest right to abseil from a tree at the left-hand end of Windy Buttress.

Windy Buttress

Home to many hard classics, this buttress is one of the jewels in the crown of Peak Limestone climbing – a must for aspiring rock athletes. The harder routes are accessed via the mid-height walkway, from which it is worth taking a look. Our first route starts from ground level on the right of the main buttress.

19» Aurora
VS 4c, 4c // 50m // ✪✪

1: From the toe of the buttress, boldly climb the wall. The climbing is easy, but the rock and protection are a little suspect. Belay.

2: From the break/ledge, swing right and climb the fine corner crack.

20» Aurora Arête
HVS 5a // 35m // ✪✪

Traverse easily into the belay on *Aurora* (VDiff). Climb the exposed arête above, drenched in exhilaration.

Descent: To descend from both routes, head right to a steep path.

Susan Hatchell on Aurora Arête (HVS 5a) **photo :** Ian Parnell

Garage Buttress

From the parking in Stoney, this is the first large buttress you meet. A selection of climbs, including several new sport routes, populate the technical lower walls and steep upper section.

21» Evasor **VS 4b,4c // 35m // ✪✪**

1: The start is easy enough, if a little unprotected. Climb up via a series of ledges, to a rib and a belay at a tree below the break.

2: Climb up and traverse left to the base of the steep groove, fortunately easier than it looks. Great climbing in an amazing position. Walk off right.

22» Pendulum **HVS 5a // 60m // ✪**

A long traverse of **Garage Buttress** and a must-do Stoney route. Most easily started from the descent path at the right-hand end of the buttress. Follow the break for several good long pitches before reversing the semi-detached pillar with interest – abseil descent from here from a tree. It is also possible to abseil off the route at a number of earlier points, should night/rain/boredom set in.

wildcat

Wildcat is a thoroughly pleasant venue with a delightful aspect overlooking the River Derwent. With a choice selection of routes from Severe to HVS, the majority of which are multi-pitch affairs, the crag is particularly rewarding for competent duos keen to rack up mileage.

Many of the routes begin down amongst the trees (with a spot of scrambling generally required to locate and access the initial climbing) before emerging onto fine grooves and open faces on the upper walls. Facing west, the crag does catch the afternoon sun – a real boon in spring and autumn – and the walls dry quickly after inclement weather.

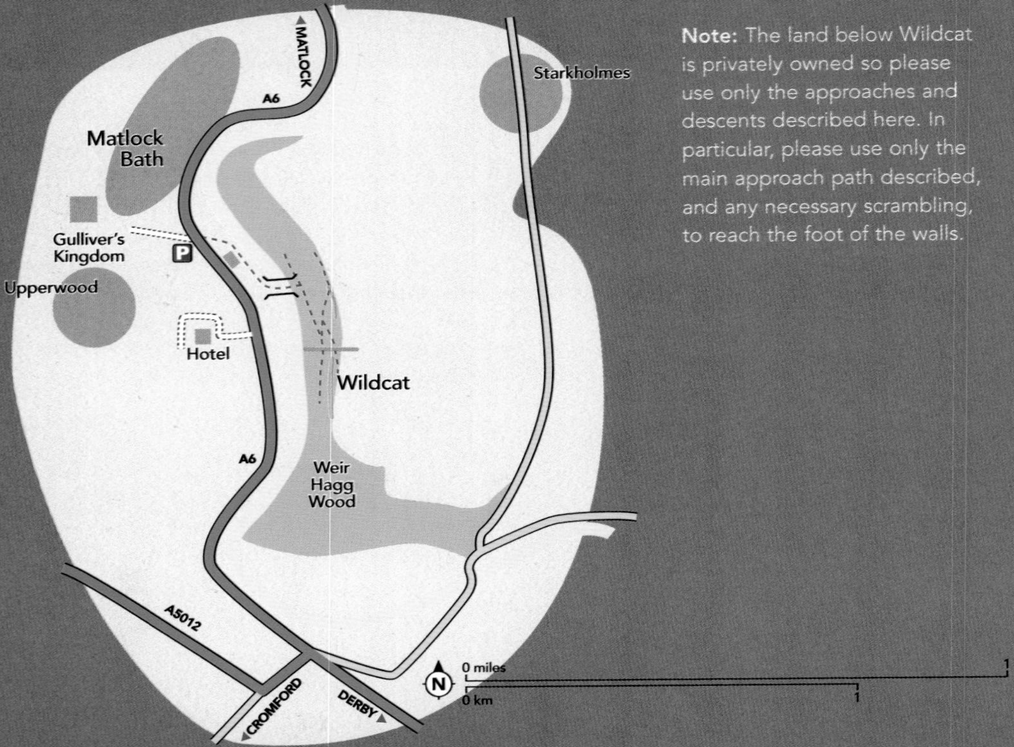

Access

Parking can be found just off the A6 in the Pay and Display car park for Gulliver's Kingdom. To access the crag, cross the main road and follow an alley on the right of the Pavilion (the large white building), passing toilets to a bridge. Cross the river and follow the path right, before forking off left onto a smaller zig-zag path, passing a broken wall, to reach **Coyote Buttress**, and then **High Crag**.

Note: The land below Wildcat is privately owned so please use only the approaches and descents described here. In particular, please use only the main approach path described, and any necessary scrambling, to reach the foot of the walls.

Jules Littlefair on Pitch 2 of Cataclysm (HVS 4b, 5a) **photo :** Stuart Littlefair

GR **SK296577**

the **routes**

Coyote Buttress

Striking grooves abound on this fine series of walls. Descend from the crag by walking off left, down a path, through an archway and then by doubling back to the crag.

1» Catastrophe Grooves
HVS 4c, 5a // 38m // ✪✪

Polished, but still super-classic.

1: Climb the crack and groove to a belay.

2: Balance up and right into the upper groove and finish more easily.

2» Coyote Buttress
HVS 5a, 5a // 38m // ✪✪

A great route taking a direct line up the crag.

1: Climb the wall left of a groove to a small belay.

2: Climb a short groove and pass a small roof on its right. Follow the left arête of the buttress and the steep crack above to finish.

3» Derek's Dilemma VS 4b, 5a // 38m // ✪

Two contrasting grooves with a testing crux.

1: Follow the groove right of a pinnacle to a belay on the right.

2: Step back left and climb the polished upper groove with difficulty.

4» Broken Toe Groove
VS 4c, 4b // 38m // ✪

1: Climb a groove left of an arête to a crack. Step right at a bulge to belay at a ledge.

2: Step back left and climb the groove right of the black streak, and the crack above.

5» Jackdaw Grooves

VS 4b, 4b // 38m // ✪✪

1: Climb a tall groove before stepping left to belay as for the previous route.

2: Step back out right and climb the wall and groove above.

6» Cat's Eye S 4a, 3a // 40m // ✪

1: Follow a crack system 3 metres right of a white groove, pass an overhang on its left and belay at the hole.

2: Climb a series of cracks out rightwards before finishing up the wall left of the corner.

High Crag

Emerging out of the trees, High Crag is the aptly named tallest section of Wildcat. Descent is as for Coyote Buttress. To access the next two routes scramble under a fallen tree to the base of a groove.

7» Sourpuss VS–, 4c // 37m // ✪

1: Start as for the next route but traverse left at the top of the first groove. Belay.

2: Head left to access the prominent, deep groove and romp up this.

8» Cat Walk HS 4a // 30m // ✪

Climb the groove and then a second groove to reach the base of a slab. Finish up the steeper groove above.

Simon Richardson on Pitch 2 of Golden Yardstick (VS 4b, 5a) **photo** : Stuart Littlefair

9» Manx **VS 4b, 4a // 36m // ✪**

1: Initially climb the left wall before heading into the deep groove proper. Belay on the right at three-quarter height.

2: Step left above the groove to finish up a short crack.

10» Golden Yardstick
VS 4b, 5a // 44m // ✪✪

1: Surmount the pedestal and climb the groove above to a belay stance in a cave.

2: Step right and then back left above the cave to access the right wall. Climb this in a great position before moving left to finish as for the top pitch of Manx.

11» Lobo **VS 4b, 4a // 40m // ✪**

1: As for the first pitch of Golden Yardstick.

2: Head off right past Ivy to a zig-zag crack. Zig and zag up this to finish on the left.

12» Lynx **HS 4b, 4a // 46m // ✪✪**

Long!

1: From a low pedestal climb up and left, past a tree, and continue diagonally across slabs to a steep groove. Climb this to a belay at a tree.

2: Continue left and join the zig-zag crack of Lobo to finish.

13» Sphynx **VS 4b, 4c // 40m // ✪✪**

1: Climb the low pedestal as for Lynx but where it moves left instead continue up and right to a groove and a tree belay.

2: Move left to a groove and climb this with tricky moves to a wide crack. Finish up this trending left.

14» Climacteric VS 5a // 40m // ★★

Starting just right of a groove and a mass of vegetation climb the wall to the overlap. Access to the steep wall above is by means of a fairly hard (crux) move around the lip. Climb the wall above, slightly left of centre. A fine and enjoyably long pitch.

15» Cataclysm HVS 4b, 5a // 38m // ★★★

One of the best on Peak limestone, this route bears the polish to prove it.

1: Follow a groove, past a tree, to an interesting belay in yet another cave.

2: Climb the superb groove above to a small overhang, before moving right to finish up cracks on the exposed upper wall.

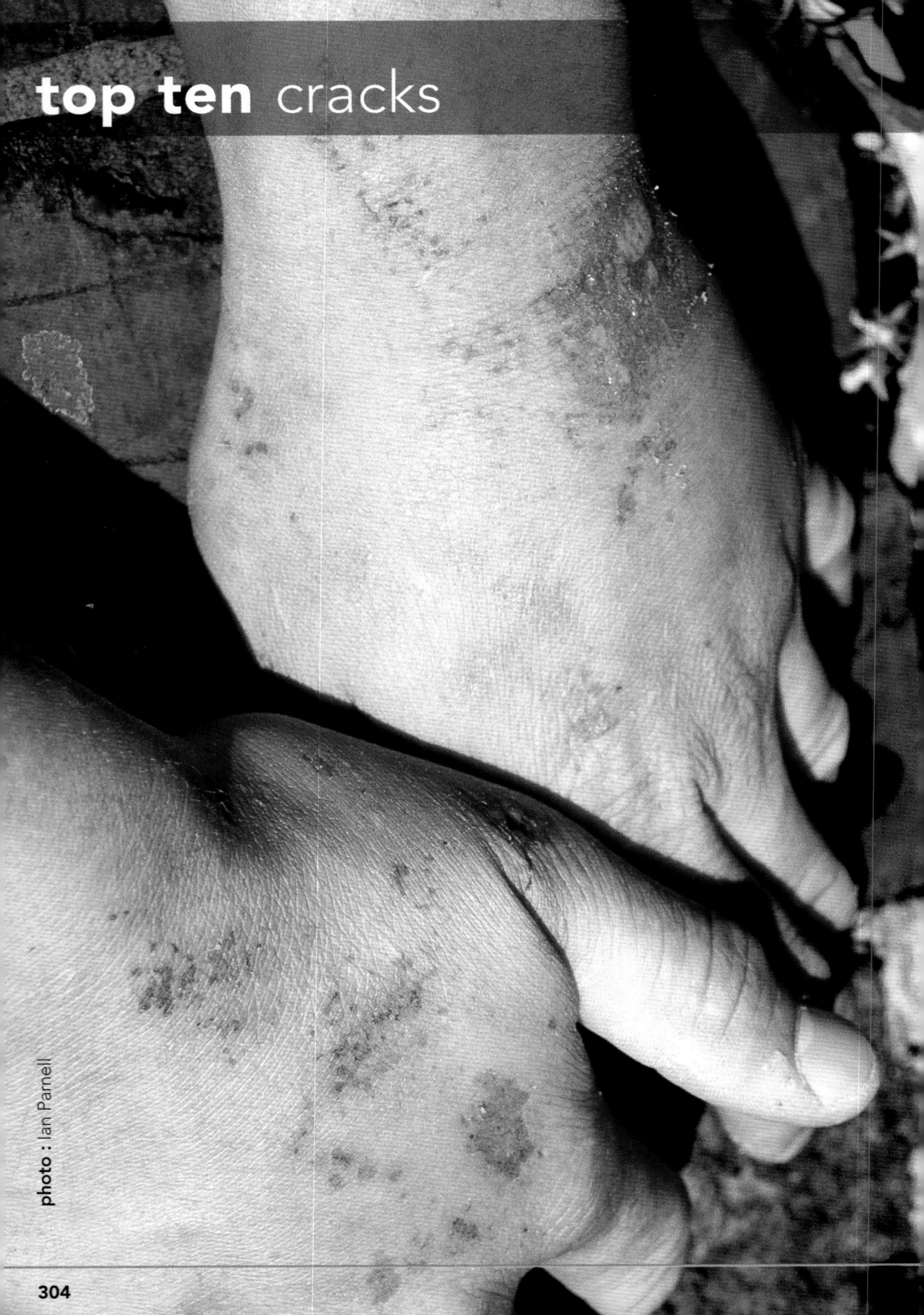

top ten cracks

photo : Ian Parnell

Angling to be the complete Fissureman?

Terrible joke we know – sorry!

01 » **The Crack** **VS 4b** // ***Castle Naze***
Of course!

02 » **Bond Street** **HVS 5a** // ***Millstone***
Hand-jamming perfection.

03 » **Jester Cracks** **VS 4c** // ***Kinder North***
Nothing to laugh about.

04 » **Mississippi Crack Variant** **VDiff** // ***Windgather***
An easier start to the excellent S crack.

05 » **Roof Route** **HVS 5b** // ***Rivelin***
Cruise it and consider yourself solid at HVS, struggle and join many others who swear blind it's E1.

06 » **Crabbie's Crack** **VS 4c** // ***The Roaches***
Steep super fun.

07 » **October Crack** **Diff** // ***Stanage North***
The wide crack is good clean fun.

08 » **Hollybush Crack** **S 4a** // ***The Roaches***
A big route through the upper tier.

09 » **Joint Effort** **HVS 5a** // ***Staden Quarry***
A full height outing with sustained climbing.

10 » **Medusa** **HVS 5b** // ***Stoney Middleton***
Top of the grade.

top ten first leads

Anna Shekratt on The Promenade (VMod) **photo**: Nick Smith

The first time you head out on the sharp end should be savoured, enjoyed and remembered.

Here are our suggestions for good first leads outdoors.

01 » Staircase **Mod** // Windgather
No worries here, good holds and gear mean the emphasis is placed on enjoying the climbing.

02 » Rivelin Slab **Mod** // Rivelin
The friendly aspect within the trees at Rivelin lends itself to first leads, and pushed grades.

03 » The Promenade **Mod** // Birchen Edge
A wonderful outing with varied and interesting climbing.

04 » October Crack **Diff** // Stanage North
Friendly and inviting, with plenty of gear.

05 » Buttress Two Gully **Mod** // Windgather
Number 2 at Windgather – there's a reason it's popular with novice climbers.

06 » Prow Cracks **Diff** // The Roaches
The cracks provide plenty of protection.

07 » Steptoe **Mod** // Burbage North
Friendly climbing through the blocky groove.

08 » Nursery Slab **Mod** // Froggatt
Although it appears broken up, the rock lends itself to plenty of opportunities for gear and holds.

09 » Slab Recess **Diff** // Froggatt
One of the best with good holds throughout.

10 » Left Twin Chimney **Mod** // Stanage Popular End
Tired of seconding your partner on the Popular End? Demand that they belay you on your first lead; right here, right now.

top ten spacewalks

Libby Peter on The Arête (HVD 4a) **photo :** Mike Robertson

The exposure is palpable, the gear perhaps distant.

Climbing can be a lonely experience
but it can take you to places never before imaginable.

01 » **Sunset Slab** **HVS 4b** // *Froggatt*
The ultimate, with gear of only psychological value on the upper section.

02 » **The Neb Finish** **VS 4b** // *The Roaches*
A route which begins halfway up the crag with tremendous exposure.

03 » **Skywalk** **VS 4b** // *Millstone*
VS access onto the big and brash Keyhole Cave wall should not be sniffed at.

04 » **Powder Monkey Parade** **HS 4b** // *Birchen Edge*
Split into three contrasting sections, the middle traverse should get the pulse going and the brain cogs racing.

05 » **The Arête** **HVD 4a** // *Hen Cloud*
HVD climbing with a 4a crux thrown in for good measure.

06 » **P.M.C. 1** **HS 4a** // *Curbar*
It's all about the top section here, with airy climbing on less than positive holds.

07 » **Flash Wall** **VS 5a** // *Kinder South*
The wide crack is good clean fun.

08 » **Scoop Face** **HVS 5a** // *Castle Naze*
Delicate padding through the delightful scoop.

09 » **Hargreaves' Original Route** **VS 4c** // *Stanage Popular End*
It is much better protected these days – spare a thought for what it must have been like pre-cams!

10 » **Plexity** **HVS 5a** // *Millstone*
A big route feel that charts a path through and around the bulging difficulties.

the tick list

- 01 » The Sloth — HVS // *The Roaches*
- 02 » Suicide Wall — HVS // *Cratcliffe*
- 03 » Joint Effort — HVS // *Staden Quarry*
- 04 » Mortuary Steps — HVS // *Stoney MIddleton*
- 05 » The Right Unconquerable — HVS // *Stanage Plantation*
- 06 » Megalithic Man — F6b+ // *Horseshoe Quarry*
- 07 » Delstree — HVS // *Hen Cloud*
- 08 » Chequers Buttress — HVS // *Froggatt*
- 09 » Great North Road — HVS // *Millstone*
- 10 » The Peapod — HVS // *Curbar*
- 11 » Croton Oil — HVS // *Rivelin*
- 12 » Rocky Variations — F6b // *Harpur Hill Quarry*
- 13 » Valkyrie — VS // *The Roaches*
- 14 » Froth — VS // *Stoney Middleton*
- 15 » Flash Wall — VS // *Kinder South*
- 16 » Topsail — VS // *Birchen Edge*
- 17 » Nozag — VS // *Castle Naze*
- 18 » Rotund Rooley — F6b // *Horseshoe Quarry*
- 19 » Altar Crack — VS // *Rivelin*
- 20 » Inverted V — VS // *Stanage Popular End*
- 21 » Central Climb — VS // *Hen Cloud*
- 22 » Excalibur — VS // *Lawrencefield*
- 23 » The Mall — VS // *Millstone*
- 24 » The Running Man — F6a+ // *Horseshoe Quarry*
- 25 » Green Gut — HS // *Froggatt*

26 » **Christmas Crack** HS // *Stanage Popular End*

27 » **Upper Tor Wall** HS // *Kinder South*

28 » **Jeffcoat's Buttress** HS // *The Roaches*

29 » **Powder Monkey Parade** HS // *Birchen Edge*

30 » **Amazon Crack** HS // *Burbage North*

31 » **Coral Seas** F6a // *Harpur Hill Quarry*

32 » **Bertie's Bugbear** S // *Wimberry*

33 » **The Niche** S // *Castle Naze*

34 » **Doctor's Chimney** S // *Stanage North*

35 » **Sail Chimney** S // *Birchen Edge*

36 » **Black and Tans** S // *The Roaches*

37 » **The Rising Sun** F5 // *Harpur Hill Quarry*

38 » **Ashop Climb** HVD // *Kinder North*

39 » **Nose Direct** HVD // *Windgather*

40 » **The Arête** HVD // *Hen Cloud*

41 » **Heaven Crack** VDiff // *Stanage Popular End*

42 » **Ash Tree Crack** VDiff // *Burbage North*

43 » **Right Route** VDiff // *The Roaches*

44 » **Renshaw's Remedy** VDiff // *Rivelin*

45 » **Paradise Crack** VDiff // *Stanage Plantation*

46 » **Inverted Staircase** Diff // *The Roaches*

47 » **Slab Recess** Diff // *Froggatt*

48 » **High Buttress Arête** Diff // *Windgather*

49 » **Left Twin Chimney** Mod // *Stanage Popular End*

50 » **The Promenade** Mod // *Birchen Edge*

climbing **dictionary**

Climbers don't half use some funny old words.

To help you understand what they're on about, we've picked out some of the more common and bizarre ones.

Aid Climbing » Climbing using placed protection to support hands, feet and body weight. Not a common practice in the UK.

'Ard » Like hard, but the correct pronunciation if born and/or bred in Yorkshire.

Arête » Opposite of *corner.*

Belay » The anchor that holds you to terra firma.

BMC » The British Mountaineering Council. Climbing's governing body (it also does hill walking and stuff) responsible for Herculean access and conservation efforts, including purchasing **Horseshoe Quarry** to secure access for climbers.

Bolt » *In-situ* protection found on sport climbs. Not to be placed on grit.

Bomber » A very good runner.

Boning » You have such a dirty mind! It actually refers to *crimping* a hold very hard.

Bouldering » Climbing for little people.

Break » A horizontal crack in the rock.

Bridge » To span, with feet, between two opposing rock walls.

Cams » Protection devices, also called *Friends.*

Chalk » Used on the hands to combat sweat and therefore improve grip.

Chimney » A wide *crack* in which the climber fully inserts him/herself in order to ascend.

Corner » Opposite of *arête.*

Crack » Fissure in the rock.

Crimp » A small finger hold.

Disco Leg » Seemingly uncontrollable gyration of one or both of the two lower limbs when experiencing a higher state of awareness during climbing. One might well refer to a climber experiencing disco leg as *Elvis.*

Dog » To dog a route is to climb it (lead or top-rope) with many rests. Also, man's best friend, apparently.

Dyno » To move quickly or dynamically – usually jumping and kicking with the feet to gain height.

Elvis » See *disco leg.*

Ethics » At the core of British and, in particular, *trad climbing.* Ensures no bolts are placed on gritstone and the rock is treated with the respect it deserves and which history dictates. Beware the 'Ethics Police', easily identified by the loud tutting noise generated when ethics are followed loosely or, worse, not at all.

Fall » One to avoid. Losing contact with the rock, and not regaining it straight away/ at all.

Free Climb » To climb using only hands and feet to generate upwards movement. See also *aid climbing.*

Friends » A term for cams, named after the original camming device, the Friend, made by Wild Country.

Gear » Protection.

Gritstone » God's Own Rock. A coarse, sedimentary rock made up of large sand grains and small stones (pebbles). Common in the Peak District and the Yorkshire Dales. Legendary friction properties which in many places compensates for the absence of *holds.*

Gurn » Uncontrollable facial expression involving sucking chin into mouth, often generated when trying *'ard.*

Highball » A boulder problem that approaches route height.

Holds » Sometimes a subtle change in the texture of the rock, sometimes a bloody great big hole.

Jam » Quite literally to jam a body part into the rock to aid upward movement: hand-jam, finger-jam, fist-jam, foot-jam, raspberry jam…

Jug » A good, incut hold. A welcome sight when experiencing *disco leg*.

Layback » To climb a feature, hands and feet all on the same plane.

Leader » To climb the route first, from bottom to top, placing gear as you go.

Limestone » In the Peak District, the shiny, white cousin of Gritstone. While technically sedimentary, it shares none of gritstone's legendary friction and climbers must instead use *Holds*. Whereas every single gritstone route is good, only a dozen or so limestone routes are worth getting out of bed for (only kidding).

Lowball » A boulder problem very close to the floor.

Mantelshelf » Usually the final move of the route, not knowing how to when tired can thus be problematic.

Mono » To place only one finger on a hold – more common on small, one finger pockets. A dirty habit, which should be frowned upon. Encouraged by physio-therapists in private practice.

Multi-pitch » A long route, requiring mid-route belays.

Natural protection » For example, *Friends*, nuts, slings – gear that can be removed by the second climber leaving virtually no trace of its presence.

Offwidth » A particularly wide crack that renders most types of *jamming* redundant. Narrower than a *chimney*, success is often reliant on the insertion of major body parts and lots of *squirming*.

Overhang » One up from *sheer* on the steepness scale.

Roof » One up from *overhang*.

Runner » Piece of protection.

Second » Literally to follow the climb after the leader, on a top-rope.

Sheer » A steep section of rock where the arms take much of body weight.

Slab » An angle of rock less than 90° off vertical, one down from *wall* on the steepness scale, ironically often harder than *overhang* for the modern, athletically fit climber.

Sit-Start » In bouldering, start with your bum on the floor.

Slap » Attaining a hand hold dynamically, common in bouldering.

Sloper » A hold requiring friction to grip on to.

Smear » A *sloper* for the feet.

Solo » Ropeless climbing.

Spandex » The one time fashion statement of choice for aspiring rock poets, reputedly adds a grade to one's climbing performance.

Sport Climbing » An imported style of climbing with bolt protection – allows focus to be placed on the physical and technical difficulties as the danger element is essentially removed.

Squirming » Poor style; sliding upwards with no regard for self-image. See *offwidth*.

Top Rope » To climb with rope protection above.

Trad Climbing » The most popular form of climbing practiced in the UK, involving the placing of natural protection and a goal to respect the rock and leave it as it was found.

Wall » A steep piece of rock, requiring good technique, strength and balance in equal measure. Typically found to be at right angles to the path.

Climbing walls

The Peak District and the towns and cities surrounding it are blessed with some of the best indoor climbing walls going, should the weather turn sour.

Sheffield

The Climbing Works
The world's largest bouldering wall
Unit B, Centenary Works, Little London Road, Sheffield S8 0UJ
Tel: 0114 250 9990
www.climbingworks.com

The Foundry
Loads of routes and steep bouldering
45 Mowbray Street, Sheffield S3 8EN
Tel: 0114 279 6331
www.foundryclimbing.com

The Edge
Top routes and a good bouldering room
John Street, Bramall Lane, Sheffield S2 4QU
Tel: 0114 275 8899
www.sheffieldclimbing.com

Glossop

Glossop Leisure Centre
Old school concrete wall
High Street East, Glossop SK13 8PN
Tel: 01457 863 223

Manchester

Manchester Climbing Centre
Recently developed wall owned by rock legend John Dunne
St. Benedict's Church, Bennett Street, Manchester M12 5ND
Tel: 0161 230 7006
www.manchesterclimbingcentre.com

Rope Race
Good low grade routes and dedicated bouldering
Goyt Lane, Upper Hibbert Lane, Marple SK6 7HX
Tel: 0161 426 0226
www.roperace.co.uk

Awesome Walls Stockport
A new wall on the edge of the Peak District.
The Engine House, Pear Mill, Stockport Road West, Lower Bredbury, Stockport SK6 2BP
Tel: 0161 494 9949
www.awesomewalls.co.uk

Further reading

Available from **www.v-outdoor.co.uk**

Peak District : Bouldering

The most up-to-date guide to bouldering in the Peak District is by Vertebrate Publishing, and covers all the main areas with nearly all of the bouldering. At the time of its publication, all problems graded Font 7a or harder were included, in addition to all the best problems below 7a.

MLTUK

Rock Climbing is an invaluable reference and learning guide for every climber, packed with essential information and techniques and also containing specific ideas for anyone wanting to help coach and instruct others. The handbook is split into sections including: all aspects of single and multi-pitch climbing; bouldering and movement skills (indoors and out); mountain scrambling and related activities; descending from climbs and solving problems; and the climbing environment, its history and development. There are also chapters on sport climbing, sea-level traversing, injury avoidance, improving technique, risk management and the law and working with young people.

It is the second of a series of manuals and has been written by Libby Peter, an international Mountain Guide and Mountaineering Instructor. ***Hill Walking*** and ***Winter Skills*** complete the series.

Rockfax

Rockfax have produced three selective guidebooks covering much of the best climbing in the Peak District: the recently updated ***Eastern Grit***, ***Western Grit*** and the mammoth ***Northern Limestone***, which also extends into the Yorkshire Dales and the southern Lake District.

Useful websites

www.v-outdoor.co.uk
Borrowed somebody else's copy of this book? *Get your own here, ya cheapskate!*

www.ukclimbing.com
News, photos and forums updated daily.

www.ukbouldering.com
A good source of general bouldering information and specific problem beta.

www.rockfax.com
Further information on the publications and a comprehensive online route database.

www.meto.gov.uk
Keep tabs on the weather – you never know!

bmc guidebooks

This superb guide will no doubt have taken you through the first stages of your love affair with the Peak District and its climbing and shown you some of the great routes on its fine cliffs. If you have climbed all the routes shown at your favourite crags, or if you are seeking harder routes, then the series of definitive guides from the British Mountaineering Council will show you all you need to know.

The new series of guides, including ***The Roaches***, ***Burbage Millstone and Beyond*** and the latest, ***Stanage***, all detail every route and boulder problem on the crags covered. The fantastic modern design is complemented well with in-depth knowledge of the areas and climbs covered, as well as historical round-ups of the climbing. Let these guides take you the next step of the way.

Stanage

The queen of gritstone crags, with a superb guidebook to match. Where beginners come for their first grapples and the top performers crank off the hardest problems. This is a guide that will get the first-time visitor to the greatest climbs, or help a long-time local find something new.

1300 routes and 400 boulder problems.

Burbage, Millstone and Beyond

An exhaustive and entertaining guide to the fantastic gritstone crags in the Sheffield Area. Covering everything from the Burbage and Millstone crags, with their fantastic procession of classics, through to the delights of Bamford and Rivelin and the lonely wilds of Derwent Edge.

2,200 routes and 750 boulder problems.

The Roaches

Covering all the gritstone crags of Staffordshire in one lovely volume, from the beautiful Roaches, the bastions of Hen Cloud and the brutal Ramshaw, as well as the myriad of lesser-known but superb venues such as The Churnet, Castle Naze, Windgather, Baldstones and Newstones. This really is a guide to bring a smile to your face.

1600 routes and 800 boulder problems.

Froggatt to Black Rocks

Due 2008. The next BMC guide is set to be the biggest and best yet, covering everything from the mighty Froggatt and Curbar crags in the north, across to the pastoral sweetness of the Cratcliffe and Robin Hood's Stride areas in the east, and down south as far as the Black Rocks area. A lifetime's worth of quality.

For more information about the full range of BMC guidebooks, visit

www.**thebmc**.co.uk/guidebooks

Where to stay

Campsites

North Lees, Hathersage: 01433 650 838

Hardhurst Farm, Hope: 01433 620 001

Eric Byne Memorial Campsite, nr Birchen: 01246 582 277

Hen Cloud Camp Site. Contact Mr Day on 01538 300 419

Camping and Caravanning Club, Blackshaw Moor: 01538 300 285

Bunkhouses

Don Whillans Memorial Hut, The Roaches. Owned by the BMC, it sleeps 12 and tends to be booked out around 10,000,000 years in advance. Contact the Booking Secretary, Michael Hunt, on 01433 639 368.

There is also a range of YHA Bunkhouses all over the Peak District. Visit **www.yha.org.uk** for more information.

B&Bs and Hotels

There is a wide range of B&Bs and Hotels in the Peak District, including a choice of excellent 5-star award-winning guest houses.

For more information about accommodation in the Peak District visit: **www.visitpeakdistrict.com**

Cafés and pubs

Cafés

Outside Café, Hathersage: 01433 651 936

Outside Café, Calver: 01433 639 571

Woodbine Café, Hope: 01433 621 407

Coleman's Deli, Hathersage: 01433 650 505

Roaches Tearoom (opposite Hen Cloud): 01538 300 345

Pubs

Millstone Inn, Hathersage

The Scotsman's Pack, Hathersage

The Little John, Hathersage

The Grouse Inn, nr Froggatt

The Olde Rock Inn, Upper Hulme

Traveller's Rest, just off the A53

Gear Shops

There are good gear shops located in most of the main locations in and around the Peak District, ideal for getting rid of all that money burning a hole in your pocket.

Outside, Hathersage: 01433 651 936

Hitch 'n' Hike, Bamford: 01433 651 013

Reaching New Heights, Leek: 01538 373 854

Mountain Fever, Stoke-on-Trent: 01782 266 137

Jo Royle Outdoor, Buxton: 01298 258 24

Alpenstock, Stockport: 0161 480 3660

CragX, The Foundry, Sheffield: 0114 276 9741

About Vertebrate

Vertebrate Publishing is an imprint of **Vertebrate Graphics**, Britain's leading graphic design agency that specialises in the outdoor leisure market. Based deliberately near the Peak District, the guidebook production team spends as much time as possible climbing, walking and cycling in the Peak District.

We have had substantial success in the design and production of specialist outdoor books. These include *Staffordshire Grit: The Roaches*, *Peak District: Bouldering*, *Hillwalking – The Official Handbook of the Mountain Leader and Walking Group Leader Schemes* (a bestselling outdoor title for three years running) and the UK's best selling mountain biking guide: *Dark Peak Mountain Biking – True Grit Trails*.

www.v-publishing.co.uk

index

index

index